THE UNDERLYING PRINCIPLES OF MODERN LEGISLATION

BY W. JETHRO BROWN

LL.D., LITT.D., LATE MACMAHON STUDENT OF ST. JOHN'S COLLEGE CAMBRIDGE; BARRISTER-AT-LAW OF THE MIDDLE TEMPLE; SOMETIME PROFESSOR OF CONSTITUTIONAL LAW IN UNIVERSITY COLLEGE, LONDON; PROFESSOR OF LAW IN THE UNIVERSITY OF ADELAIDE.

THE LAWBOOK EXCHANGE, LTD.
Clark, New Jersey
2006

ISBN-10: 1-58477-652-8
ISBN-13: 978-1-58477-652-9

Printed in the United States of America on acid-free paper

THE LAWBOOK EXCHANGE, LTD.
33 Terminal Avenue
Clark, New Jersey 07066-1321

Please see our website for a selection of our other publications and fine facsimile reprints of classic works of legal history:
www.lawbookexchange.com

Library of Congress Cataloging-in-Publication Data

Brown, W. Jethro (William Jethro), 1868-1930.
The underlying principles of modern legislation / W. Jethro Brown.
p. cm.
Originally published: London : John Murray, 1912.
Includes bibliographical references.
ISBN 1-58477-652-8 (alk. paper)
1. Legislation--Great Britain. 2. Legislation. I. Title.
KD4230.B76 2005
349.41--dc22 2005015136

THE UNDERLYING PRINCIPLES OF MODERN LEGISLATION

BY W. JETHRO BROWN

LL.D., LITT.D., LATE MACMAHON STUDENT OF ST. JOHN'S COLLEGE CAMBRIDGE; BARRISTER-AT-LAW OF THE MIDDLE TEMPLE; SOMETIME PROFESSOR OF CONSTITUTIONAL LAW IN UNIVERSITY COLLEGE, LONDON; PROFESSOR OF LAW IN THE UNIVERSITY OF ADELAIDE.

LONDON
JOHN MURRAY, ALBEMARLE STREET, W.
1920

First Edition (10/6) - - - January, 1912
Second Edition - - - - July, 1912
Third Edition (6/-) - - - - July, 1914
Fourth Edition (6/-) - - October, 1915
Fifth Edition (6/-) - - - April, 1917
Sixth Edition - - - July, 1920

Sherratt & Hughes, Printers, Manchester

TO MY READER

PREFACE.

In the present work, though I refer especially to British politics, I have drawn illustrations from many sources. The experiences of a somewhat nomadic existence have convinced me that no one who wishes to understand the course of legislation in any one country can afford to ignore the trend of political and industrial progress in other lands.

My primary purpose has been to state the principles that underlie the course of legislation. My occasional incursions into the field of present politics have been chiefly prompted by the belief that the meaning and value of a principle can be most effectively illustrated by a reference to problems whose data are derived from the facts of immediate experience. An acceptance of my statement of legislative principles need not involve an endorsement of conclusions I sometimes venture to express regarding the issues that divide the political parties of our time. If I am so fortunate as to convince the reader that a review of the course of legislation reveals the presence of principles which lie deeper than the antagonisms of parties or the conflicts of the schools, I shall endure with fortitude the charge of occasional error in my attempt to interpret these principles in relation to problems of the moment.

My readers will probably vary in their opinion of the value of the principles for the purposes of practical statesmanship. One point will be conceded by all. While the principles which have guided legislative action in the past may not solve all our problems, they represent the wisdom which lies in the accumulated thought and experience of the generations. They serve not only to make intelligible the content of that law which must be understood if it is to be reformed in any worthy sense, but also to provide the social reformer with an intellectual equipment which should be of service in assessing the relative value of the many proposed solutions of existing problems. I do not think that it would be presumptuous to say that the contributions of those who approach the study of social questions from a more or less Utopian point of view vary in value in direct proportion to the writer's grasp of principles and ideals which are implicit in existing laws and institutions. "Statesmen," said Burke, "instead of exploding general prejudices employ their sagacity to discover the latent wisdom which prevails in them."

In my Preface to the first edition, I stated that, in the hope that this work might be of some service as a University text-book, I had given to certain subjects a fuller treatment than would be permissible in a work addressed solely to experts. I may be allowed to repeat my opinion that, whatever may be the value of my own work for the purpose just indicated, the claim of the theory of legislation to a place in the curriculum of the University stands in no need of statement or defence. The question of to-day is rather whether every candidate for a degree ought not to take this subject at some stage in his course. Those who attach as much importance as I do to the democratising of our institutions and to the constant widening of the sphere of positive law will incline to answer this question in the affirmative. But, however the question be answered, no one can doubt that the study of the principles of legislative action will receive increasing attention in the Faculties of Arts and Law. Upon students in the latter Faculty the subject has special claims. It is only when we view the statute-book in relation to legislative ideals and purposes that we are able, as Jhering would say, to pass from the *formulated* law to the *real* law—from the letter which killeth to the spirit which giveth life. The mere bulk of our modern law compels the lawyer to pass beyond legal rules to ultimate elements or conceptions; and in the course of this endeavour he is constrained, both by the necessities of thought and the trend of judicial interpretation, to reflect upon the ends which law serves and the principles to which it gives expression.

In the reviews of the first edition of this work, a very generous appreciation was qualified in some cases by the complaint that I had often failed to indicate my own views as to the best solution of a particular problem. But, in a University text-book, the writer ought to be careful in expressing personal opinions about problems of which the precise solution is very debatable. In a work now in the Press on "The Control of Monopolies" I have allowed myself a greater latitude of expression.

W. JETHRO BROWN.

UNIVERSITY,
ADELAIDE,
March 1914.

TABLE OF CONTENTS.

CONTENTS

PROLOGUE

THE CHALLENGE OF ANARCHY.

PART I.—THE STATEMENT OF PRINCIPLES

CHAPTER I

LEGISLATIVE IDEALISM IN THE NINETEENTH CENTURY.

CHAPTER II

NATIONAL LIFE AND THOUGHT IN THE NINETEENTH CENTURY.

CHAPTER III

FUNDAMENTAL PRINCIPLES.

CHAPTER IV

THEORETICAL FORMULATIONS OF THE SOCIAL UNITY.

PART II.—THE PRINCIPLES IN APPLICATION

CHAPTER V

THE TRUTH IN *LAISSEZ FAIRE* (I.)—PARENTAL GOVERNMENT AND CLASS LEGISLATION.

CHAPTER VI

THE TRUTH IN *LAISSEZ FAIRE* (II).—COMPETITION.

CHAPTER VII

THE RIGHTS OF THE INDIVIDUAL (I.)—THEORY.

CHAPTER VIII

THE RIGHTS OF THE INDIVIDUAL (II.)—ILLUSTRATIONS.

PART III.—THE OUTLOOK

CHAPTER IX

THE OUTLOOK: PROBLEMS OF TO-DAY AND TO-MORROW.

THE UNDERLYING PRINCIPLES OF MODERN LEGISLATION

PROLOGUE.

THE CHALLENGE OF ANARCHY.

"One might succeed in explaining to the dullest of men the most difficult of problems, if he had no previous conception in regard to them; but it is impossible to explain to the cleverest man even the simplest matters, if he is perfectly sure that he knows everything about it."

—TOLSTOY.

A BRUSSELS police officer, on being informed that the militant member of the British House of Commons, whom he had arrested, was no anarchist, but a "mere socialist," replied that he failed to see the difference. Many will regard his mistake as excusable and his action as commendable. To the student of social institutions, the incident will serve as a reminder that anarchy and socialism, though radically opposed in their methods and ideals, rank together as great schemes of social reconstruction which claim to have discovered a solution of the problems of our age.

The earnest investigator will find additional reasons for being interested in anarchy apart from the fact that it is one of two great theories for the reconstruction of society. He will be aware that anarchy, no less than socialism, can boast its acute and original thinkers, its numerous and militant societies, and its multitude of unconscious adherents who, at the very moment that they condemn its central doctrine, may be engaged in advocating principles by which that doctrine is justified. He will remember also that anarchy has the merit of challenging ideas whose eternal validity is apt to be taken for granted. Men are born under government, live under it, and die under it, for the most part without troubling themselves to consider whether government is a good thing or not. But what, it may well be asked, is the good of our interminable discussions about the sphere of the State if we lack a clear and consistent idea of the right of the State to have any sphere at all?

Few of the great causes that have inspired devotion in the past have suffered so much as anarchy from the uncritical depreciation that confuses essentials with accidental associations. I propose to give several examples. Perhaps the most striking relates to the methods adopted for bringing the new social order into being. To the popular mind, the stiletto and the bomb are the very symbols of anarchy. The means employed by some anarchists for the purpose of achieving the end in view are mistaken for the end itself. The explanation is simple. While the annals of a certain type of crime absorb popular interest, the abstract treatises on the nature of man and society which explain that type, and may even seek to justify it, are allowed to slumber in the dust of our libraries; and anarchy is regarded, not as a theory of social reconstruction, but as a gospel of violence and crime. So we may even read, in our morning paper, of anarchists in India! The fact is overlooked that the native revolutionaries who employ the methods of violence merely desire to substitute one set of political institutions for another.

In part, of course, the anarchists themselves, or some of them, are to blame. He who commits a crime in order to serve a noble purpose ought not to be surprised if an undiscriminating public overlooks his purpose in its horror of the crime. Many readers will remember the assassination of the Tsar Alexander II. A bomb had wrecked the carriage in which he was riding, but the Tsar leapt to earth apparently unharmed. Some one rushed forward. "Your Majesty is safe?" "Yes, thank God," was the response. "It is too soon to thank God," said an anarchist, who threw a second bomb with fatal effect. The blameless President M'Kinley was shot by a man to whom he had extended his hand in friendly greeting. At Geneva, on the afternoon of Saturday, 10th September, 1898, an assassin plunged a stiletto in the heart of a defenceless woman whose only crime was that of being an Empress. We cannot forget deeds such as these; nor can we forget that they have been promoted by anarchist organisations, and even defended by anarchist thinkers of ability and repute. Johann Most, for example, has won distinction as an exponent of the gentle art of assassination. A Congress, held in London in July 1881, resolved that all means were permissible for the annihilation of rulers, ministers of State, the nobility, the clergy, the most prominent capitalists, and other exploiters; and that accordingly great attention should be given to the study of chemistry and the preparation of explosives.[1]

Those who, under whatever pretext, commit or plot murder in cold blood, have much to answer for. Yet we can no more reject anarchy because ill deeds have been done in its name than we can reject liberty for the same reason, or than we can repudiate Catholicism because of the Inquisition. In actual fact, anarchy did not originate as a theory of violence; and those anarchists who have advocated violence have done so as a temporary means and on the plea of an overwhelming necessity. The appeal to violence originated in Russia, where men, opposing force to force, struck in a blind fury of protest at a despotism that seemed unassailable by any other weapon. While we repudiate the nihilist and his imitators in other parts of the world, we must remember that the real problem for consideration in relation to anarchy is the practicability and merits of a certain form of social organisation, and

1. Zenker, "Anarchism," 231.

not the means proposed by some misguided enthusiasts for bringing that organisation into existence. The absence of any essential connection between anarchy and violence is sufficiently proved by the attitude of many acknowledged exponents of anarchist doctrine. "The kingdom of truth," said Godwin, "comes quietly . . . . I had rather convince men by argument than seduce them by example."[1] "When once ideas have originated," said Proudhon, "the very paving stones will rise of themselves unless the government has sense enough to avert this. And if not, then nothing else is of any use." "The Social revolution," declares Benjamin Tucker, "must come by passive resistance." Tolstoy, greatest of all the anarchists, looks forward to the realisation of the new order as a result of the gradual recognition of the contradiction between civic institutions and the Christ Law.[2] In an interview with some representatives of the revolutionary party, Tolstoy was confronted by the following statement from the party manifesto: "Hatred for the landowners is the first and most sacred sentiment a father should teach his children." He answered:

"Such words are base. If the moral sense exists in men at all, it expresses itself in love—love of God, of one's neighbour, of humanity without exception. For every man is my brother. If I hate the landowner, I invite a like hate in return. When I seek to justify my hate I am denying the very foundations of all morality."[3]

The confusion of anarchy with assassination recalls the philosophical theory of the anarchist Stirner.

"Might," he declared, "goes before right and quite rightly . . . . What I have the might to be I have the right to be. I deduce all right and all title

1. "Political Justice," i. 94.

2. Tolstoy, "The Kingdom of God is Within You," 38 *et seq.*, 223–43. *Cf.* Eltzbacher, "Anarchism." The latter work, which consists of excerpts from anarchist literature, might be styled "A Bible of Anarchy." It will be found invaluable to all students of the subject.

3. *Mercure de France*, 16 Mars, 1910, 271, freely translated.

from myself; I am entitled to everything that I have might over. I am entitled to overthrow Zeus, Jehovah, or God, if I can; if I cannot, then these Gods will always remain in the right and might as against me. . . . One gets farther with a handful of might than with a bagful of right."[1]

But the theory of Stirner is anything but typical. Anarchism, as ordinarily presented, is a protest against the rule of might. It is an appeal from the might of rulers to the sense of right in the individual; from the coercion of the State to the conscience of the citizen; from the law that is penally enforced to the law that is voluntarily accepted. The plausibility of the theory of Stirner consists in the fact that, if we make the individual the judge of right, we may seem to enthrone the individual who can force his will on others, in a world where different interpretations of right are inevitable. But more representative anarchists do not believe that the enthronement of the individual would mean the enthronement of force. On the contrary, they believe that the power of moral ideas in the anarchist community, the restraining influence of a due regard for the claims of others, would be more potent than at present.

The illusion just referred to finds some justification in anarchist literature. So much can scarcely be said of the illusion that anarchy, in rejecting the State, also rejects society and associated effort. Although, as we are frequently reminded, Godwin condemned the orchestral concert as a degrading denial of individual independence, we should display a strange lack of discrimination if we regarded this condemnation as more than an indication of Godwin's musical taste. Throughout anarchist literature, a distinction is drawn between society and the State—between voluntary groups of human beings, united by co-operation for the promotion of common interests, and the organised

1, Quoted, Eltzbacher, "Anarchism," 98—100.

State, with its agencies for compelling individuals to live according to certain rules whether they approve of them or not.

"Society and government are different in themselves, and have different origins. Society is produced by our wants, and government by our wickedness. Society is in every state a blessing; government, even in its best state, but a necessary evil." [1]

"The life of Society," says Benjamin Tucker, "is inseparable from the lives of individuals. Society has come to be man's dearest possession." [2]

No account of popular misconceptions about anarchy would be complete without reference to the illusion that it is hostile to law in the sense of rules of conduct generally observed among men. Although some anarchist writers express the strange opinion that men can dispense with rules of conduct, each man doing as he thinks best under the particular circumstances, anarchists in general are not guilty of so puerile an assumption.

"Imagine," exclaims Mr. Bernard Shaw, "leaving the traffic of Piccadilly or Broadway to proceed on the understanding that every driver should keep to that side of the road which seemed to him to promote the greatest happiness of the greatest number!" [3]

The protest of anarchy is not against rules of conduct, but against the enforcement of such rules by the might of society without regard to their approval by the individuals upon whom they are enforced. We can only accuse anarchy of lawlessness if we limit the term "law" to State-enforced rules.

"Dogs," exclaimed the railway porter immortalised

1. Godwin, "Political Justice," i. 79, quoting Paine, "Common Sense."
2. Quoted, Eltzbacher, "Anarchism," 194.
3. "The Sanity of Art," 48. Needless to say, Mr. Shaw is not an anarchist, though his views on some subjects display anarchist tendencies.

in *Punch*, "is dogs; cats is dogs; rabbits is dogs; but this 'ere tortoise is a hinsect." Some readers will be tempted to challenge my definition of anarchy as no less arbitrary. In point of fact, however, underlying all the divergencies of anarchist opinion and all the criminalities or absurdities of isolated anarchists, there is one common and fundamental conviction which is neither criminal nor absurd—the conviction that the best social order is one where men live their lives, not under the compulsory regulation of the State, but in voluntary co-operation. Both the negative and the positive aspect of this conviction call for some explanation.

Negatively, anarchy means the repudiation of the claim of the State to impose its will upon the citizen by force. The right of a society to promote the common good of its members is not called in question; what is denied is the claim of society to force upon individuals its own interpretation of that good. The anarchist is the sworn foe, not of all government, but of government which is not based upon the free and full consent of the individual. The qualified character of this repudiation of the State deserves careful notice. Apart from the vigilance committee for dealing with cases of flagrant criminality, most anarchists expressly or implicitly sanction a measure of compulsion in the sphere of contract and property. "*Contracts must be kept!*" The statement implies a coercive law. As regards property, while some reject the conception altogether, others retain it in one form or another. According to Tucker, every individual is to be guaranteed the product of his labour; according to Bakunin, private property is to be allowed in the objects of consumption; according to Kropotkin, there may be social property, but no private property. What then, it may be asked, is the distinction between the State, as the term is ordinarily understood, and a social order in which contractual obligation may be enforced, and some forms of private property may be protected?

The distinction lies in the fact that the State coerces the individual whether he consents to the coercion or not, whilst the anarchist community repudiates all coercion save in so far as the individual must be held to have consented to it:—for example, by promising to perform acts or to conform to rules, or by voluntarily enrolling himself as a member of a community of whose usages and institutions he approves. It is sometimes said that existing governments derive their authority and power from the consent of the governed. According to the anarchist, the attitude of the governed is one of passive toleration rather than actual consent; and, apart from other conditions, the mere magnitude of modern communities makes the presumed consent of the individual a fiction.

From the positive point of view, anarchy means self-government. "Why speak of anarchism?" asks Egidy. "Why not say at once *self-discipline*?" "Civilisation," says Tucker, "consists in teaching men to govern themselves by letting them do it." The logical kinship of such views to the theory of the early Protestants will be apparent; but the claim is more comprehensive. Although Luther in "The Babylonish Captivity" went so far as to urge the central dogma of anarchy that no man should be ruled save by his own consent, most of the early Reformers were only concerned with self-government as a means to spiritual freedom. They were content to substitute the priesthood of the believer for the priesthood of a Church. The anarchist takes a wider view; he seeks to realise freedom in general. While the early Protestant proclaimed the right of the individual to worship God according to the dictates of his own conscience, the modern anarchist proclaims the innate and imprescriptible right of the individual to govern himself in all the affairs of life.

Thus, in the Kingdom the anarchist seeks to establish, law is self-imposed, and all associated effort is the result of voluntary co-operation. I pass to the arguments by which this conception of the ideal social order is justified. It would be superfluous to warn the reader against regarding my statement of these arguments as complete. Not only has each anarchist his own intellectual armoury, but the exceeding difficulty of doing justice to opinions that challenge a long-established order of things will be readily admitted by any one who has seriously attempted the task. The conviction that political institutions are a part of the eternal order of nature is so deeply rooted in all our ideas about social life that an adequate statement of the case for the anarchist would require a comprehensive treatise. I shall only endeavour to present it in the barest outline, stating as clearly and as forcibly as I can what appear to me to be the more important arguments.

I shall begin with a phase of the subject about which most people are in agreement—the failure of human governments to secure social justice. In theory, the State exists to promote the general interest; in historical fact, governments have sought to promote, first and foremost, the interests of a governing class. Even where they have aimed at the common good, their view of the nature of that good has been determined by class institutions and prejudices. Under modern democracies, it is true, there is to be found a clearer appreciation of the ends which governments ought to serve. Nevertheless, the ignorance and self-interest of rulers, the empire of traditional conceptions over the minds of the multitude, the ambitions of some, and the general inertia of many, so affect the course of legislation as to suggest the disturbing question whether government is not responsible for more evils than it prevents. How many individuals, even in the most democratic communities, can be trusted not to employ their political power in the interest of themselves or their class? If we are to judge an institution by its fruits, what shall be said of human government when we regard impartially its most distinctive product—our system of property? When Paley, surely one of the least revolutionary of philosophers, began his defence of that system, he wrote, in a famous passage:

"If you should see a flock of pigeons in a field of corn, and if (instead of each picking where and what it liked, taking just as much as it wanted, and no more) you should see ninety-nine of them gathering all they got into a heap; reserving nothing for themselves, but the chaff and refuse; keeping this heap for one, and that the weakest, perhaps the worst, pigeon of the flock; sitting round, and looking on, all the winter, whilst this one was devouring, throwing about, and wasting it; and if a pigeon more hardy or hungry than the rest touched a grain of the hoard, all the others instantly flying upon it, and tearing it to pieces; if you should see this, you would see nothing more than what is every day practised and established among men."[1]

To some readers this analogy may seem wholly remote from fact. I do not think the impartial historian would so regard it.

"I contend," said Thorold Rogers, "that from 1563 to 1824 a conspiracy, concocted by the law and carried out by parties interested in its success, was entered into to cheat the English workman of his wages, to tie him to the soil, to deprive him of hope, and to degrade him into irremediable poverty."[2] . . . "We have been able," he adds in a later chapter, "to trace the process by which the condition of English labour had been continuously deteriorated by the acts of government. It was first impoverished by the issue of base money. Next it was robbed of its guild capital by the land thieves of Edward's regency. It was next brought into contact with a new and more needy set of employers—the sheepmasters who succeeded the

1. "Works," ii. 70. *Cf.* Anatole France's chapter on "The Origin of Property" in "L'île des Pingouins."
2. "Six Centuries of Work and Wages," ch. xiv.

monks. It was then, with a pretence and perhaps with the intention of kindness, subjected to the quarter sessions assessment, mercilessly used in the first half of the seventeenth century, the agricultural labourer being still further impoverished by being made the residuum of all labour. The agricultural labourer was then further mulcted by enclosures, and the extinction of those immemorial rights of pasture and fuel which he had enjoyed so long. The poor law professed to find him work, but was so administered that the reduction of his wages to a bare subsistence became an easy process and an economical expedient."[1]

I have quoted the opinions of a philosopher and of an historian, neither of whom can be suspected of a bias towards anarchy. These opinions may be read with advantage in the light of the facts of our own time as narrated in journals that represent the classes supposed to be most interested in the maintenance of the existing order. A recent article in the *Times* has dealt with the social and economic conditions now prevalent in the most advanced of modern republics. The United States—with its highly-developed industrial organisation, its vast resources, and its colossal fortunes—includes among its inhabitants, in fairly prosperous years, not less than 4,000,000 paupers. If we divide the entire population into 3,000 parts, one of these parts will own more than a fifth of the total wealth of the whole country. In other words, twenty per cent. of the nation's wealth is owned by less than one-thirtieth per cent. of the population. In New York City, with its brilliant society, its boundless luxury, and its profligate extravagance, two-thirds of the inhabitants live in tenement houses. In these tenements are 3,000,000 living-rooms into which, as they have no windows, no ray of sunlight ever comes. One in every ten of this city's inhabitants receives a pauper's burial. In 1903, in the borough of Man-

1. "Six Centuries of Work and Wages," ch. xvii.

hattan alone, 60,000 families were evicted from their homes.[1] If we turn to Great Britain we find that, of 400,000 persons who die annually, five-sixths leave no property at all; while, of the £300,000,000 which passes at death each year, one half is left by less than 2,000 people. According to statistical data available for 1911, one-ninth of the population possessed one-half of the national income, while at least thirty-two per cent. of men employed in regular occupation received less than twenty-five shillings a week. In the report of Sir Charles Cameron on the public health of Dublin, published October 17th, 1913, there are more than 21,000 single room tenements in the city of Dublin. "It is now admitted," comments the *Times*, "by all classes in Dublin that the state of the slums is a civic disgrace and danger."

We are all more or less familiar with the existence of such facts as I have quoted—too familiar, it may be, to feel the shock of them. Our sensibility is so dulled by their frequent repetition that we are only too inclined to take them for granted and pass on our way. If we are so far affected as to feel uncomfortable, we perhaps seek an anodyne in pious reflection on the mysterious dispensations of Providence, or we possibly lament the inexorable character of natural and economic laws. Quite a number of plausible excuses are available if the mind be fixed upon the goal of convenient conclusions. But, however disagreeable may be the facts to which I have referred, I must ask the reader to consider them fairly, without shifts or evasions. It is only thus that we can hope to understand the anarchist point of view. "We know," said Reclus, "that we are defending the cause of the poor, the disinherited, and the suffering."[2] No doubt the language of anarchist attack is often extreme, but rhetorical exaggeration is a frailty to which all reformers are liable. The real question is, not whether

1. The *Times*, weekly edition, 28th August, 1908.
2. *Contemporary Review*, May, 1884, 637.

the language of censure is wholly true, but whether it is sufficiently near the truth to explain a deep antipathy to existing institutions.

A few extracts will serve to illustrate the view taken by anarchists of the institution of private property as it has developed in modern States.

"What men aim at in life," said Tolstoy, "is not to do what they think good, but to call as many things as possible 'mine.' . . . It is a crime that tens of thousands of hungry, cold, deeply degraded human beings are living in Moscow, while I with a few thousand others have tenderloin and sturgeon for dinner, and cover horses and floors with blankets and carpets." [1]

"The ignorant," wrote Reclus, quoting the Mahabharata, "are not the friends of the wise; the man who has no cart is not the friend of him who has a cart. Friendship is the daughter of equality; it is never born of inequality." [2]

"Laws," exclaimed Proudhon, "are cobwebs for the powerful and rich, chains which no steel can break for the little and the poor, fishers' nets in the hands of the government." [3]

"We enact many laws that manufacture criminals," protests Tucker, "and then a few that punish them." [4]

In the nineteenth century, says Doctor Leete in Bellamy's story,

"fully nineteen-twentieths of the crime, using the word broadly to include all sorts of misdemeanours, resulted from the inequality in the possessions of individuals; want tempted the poor, lust of greater gains, or the desire to preserve former gains, tempted the well-to-do. Directly or indirectly, the desire for money, which then meant every good thing, was the motive of all this crime, the tap-root of a vast poison growth, which the

1. Quoted Eltzbacher, "Anarchism," 250-2.
2. *Contemporary Review*, May, 1884, 636.
3. Quoted, Eltzbacher, "Anarchism," 70.
4. *Ibid.*, 193.

machinery of law, courts, and police could barely prevent from choking civilisation outright."[1]

The anarchist attacks government on other grounds than the inequities of our existing system of property. He shows how large a part has been played in the history of political institutions by force, violence, fraud, and class interest; he dwells upon the corrupting influence of power upon those who possess it; and he asserts as inevitable the tendency of rulers to magnify their office, to enlarge their competence, and to displace the self-government of the individual by the coercion of law. The mutual oppression of one another by members of a society, urged Tolstoy, is only rendered possible by a highly artificial organisation, created with the help of scientific progress, in which all men are bewitched into a circle of violence from which they cannot free themselves. At present this circle consists of four expedients. The first is intimidation. It

"consists in representing the actual organisation of the State as something sacred and immutable. . . . The second expedient is bribery, and consists in taking the property of the labouring classes and distributing it among the officials, who, in consideration of this, are bound to maintain and increase the bondage of the people. . . . The third expedient is hypnotism, and consists in retarding the spiritual development of men, and, by means of various suggestions, influencing them to cling to the theory of life which man has already left behind, and upon which rest the foundations of governmental authority. . . . The fourth expedient consists in this: certain individuals are selected from among the mass of enslaved and stupefied beings and are made the passive instruments of the cruelties and brutalities indispensable to the government."[2]

The indictment which the anarchist brings against

1. "Looking Backward," ch. xix. Although Bellamy's ideal society was not a state of anarchy, much of the destructive part of his argument is fairly expressive of anarchist opinion.

2. "The Kingdom of God is Within You," 200-3 (abbreviated).

governments is nowhere on surer ground than when the subject of censure is militarism. A budget, the memory of a disastrous war, the novels of a Zola or a Tolstoy, enable us to realise something of the evils of warfare—its cost in blood and money, the armaments for which the fear of war is responsible, and the stimulus to national hate that is afforded by wars, by the possession of vast armaments, and by the pursuit of a "vigorous foreign policy." Few of us realise what ingenuity is directed by modern governments to the aggravation of such evils. Intoxicated by the sense of power and fascinated by the lure of foreign conquest, they are restrained from war less by a desire for peace than by the fear of defeat. "By far the greater proportion of the debt of Europe," writes Mr. Charles Booth, "has been contracted for munitions of war." In the year 1908 of the Christian era, when British politicians were wrangling about a proposal to set apart £6,000,000 to provide pensions for the aged poor, the net expenditure for the army and navy was just under the enormous sum of £60,000,000! Later years have added enormously to that sum. According to the anarchist, such things result less from the frailties of average human nature, than from the incompetence, the corruption, the ambition, or the greed of governments. Even if one government should wish to avoid war and the burden of great armaments, it would be powerless to give effect to that wish in a world of governments armed to the teeth. Although most nations might really desire to achieve reform in this direction, the greed of a single government would set the pace to others.

"It is the nature of a government," wrote Tolstoy, "not to be ruled, but to rule. And as it derives its power from the army it will never give up the army, nor will it ever renounce that for which the army is designed—war." [1]

1. "The Kingdom of God is Within You," 152.

Rulers, he maintained, are less interested in the condition of the people than in the glory of foreign conquest. They deliberately thwart demands for domestic reform by diverting national enthusiasm into the channel of international conflict. The facts of the present, no less than the history of the past, make this charge difficult to disprove. The reform movement in Germany to-day finds itself confronted by a Court and a Bureaucracy which are not indisposed to profit by their knowledge that the most effective check to domestic reform is the pursuit of a vigorous foreign policy. If that check should prove insufficient, the German government would have only to find some pretext for a foreign war in order to drown the cry of civic patriotism in an exultant appeal to arms. I suppose no one will question that the war between Russia and Japan—with its terrific slaughter, its devastation of territory, and its frightful exploitation of national resources—was the work of the Russian government, not of the Russian people. If we reflect upon the condition of Europe to-day, if we think of the enormous sums spent annually on armaments while multitudes at home starve or perish, we can understand why the anarchist regards such a condition of things as a more powerful indictment of government than could be written by the hand of man. "We are being ruined," it was said at the Peace Congress in 1890. "We shall perish with hunger to have success in murder."

"It looks," said Signor Moneta, "as though the folly of the rulers had passed into the ruling classes. Now they no longer fight because one king has been rude to another king's mistress, as in the days of Louis XIV., but by exaggerating the importance of national dignity and patriotism—emotions which are natural and honourable in themselves,—and excitng the public opinion of one country against the other, they have arrived at such a pitch of sensitiveness that it is enough to say, for instance (even if the report were proved false), one country has refused to receive the ambassador of another, to precipitate the most frightful and disastrous war."[1]

Moltke has defended war as a means of emancipating the human spirit from the bondage of materialism. Less distinguished apologists have maintained the same line of defence. Even expounders of the Christian Faith have taught us how to reconcile that Faith with a Gospel of enmity.

"So!" exclaimed Tolstoy, quoting Maupassant, "Assembling in herds by the hundred thousand, marching night and day without rest, with no time for thought or for study, never to read, learning nothing, of no use whatsoever to any living being, rotting with filth, sleeping in the mud, living like a wild beast in a perennial state of stupidity, plundering cities, burning villages, ruining whole nations; then to encounter another mountain of human flesh, rush upon it, cause rivers of blood to flow, and strew the fields with the dead and the dying, all stained with the muddy and reddened soil, to have one's limbs severed, one's brain scattered as wanton waste, and to perish in the corner of a field while one's aged parents, one's wife and children are dying of hunger at home,—this is what it means to be saved from falling into the grossest materialism! . . . We have seen war. We have seen men maddened, returned to the condition of brutes, we have seen them kill in wanton sport, out of terror, or for mere bravado and show. Where right exists no longer, and law is dead, where all sense of justice has been lost, we have seen innocent men shot down on the highway, because they were timid and thus excited suspicion. And this is what they call saving men from the most shocking materialism! To invade a country, to kill the man who defends his home because he wears a blouse and does not wear a kepi, to burn the dwel-

1. "The Kingdom of God is Within You," 133-4.

lings of starving wretches, to ruin or plunder a man's household goods, to drink the wine found in the cellars, to violate the women found in the street, consume millions of francs in powder, and to leave misery and cholera in their track. This is what they mean by saving men from the most shocking materialism!"[1]

Two counts in the anarchist indictment have now been considered—the social injustice of which governments are guilty and the militarism which they foster. It would be easy to show that these perversions of the ends of government are peculiar to no age or people; and that "the social problem" is no new problem, but existed in Greece and in Rome, and has existed in every developed State of which we have any knowledge. Wherever political institutions are to be found we can trace the debasing influence of power upon those who exercise it. We can see governments false to the purposes they profess to serve, individuals exploiting legal institutions for selfish ends, and the many suffering in poverty while a few revel in extravagance. If we can escape from the attitude of mind which takes traditional institutions for granted, and can reflect seriously upon the injustice and wrong which have everywhere accompanied political institutions like an attendant spectre, we shall understand, if we do not share, that distrust of government to which the anarchist of our day gives effective expression. Although its causes are familiar to all, the anarchist may claim to be more sensible of their existence, if not more anxious to discover a means for effecting their remedy, than those respectable members of society who regard his indictment as exaggerated and his remedy as impossible. I shall now pass to consider an argument that is more distinctive of anarchist teaching—the argument that government by the State is open to the fatal objection that it makes

1. "The Kingdom of God is Within You," 157-8. *Cf.* Maupassant, "Sur l'eau," 68–76. As might be anticipated, the passage loses much in the translation

self-government impossible. Self-government implies the rule of each individual by himself; political institutions display the control of individuals by rulers who, at best, represent popular majorities.

Before stating this argument in greater detail, it may be well to dwell for a moment on the truth, accepted by ethical enquirers of very different schools of thought, that the ideal source of law must be found in man himself.

> " It is the very essence of moral duty," said T. H. Green, " to be imposed by a man on himself. The moral duty to obey a positive law, whether a law of the State or the Church, is imposed, not by the author or enforcer of the positive law, but by that spirit of man which sets before him the ideal of a perfect life." [1]

From this standpoint, the Christian who affirms the obligation of absolute submission to divine law must be taken to have assumed that man only attains to the full stature of his being when he has so disciplined his soul as to make it a willing instrument of God's will. As St. Augustine teaches, God has so made man for Himself that our own wills are by nature inwardly restless until they rest in harmony with His. Perfected manhood implies obedience to laws which, whether divine or human in origin, are set by man to himself.

If, then, the moral law is only fulfilled when its rule of life is self-imposed, a practical question arises for consideration. What social system is best adapted to secure self-discipline among men? The answer of the anarchist is simple and emphatic. Self-discipline is to be promoted by allowing the individual to govern himself. " Civilisation," says Tucker, " consists in teaching men to govern themselves by letting them do it." The fact that men cannot live together without exercising a mutual restraint upon one another's actions is not called in question. The existence of such

1. " Prolegomena to Ethics," 354.

restraint is admitted to be inevitable and, within limits, useful. But when the social group attempts to induce conformity to type by means of physical force, it is charged with the guilt of destroying that moral autonomy which should be its chief care.

"The persuasive influence of public opinion seeks to win men to adopt for themselves the common rule; the employment of physical force saps the foundations of the moral life."

To the anarchist, it seems that men in the past have been content to affirm the importance of self-government as a moral idea, while submitting in fact to the control of institutions that make the realisation of that ideal impossible. He contends that all existing forms of political society are based upon force, since they imply the coercion of the individual by the Government. Even the most democratic State involves the coercion of the minority by the majority. "Behind the ballot, there is the bullet." What is the good, he argues, of talking about self-government as an ideal while denying it as a fact? The compulsion of the individual by an external authority is unnecessary, inexpedient, and morally wrong. (1) It is *unnecessary*, because experience shows that men are never more ready to obey rules of conduct than when obedience depends upon their individual sense of honour and their social reputation. No debt is more scrupulously regarded than the debt of honour. Even to-day men obey the rules of the State less through fear of the civic penalty than through fear of public censure.[1] (2) It is *inexpedient*, because it violates the fundamental principle that forms of social control should be subservient to the development of individual character. "Law," said Reclus, "instead of appealing to man's better part, appeals to his worst; it rules by fear."[2]

1. *Cf.* Godwin, "Political Justice," ii. 729.
2. *Contemporary Review*, May 1884, 636.

"As long as a man," said Godwin, "is held in the trammels of obedience, and habituated to look to some foreign guidance for the direction of his conduct, his understanding and the vigour of his mind will sleep. Do I desire to raise him to the energy of which he is capable? I must teach him to feel himself, to bow to no authority, to examine the principles he entertains, and render to his mind the reason of his conduct." [1]

(3) Finally, the compulsion of the individual by an external authority is morally *wrong* because it involves an invasion of the rights of manhood. If one man has no right to tax another without his consent, then a majority has no right to tax a minority without their consent. No man, no group of men, can impose a rule on another against that other's will. The inviolable sanctity of the individual is, in fact, the very heart and centre of anarchist teaching. Our supreme law, says Proudhon, is Justice; and

"Justice is respect, spontaneously felt and mutually guaranteed, for human dignity. . . . In consideration of what do I owe my neighbour this respect? It is not the gifts of nature or the advantages of fortune that make me respect him; it is not his ox, his ass, or his maid servant, as the decalogue says; it is not even the welfare that he owes to me as I owe mine to him; it is his manhood." [2]

No account of anarchy would be adequate unless it dealt with a question to which I shall now refer. What is to be done with the criminal in anarchist society? Though some crimes will disappear with the abolition of our system of property, others are certain to remain. How is the criminal to be dealt with? Many anarchists advocate the stern measures of the Vigilance Committee. But Tolstoy based his answer to this question, as indeed his whole doctrine of

1. Godwin, "Political Justice," ii. 776.
2. Quoted, Eltzbacher, "Anarchism," 67-8.

anarchy, upon the express commands of Christ. Those commands, he urged, indicate that forgiveness, not violence, is the weapon by which wrong in the world is to be overcome. No part of anarchist teaching is more deserving of sympathetic examination. For, in the first place, although all men do not agree in regarding Christ as divine, all acknowledge His claims as a prophet and teacher. He knew men as well as loved them. His insight and broad sympathy, no less than the moral beauty of His teaching, give to His precepts a unique authority. If, as Tolstoy believed, the gospel of Christ was a gospel of anarchy, the validity of the popular assumption as to the need for State control is seriously challenged. And, in the second place, no careful student of Tolstoy's writings will deny that this prophet of the latter days displayed a rare capacity for assimilating and expressing the spirit of Christ's teaching. He had that which most men find so difficult to gain—Christ's sense of moral values. He did not put a Church first, or religious ordinances first. Nor was he enslaved by the traditional conceptions that often lead even good men to place an entirely wrong emphasis upon the relative value of different moral rules. For him, as for the Master, love was the supreme law. I shall not soon forget an address I once heard on the value of religious ordinances. It concluded with this remarkable admission :

" I do not wish to underestimate the importance of the duty of charity. If I met a beggar in need of help, I should feel it my duty to assist him—*provided, or course, he was baptised!*"

I quote these words, not because I am so foolish as to suppose that they are typical of the modern clerical attitude, but because they serve to illustrate in an extreme form a failure in moral perspective which is more common in the literature of orthodox Christianity than in the writings of Tolstoy. I do not doubt that this excommunicated sinner understood Christ better, and was more actively concerned to fulfil the law of Christ, than the dignified ecclesiastics who denied him the rites of the church.

The express commands of Christ upon which Tolstoy based his social faith have been a source of endless perplexity to multitudes in their attempt to apply the Christian ethic to everyday practice:

"Love one another; Resist not evil; Give to him that asketh of thee, and from him that would borrow of thee turn not thou away; Whosoever shall smite thee on the right cheek, turn to him the other also; If any man will sue thee at law and take away thy coat, let him have thy cloak also."

Tolstoy maintained that these simple commands had been transformed and perverted to suit the world.

"Men, if they are inimical to Christianity, utterly deny the sense of Christ's doctrine; but if they are leniently inclined, then, from the height of their superior wisdom, they amend it, taking for granted that Christ would have said what they think He meant, had He known how to express Himself."[1]

No one will deny, I suppose, that the Christian layman of to-day is too often distinguished less by his zeal in carrying out Christ's plain commands than by his ingenuity in explaining them away. Are there not individuals who remain without the Christian pale because they cannot accept the Christian ethic as Christ taught it? Tolstoy has related how his whole interpretation of the Christ law was illumined by the text, "Ye have heard that it was said, eye for eye, and tooth for tooth. But I say to you, *Resist not evil.*" This passage

"became the key of the whole. I needed only to take

1. "The Kingdom of God is Within You," 94.

these words simply and downrightly, as they were spoken, and at once everything in Christ's whole teaching that had seemed confused to me, not only in the Sermon on the Mount, but in the Gospels altogether, was comprehensible." [1]

Although most people will feel some degree of sympathy with each step in the anarchist's argument, his conclusion that governments should be abolished finds few supporters. What are the prospects of the conversion of the multitude to anarchist belief in the near future?

I think that only one answer to this question is possible. Anarchists in general strangely misread that logic of the course of events against which ideals have so often proved powerless in the past. They predict that the State must soon cease to be. They proclaim the swift inauguration of a new social order where all shall be free, none shall be oppressed, all shall work, no one shall be poor, and every one shall enjoy the fruits of his toil. After the revolution, says Kropotkin,

"the workers will go away from the city and return to the country. With the help of machinery which will enable the weakest among us to support it, they will introduce into the methods of cultivation a revolution similar to that introduced into the ideas and conditions of those who were before but slaves. Here hundreds of acres will be covered with glass houses, and men and women will tend with gentle hands the young plants. Elsewhere hundreds of acres will be cleaned and broken up by machinery worked by steam, improved by manures and enriched by various growths. Laughing troops of workers will in due time cover these fields with seeds, guided in their work and in their experiments by those who understand agriculture, but all of them continually animated by the powerful and practical spirit of a people that has woke up from a long sleep and sees before it the happiness of all, that

1. Tolstoy, "What I Believe."

lighthouse of humanity shedding its rays afar. And in two or three months an early harvest will relieve their most pressing needs, and provide with food a people who after centuries of silent hope will at last be able to satisfy its hunger or eat as its appetite desires." [1]

What countenance is lent to such forecasts by the actual course of events? The anarchist foretells the speedy abolition of the State. But if there is one fact about modern social progress more evident and indisputable than all others, it is the progressive widening of the area of State regulation and compulsion. The anarchist, conscious of the increasing difficulties in the way of the realisation of his ideals as social communities grow larger, predicts the multiplication of small communities which are to be free and independent of one another. But the general trend of social evolution has been, and is, in the direction of social organisation on a vast scale. Finally, the anarchist, realising that the highly complex community, with its elaborate division of labour, involves increasing restraints upon each in the alleged interests of all, predicts a new era in which the separation of mental from bodily labour will come to an end and poets and scientists will print their own writings. But the actual course of social evolution is in the direction of an increasingly elaborate division of labour as a means to promoting the social and economic efficiency of each individual. The great facts of social progress, the stubborn, relentless, invincible realities of the social trend, are thus in absolute disaccord with anarchist prophecy. Whether we regard this disaccord as unfortunate or fortunate, we cannot ignore it.

The present trend of social evolution, then, suggests that the abolition of political institutions is unlikely to be effected within any measurable period. As a gospel of reform, anarchy is impracticable. But

1. Quoted, Zenker, "Anarchism," 152-3.

the further question whether anarchy would be desirable, if it were practicable, is still worthy of brief notice. The argument of Tolstoy would be dismissed by some critics as irrelevant. "If Christ taught anarchy, so much the worse for Christ!" A better answer may be found when we remember that Christ's gospel was not designed to solve the problems of social organisation.

"He does not give us," writes Archdeacon Peile, "rules for dealing directly with the social problems of to-day. He did not deal directly with the social and industrial problems of His own time, and seems to have taken little interest in them.[1]

"Christianity," writes Principal Forsyth, "has not a theory of the State. It accepts what it finds to its hand historically in each age, and it applies to its development its own ethical standard. It deals, not with the structure of the polity, with the constitution, but with the ethics of politics. It works by a principle, not a programme."[2]

Those who desire to avoid the error of reading into Christ's message more than was actually meant would do well to ponder the oft-quoted words:

"And He saith unto them, Whose is this image and superscription? They say unto Him, Caesar's. Then saith He unto them, render therefore unto Caesar the things which are Caesar's; and unto God the things that are God's."

Apart from the fact that Christ does not affect to deal with the problems of political organisation, it is at least doubtful whether the commands to which Tolstoy refers mean more than that a man should love his enemy. True, they may be regarded as enjoining both an inward state of feeling and an external mode

1. "The Reproach of the Gospel," 103-4.
2 *Contemporary Review*, July 1910, 82.

of expression. But before we put such an interpretation on Christ's teaching, we must remember that He conceived Himself as having a message for all ages and all peoples. A prophet whose ambition soars so high necessarily ignores that logic of circumstance which must enter into the calculations of individuals who have to take account of conditions of time and place. The disciple who seeks to live by the Christ law must recognise that the supremely important thing is to interpret that law in the spirit, rather than to regard it as a positive prescription for immediate and literal application. It is at least arguable that, in a world where the vast majority are still unregenerate, the injunction to return good for evil is fully and loyally observed by the individual who, whether he suffers a wrong without resistance or assists in the repression of wrong, has cleansed his heart of all hatred and revenge. So interpreted the Gospel message is a stern doctrine, perhaps " a rapture too severe for weak mortality "; but it is far from being a Gospel of anarchy.

Two answers, then, have been suggested to Tolstoy's interpretation of the Gospel message :— Christ does not deal with the problems of political organisation; and the whole character of His message as one for all ages and peoples necessarily imposes upon individuals who seek to apply it the obligation of a broad and liberal interpretation, with a view to giving such practical form to the spirit as the particular circumstances of time and place may admit. With regard to the latter of these answers, note should be taken of Tolstoy's own admission that the precept of non-resistance to evil represents a moral ideal that can only be actualised under particular conditions. He denied, not the utility of governments in the past, but the need of them in the present. He held that Christ's teaching had become so far assimilated by the human spirit that man was inwardly conscious of a contradiction between Christian doctrine and civic institutions; and he regarded the attainment of this consciousness as a proof that men were ready to pass from the pagan social order to the Christian or divine order.

"To every man in our time it must be clear that true Christianity, the doctrine of humility, forgiveness, love, is incompatible with the State and its haughtiness, its deeds of violence, its capital punishments and wars."[1]

What, however, seemed so clear to Tolstoy does not appear so clear to other people. Most of those who have given any serious thought to the matter will agree that, even in our own day, the teaching of Christ can only be understood aright when it is regarded, not as presenting a form of polity, but as upholding an ideal of individual duty; not as a complete compendium, defining the whole code of man's duties and admitting of literal application under all conditions of time and place, but as a broad principle of conduct, concerned with the spirit of men's relationships to others, rather than with the precise form in which that spirit may find expression.

But if we put on one side, as at least inconclusive, the argument from the teaching of Christ, our answer to the question whether anarchy be desirable must depend upon our view of human character. Human character, according to most anarchists, is essentially good, not evil; noble, not ignoble; loyal, not disloyal; industrious not idle; dominated by love, not by hate. Such evil attributes as we find in man to-day are regarded as due supremely to a governmental tyranny and the institutions which that tyranny has fostered or created. The individual is good; the State alone is evil. The real facts appear to be that a State is what its citizens make it; that a community has as good a government as it deserves; and that the life of the individual is a continued struggle between the elements

1. "The Kingdom of God is Within You," 246-8.

of good and evil, between loyalty and disloyalty, industry and indolence, love and hate. Man's progress towards a perfect life consists in the gradual subordination of that which is evil to that which is good. He is evolved in the course of long ages from the beast; in the process of that evolution he slowly acquires self-consciousness and a sense of moral responsibility; but in all stages the marks of his humble origin are as apparent when we regard his moral character as when we regard his physical frame. Always and everywhere the struggle between good and evil continues; always and everywhere the enthusiastic visionary who imagines that some new reform in human institutions will eradicate evil and leave the good triumphant is doomed to tragic disillusionment. When Egidy proclaims the possibility of a new social paradise which is to be inaugurated by getting rid of political institutions, he makes the significant addition: "Of course, the 'old Adam' must be left outside." But, as Zenker retorts, it is not so easy to leave the old Adam outside.

No, it is not so easy to leave the old Adam outside. The anarchist does well when he affirms the fact of human worth; his mistake consists in slurring over the fact of human frailty. The mistake is a serious one, because it leads to false conceptions of liberty and of the best means for its realisation. The maxim of anarchy is "Do as thou wilt." But "He who is to be a law unto himself should have a perfect self." Experience shows that the maxim of anarchy is dangerous even in the modified form which was advocated by *laissez faire* politicians of a past generation. The time may come when man may be trusted to do as he likes; but, as Renan pointed out, that ideal is a long way off, and there could be no surer means of removing it to an indefinite distance than for the State to withdraw its controlling influence too soon. If we deal with human character and needs as we find them, we are driven to the conclusion that stern discipline is necessary, not merely in order to restrain the free action of some in the interest of the free action of many, but also to promote the well-being and liberty of the very individuals whose free action is being restrained.

"A thousand years see the rise and fall of many generations, yet they are but a short period in the history of the Race; and on the most flattering estimate of progress the most we can claim for Humanity in Science and Morals is that it is emerging from a troublesome childhood into a somewhat petulant youth. *Discipline may be changed and modified to suit with growth, but it cannot safely be relaxed.* We still need the help and guidance of external coercion, because the rules and limitations which seem to hamper free achievement are really what make any achievement possible for most of us." [1]

Because human government is subject to multitudinous imperfections, the anarchist would abolish all forms of political control; concluding, as is not unnatural, that if there were no government there could be no bad government. Because the existing system of property is grossly inequitable, he is disposed to urge its complete abolition; concluding, as is also not unnatural, that if there were no private property there could be no such crime as theft. Such methods of dealing with the complex problems of social life have the merit of an apparent simplicity; but, if they were applied consistently, society would soon pass into the stage reached by the man who sought to give effect to an ancient injunction about sacrificing "the offending member," only to discover that he would soon have no member left. A divine discontent with existing ills is admirable; but not less admirable is a sense of proportion in the choice of remedies. The anarchist displays the former virtue in a rare degree; his sense of proportion is conspicuous by its absence.

If the anarchist scheme of social regeneration is

1. Peile, "The Reproach of the Gospel," 130.

neither practicable nor desirable, how are we to explain its present influence? Those who would place anarchist literature in the archives of criminal research have their own answer to this question; but I do not think it is a correct one. The lives of the leaders of the movement may suggest a misguided philanthropy; they certainly do not justify the imputation of criminality. The real explanation of the influence of anarchist doctrine to-day must be found in the important truths underlying that doctrine. An attempt to state these truths will conclude my prologue.

In the first place, although the anarchist may be wrong in his remedy for existing social ills, he is fundamentally right in insisting upon their reality and gravity. Our wars, our armaments, the character of our foreign policies, the inequities of our system of property, and the abiding tragedy of the proletariat—these are sinister and significant facts. They cannot be denied; and they are capable of making a powerful appeal to the popular imagination. They need to be met by action rather than by argument. Argument may demonstrate that the remedy of the anarchist would only aggravate the diseases he seeks to cure; but the true and effective answer to anarchy must be found, not in dialectics, but in a persistent policy of reform. The believer in political institutions should seek to make them more worthy of popular allegiance. He should strive for the promotion of international arbitration as a solution of international difficulties. He should seek to realise, with Victor Hugo, that homicide does not become glorious simply because many are killed instead of one; and that theft does not become beautiful simply because it attacks the territory of a people instead of the property of a private individual. Above all, he should seek to realise the urgency of the social problem as it confronts us to-day. Anarchism confronts our sense of citizenship with a challenge which we should do well to take seriously. Many who despise the anarchist are beneath rather than above him. The anarchist sees great evils, and seeks to remedy them; his censor is too often the type of person who is indifferent to social maladies because he does not happen to suffer by them. Truth to tell, the enemy to the existing social order is not the anarchist, but the individual who thinks only of himself or of his class—the man of wealth to whom personal comfort and parade are everything and social obligation nothing, the labourer who preaches a class war, the elector who will never go to the polls. These are infinitely more dangerous to the social order than the anarchist. From the anarchist we have much to learn; from the man who can think of nothing but vested interests, or is seeking to promote hatred in our social relations, or is wholly indifferent to the problems our statesmen are seeking to solve, we have much to fear.

In the second place, although the anarchist may be wrong in thinking that men can afford to dispense with the controlling influence of the State, he is fundamentally right in insisting upon the importance of self-government as an ideal to the realisation of which the efforts of the ruling powers should be directed. Political institutions are necessary as a means to realising the conditions through which the better self can become conscious and operative among men; but this end can only be attained when the institutions are so framed as to enable and teach men to govern themselves. When the anarchist bids us resist all forms of tyranny, and think for ourselves instead of taking our rule of life from the State or public opinion, he is declaring a message of which our generation stands much in need. The bloody struggles by which democratic institutions have been gained are past. We have not fought for those institutions: we have inherited them; and we are less conscious of their value than of their limitations. We see that the possession of them has not solved all our difficulties; we may even be inclined, in a spirit of petulance, to doubt whether they are worth troubling about. Some look upon democracy as a colossal blunder. Others think it no shame to submit to the tyranny of the many as long as they escape the tyranny of the few; and they display a growing disposition to look to the State as an earthly providence which is to guide and direct them in all their ways.

In the third place, we might borrow with advantage something of that faith in man's responsibility to the call of the good which, though often associated with foolish extravagances as it is presented to us by exponents of anarchy, has formed part of the message of the world's greatest teachers. If the commands of Christ cannot be recommended for universal acceptance in their literal sense, they stand nevertheless for ideas that have their value for all ages and peoples—for the patriot not less than for the anarchist; and for the State in its system of penal discipline not less than for the private citizen in his daily life. Of the moody, spasmodic, and unreflecting sentimentalism that condones wrong-doing, we have indeed enough and to spare. What is lacking is a recognition of the immense possibilities of a policy that shall subordinate punishment to the purpose of reforming the character of the wrong-doer, and shall not overlook the value of other means for promoting this purpose—especially the appeal to higher impulse.

Finally, the services of the doctrine of anarchy are not limited to the truths to which it gives expression. Perhaps its supreme service is to be found in its challenge to traditional assumptions in politics—to somnolent convictions, or, as Mill would say, "to the deep slumber of decided opinion." Any one who has faced that challenge fairly, and has sought to balance its strength and weakness, will approach the study of the principles of legislation with a new interest and a wider outlook. Such, at least, is the belief of the writer who now submits the results of his own study to the reader's consideration.

PART I

THE STATEMENT OF PRINCIPLES.

CHAPTER I

LEGISLATIVE IDEALISM IN THE NINETEENTH CENTURY.

MODERN politics divide into two grand problems—the organisation of the State, and the definition of its functions. The first problem includes such questions as the following:—Is the ideal polity aristocratic or democratic? How should representative legislatures be constituted? Who should be entitled to vote at general elections? What is the best method of conducting elections? Within what limits, if at all, should the Referendum and the Initiative be employed for the purpose of giving effect to the popular will? Should the executive be elected for a fixed term, or be immediately dependent upon the will of Parliamentary majorities?

The second problem includes such questions as the following:—What things are best done by the State and the individual respectively? How far is the State justified in controlling the actions of the individual citizen in his own or the general interest? Within what limits is it wise to allow individuals to work out their own salvation on their own lines? How far, if at all, is the State called upon to promote morality and religion? Should the industrial system of the community be State-owned, or merely State-regulated? If the latter, what degree of regulation is desirable?

The history of politics in the nineteenth century is the story of an endeavour to provide a provisional solution of the problems just indicated. The results of that endeavour can be seen in innumerable statutes which testify to a legislative activity without parallel in the whole range of history. The political institutions of Christendom were transformed; democracy succeeded to aristocracy; and far-reaching changes were effected in the laws defining the functions of government and the liberty of the subject. A movement so remarkable suggests a question of more than speculative interest. Can we discover in the legislation of the nineteenth century the predominating influence of any one ideal?

I believe that, so far as British politics are concerned, the question can be answered in the affirmative. This statement is advanced subject to three explanations. In the first place, the ideal is unconscious, rather than conscious. It is something whose nature is being slowly realised, something that finds expression in action long before it has been formulated in speech. It is

> "specially characteristic of our English habit in politics," writes Mr. J. H. B. Masterman, "that we first do things and then start theories to account for our doing them. No great revolution in England has ever been started by political philosophers; but political philosophers have always been found to justify revolutions already made." [1]

This, of course, must not be taken too literally. If so taken, it does less than justice either to the multitude or to the political philosopher. The British constitution has not been built "as bees construct honeycomb without undergoing the degradation of knowing what they are about." Nor, again, have political philosophers been without influence upon the course of events. The theoretical justification of the Puritan Revolution, for example, is to be found in the works of Locke; but Locke was not without predecessors who exercised a very important influence upon the movement which he defended. At the same time, the most important work of political philosophers in England has undoubtedly

1. "Parliament and the People," 3.

been, not to originate ideas, but to interpret them; to make explicit what was already implicit in the popular consciousness; to formulate in an ordered system of faith the vague and often conflicting expressions of popular aspiration. Certainly, in the politics of the nineteenth century, the originality of successive generations of thinkers is often imaginary—the result of taking the opinion and conduct of a preceding generation at their surface value. If we would realise the nature of the deeper purposes of the national life, we must look beyond conduct, and beyond popular professions or party creeds, to that innermost spirit which conduct, professions, and creeds only serve to reveal. When I assert the dominating influence of a single ideal in the politics of the nineteenth century, I mean that a real unity of development underlies the political and legal change of the period; and that we have to deal, not, as one eminent writer suggests, with successive and unrelated currents of opinion, but with a single movement, in the course of which there has been a progressive realisation of the nature of the goal towards which the national life is slowly travelling.

In the second place, all national ideals operate in a medium of social and economic necessities. As these necessities vary in character, loyalty to a traditional ideal assumes new forms. In asserting a continuity of development in the legislative idealism of the nineteenth century, I do not mean to deny that special aspects of the national ideal have been brought into prominence in successive generations by the conditions of the time. The pressure of some immediate necessity, a scientific discovery, a war, a famine, or the exigencies of party politics, have served to give some new direction to the current of the nation's thought. Only a careful analysis can determine whether the new direction thus given involves a departure from ancient ideals, or is merely an attempt to realise a traditional aspiration under new conditions. If, as I believe to be the case, the latter is the truer explanation of the course of events in the nineteenth century, it should be possible to trace an essential unity of development where contemporary generations or parties saw nothing but conflict.

In the third place, a political ideal, whether it be conscious and reflective, or merely something where nature is being slowly realised, will never be interpreted and applied by fallible human nature with logical consistency. It is not, like a generalisation of Natural History, subject to the limitation that it must harmonise with *all* the facts. It may be real and potent although particular legislative Acts are inconsistent with it. Its value for the historian depends, not upon its being a composite photograph, but upon its serving as a clue to the general course of legislation.

Broadly speaking, the legislation of the nineteenth century may be divided into three groups of statutes according as the immediate purpose of the legislature has been to establish democratic institutions, to secure to the citizen an immunity from undue State interference, or to extend the sphere of social control and individual responsibility. These purposes are to some extent concurrent; but they acquire their maximum influence in the order indicated. The object of the present chapter is to show that each of these purposes is no more than a special phase of a general movement towards liberty—that liberty is sought at one time in a form of polity, at another time in an emancipation from the fetters of an archaic regulation, and at yet another time in an extension of the forms of governmental control. Whether this can be done without a distortion of historical facts can only be determined after a review of the general course of legislation.

I.—Popular Government.

The outstanding feature of politics in the earlier part of the nineteenth century is the attempt to remodel the structure of the State. In ostensible form, the national ideal is the democratic constitution. If, however, we ask why the democratic constitution appeared so desirable, it is not easy to find a simple and definite answer. In part, the attractive power of democracy consisted in its promise of securing a more widely diffused material well-being. But there was undoubtedly present a belief that self-government in itself, apart from any material gains it might bring, was a thing worth striving for. That the citizen should have a share in the control of the national destinies, a voice in determining the laws by which he was governed and the taxes towards which he contributed—this desire was present in varying degrees in different classes and individuals, and constituted the more distinctive aspect of democratic idealism. To say so much is to say that the democratic ideal was essentially an ideal of liberty. The student of the history of the period is impressed by the abounding confidence in the efficacy of constitutional machinery. Democracy was not only a theory of liberty, to many it was almost the last word to be said about liberty. James Mill

"felt," wrote John Stuart Mill in his Autobiography, "as if all would be gained, if the whole population were taught to read, if all sorts of opinions were allowed to be addressed to them by word and in writing, and if by means of the suffrage they could nominate a legislature to give effect to the opinions they adopted."[1]

II.—*Laissez Faire*

Whatever may have been the hopes of those individuals and classes through whose co-operation democratic institutions were established, the identification of the liberty of the subject with free political institutions could only be provisional. Such an identification mistakes one aspect of liberty for the whole. Many writers have even contended, as John Wesley contended, that democracy is the foe to liberty. In

1. "Autobiography," 106-7. Quoted, Dicey, "Law and Opinion in England," 161.

reality, while a completely free people must be self-governed, the value of democratic institutions at any particular stage in the history of a nation, will depend upon the conditions then prevailing. The larger the State, and the more complicated its structure, the greater will be the demand on the character of the electorate. Whether a people will be more free under a democracy than under an aristocracy must depend upon the use the democracy makes of its power. In a word, a theory of liberty should throw light upon the *functions* as well as upon the *structure* of government. The recognition of this fact in nineteenth-century politics led to the gradual popularisation and ultimate triumph of a theory of liberty which had long been in the field, and which now came to be associated with the names of eminent thinkers and statesmen, and to exercise an increasing influence over the course of legislation. Its nature may seem at first sight to illustrate the irony of things. To an unbounded confidence in the blessings of popular government there succeeded a theory of liberty as implying the minimum of government of any kind. This, however, would be a superficial account of a movement whose great exponents, conspicuously Bentham and John Stuart Mill, were also ardent defenders of democratic institutions. The real significance of the movement can only be ascertained after an examination of the meaning and historical origins of the doctrine of *laissez faire*. This doctrine constituted the form in which the theory of liberty under immediate examination became a practical force in the politics of the time.

The doctrine received an express sanction in a Report of a Select Committee of the House of Commons in 1811. The Report condemns, in emphatic terms, any "interference of the legislature with the freedom of trade, or with the perfect liberty of every individual to dispose of his time and his labour in the way and on the terms which he deems most conducive to his own interest." A later economist has defined the doctrine as the policy of allowing people to manage their own affairs in their own way, so long as they do not cause mischief to others without the consent of those others.[1] Superficially, this definition may seem undistinguishable from anarchy; but political institutions are assumed, and their authority is unquestioned, although the doctrine purports to express the just scope of that authority. In brief, the doctrine implied certain views both as to the end of government and as to the means by which that end was to be gained. The end was to secure the free play of individual interests; the working out by the citizen of his own destiny on his own lines. The means were the reduction of State interference to a minimum, the avoidance of paternalism, the removal of restrictions on freedom of thought and speech, the clearing away of feudal wreckage—in a word, the progressive substitution of self-help for State aid and State control. I think it was Montaigne who said "*Laissons faire un peu la Nature.*" The injunction aptly expresses the germ of the ideas that underlay the doctrine of *laissez faire.* The upholders of that doctrine had a not altogether unwholesome scepticism as to the powers of the human intelligence in directing or controlling the course of social development.

The historical origins of the doctrine have been variously stated. To some it has seemed the result of fundamental traits of the national character. To others, it has seemed a legacy bequeathed to politics by the philosophic individualism of the eighteenth century. To others, again, it has seemed a product of economic conditions. In reality, facts and opinion were acting and re-acting upon one another; now one, now the other, being the propelling force. Both facts and opinion were complex. In the complete scheme of causes we must find a place for national temperament, industrial change, economic theory, philosophic thought, democratic ideas, and the theory of biological evolution.

1. Sidgwick, "Elements of Politics," 2nd ed., 137 note.

The national temperament, though a very important factor, calls for little comment. It is sufficient to say that, at any rate in contrast with Romance nations, the English character offered a soil that was singularly adapted to the growth of individualistic politics. A factor of more immediate significance was the industrial change which accompanied the progress of mechanical invention. England was the first country to profit by the new conditions, and the first to recognise the resulting need for an alteration in legislative policy. Partly as a result of freeing her industry from the shackles of archaic regulation, she was enabled to out-distance foreign rivals. The wisdom of a policy of governmental non-interference seemed to be finally demonstrated by the unprecedented development of national wealth and industry that succeeded the repeal of the Corn Laws. Political economists, following in the wake of Adam Smith, supported that policy by the logic of the schools. In reversal of traditional ideas as to the end of political society—ideas that centred round questions of foreign policy, diplomatic interventions, balance of power, democratic institutions, etc., and only recognised national prosperity as a means of promoting national power—they proclaimed that the increase of the national wealth was the first condition of the nation's good, and should be the foremost object of its policy. They were, however, so far under the influence of individualistic theories about the nature of political society as to identify the national wealth with the aggregate sum of the wealth of private individuals. Bagehot declared that every treatise on political economy which he had read in his youth began with the supposition that two men were cast on an uninhabited island. As a result of the combination of such views as to the purposes of government and the nature of society, economists maintained that the policy of allowing individuals to have free play in the pursuit of gain was the best means both of increasing the aggregate sum of wealth and of promoting the national happiness. Democratic ideas, for some time at least, were in accord with the attack upon State interference—a result that may be attributed to the character of the statute book.

"It might perhaps be expected," writes a modern economist, "that we could learn a good deal about labour legislation from the English statute book, which now covers in almost unbroken continuity an interval of 650 years. There is no want of such legislation in that great book; in fact there is over-abundance, and we may learn something from the failure and futility of much that has been enacted by English Parliaments. But the great lesson which we learn, and it is an impressive one, is that legislation with regard to labour has almost always been class-legislation. It is the effort of some dominant body to keep down a lower class, which had begun to show inconvenient aspirations." [1]

Finally, the bias derived from the national temperament, the need arising from the changed conditions of industry, the individualistic theory of economists and philosophers, and the aspirations of democratic reformers—all received a new and powerful ally in the Darwinian theory of natural selection. That theory, by demonstrating how the free and unfettered struggle between individuals in the past had contributed to the development of the species, gave to the prevailing doctrine a new authority and an ethical justification.

Thus the stream of intellectual tendency, which had its immediate source in industrial change, received at various stages in its course tributary streams which served to increase its volume and force. The resulting influence upon legislation was most marked in the earlier decades of the nineteenth century. The greater fluidity of capital was assured by various Companies' Acts and the repeal of usury laws. Manu-

1. Jevons, "The State in Relation to Labour," 34-5.

facturers were gradually liberated from various restrictions, which, though originally designed to secure a certain standard of quality in the goods manufactured, had come to be regarded as vexatious. The repeal of the Statute of Apprentices in 1814 and of the Combination laws in 1824–25 inaugurated a new era of freedom for the workers. Acts were passed for promoting freedom of discussion and religious liberty. Lastly, under the guiding genius of Bentham, a long series of acts was passed which abolished many of the costly anomalies which had hitherto degraded or impeded the administration of justice.

III.—State Control.

The progress of events soon demonstrated that *laissez faire*, however plausible as a theory of liberty, was not a way of national salvation. The doctrine had taught, *inter alia*, that national industry should be free from State control. But the factory movement, which at first supported, ultimately refuted, this conclusion. Under the industrial organisation inherited by the eighteenth century from the past, the master had lived in a quasi-family relation with apprentices. These apprentices were masters in the making. Scientific and mechanical advance in the later eighteenth century and throughout the nineteenth century, gradually substituted the factory for the home as the industrial *milieu*. The conditions that made the factory possible made home industry unprofitable. In the earlier stages of the movement, the thought of statesmen had been directed to the work of abolishing the archaic system of regulation. As the movement developed, experience demonstrated that modern no less than feudal industry required its system of State regulation. The factory meant costly machinery, and therefore large capital. If the capital could have been provided by the workers themselves, the result would have been the establishment of co-operative industry. But before the beginnings of the factory movement, the tendency towards the concentration of wealth in the hands of a few had been so marked that the acquisition of the instruments of production by a "capitalistic class" was inevitable. The worker suffered in two ways: the intimate relation between master and apprentice was destroyed, and the worker was no longer a master in the making. As a consequence, it became increasingly difficult to discover in the national industry that competition between free and equal individuals at which the policy of *laissez faire* had professed to aim. The man with capital was master of the situation; the workers were held in the grip of economic circumstance. As early as 1820, Sir Walter Scott wrote:—

"The manufacturers are transferred to great towns, where a man may assemble five hundred workmen one week and dismiss them next, without having any further connection with them than to receive a week's work for a week's wages, nor any further solicitude about their future fate than if they were so many old shuttles." [1]

The antagonism between the interests of the manufacturers and the interests both of the workers and of the general community became more and more acute. The manufacturers pursued immediate gain, although that gain might be won by methods that inflicted immediate misery upon the workers, exhausted the national vigour, and wasted the national resources. It was to the interest of the manufacturer, for example, that he should be free to overwork and underpay his workpeople, to increase the hours of work, to employ women who ought to be engrossed in the care of the home, to employ children without regard to their preparation for earning a livelihood in the future, and to ignore laws of sanitation that were essential to the comfort and health of the worker. Later critics of *laissez faire* have pointed out that the conditions

1. "Familiar Letters," vol. ii., letter to Morritt, 19th May, 1820. Quoted, Dicey, "Law and Opinion in England," 120.

prevailing in the factories before Lord Shaftesbury's legislation were fatal to the efficiency of labour, and were therefore prejudicial in the long run to the real interest of the manufacturers as a class. While the justice of this criticism will not be called in question to-day, there is little evidence of its recognition in the records of the period.

Theoretically the evils to which I have just referred might have been palliated, if not prevented, either by effective combination among the workers, or by the controlling influence of public opinion as expressed through philanthropic societies. But experience proved that such means were hopelessly inadequate. In proportion as the factory system developed, the freedom that the *laissez faire* politician had extolled was seen to involve for great masses of the community little more than a freedom to perish. "Every man for himself and the devil take the hindmost!"—a phrase happily paraphrased by Dickens: "Every man for himself and God for us all, as the elephant said when he danced among the chickens." Coleridge, stung to vehement rhetoric by the sacrifice of human life in the lead manufactories, struck a sterner note. "Free labour," he exclaimed, "means soul murder and infanticide on the part of the rich, and self-slaughter on that of the poor." Mr. Sidney Webb has thus described the white slavery of the period:—

"Women working half-naked in the coal mines; young children dragging trucks all day in the foul atmosphere of the underground galleries; infants bound to the loom for fifteen hours in the heated air of the cotton mill, and kept awake only by the over-looker's lash; hours of labour for all, young and old, limited only by the utmost capabilities of physical endurance; complete absence of the sanitary provisions necessary to a rapidly growing population; these and other nameless iniquities will be found recorded as the results of freedom of contract and complete *laissez faire* in the impartial pages of successive blue-books reports."

The existence of conditions so appalling might seem a sufficient refutation of the *laissez faire* doctrine; but that doctrine was deeply rooted in national thought. It had been suggested by necessities which, if transient, were none the less real; it had been associated with the names of eminent thinkers, economists, scientists, and democratic reformers; and its application had largely contributed to the industrial triumph of England over continental rivals. There ensued a period of conflict. Evidence of the conflict can be seen in the progress both of political thought and of legislative action. In thought, it is sufficient to refer to the names of John Stuart Mill and Harriet Martineau. The former, in his essay "On Liberty," had said: "Mankind are greater gainers by suffering each other to live as seems good to themselves than by compelling each to live as seems good to the rest." [1] The same author, in the "Autobiography" written many years after, spoke of himself as looking forward to a time

"when the rule that they who do not work shall not eat will be applied not to paupers only, but impartially to all; and when the division of the produce of labour, instead of depending, in so great a degree as it now does, on the accident of birth will be made by concert on an acknowledged principle of justice." [2]

Similarly, Harriet Martineau, "expositor and prophetess of the sternest Benthamism," declared in her "History of the Thirty Years' Peace":

"No man with a head and a heart can suppose that any considerable class of a nation will submit for ever to toil incessantly for bare necessaries—without comfort, ease, or luxury, now—without prospect for

1. Introduction to essay "On Liberty."
2. Quoted, Dicey, "Law and Opinion in England," 427.

their children, and without a hope for their own old age. A social idea or system which compels such a state of things as this, must be, in so far, worn out. In ours, it is clear that some renovation is wanted, and must be found." [1]

The "History of the Thirty Years' Peace" was published in 1849. The extract just quoted stands in strange contrast with the attitude which the writer had adopted in 1833 with regard to proposals to regulate the conditions of child labour. Such regulation she had opposed on the ground of its conflict with the immutable laws of political economy!

The struggle between traditional policy and national needs was further illustrated by the controversy that raged round the Factory Laws. When Lord Shaftesbury endeavoured to redeem men, women and children from the degradations of the factory and the mine, he found himself in open conflict with the Liberal statesmen of his time.

"Bright," he wrote in his diary, "was ever my most malignant opponent. Cobden, though bitterly hostile, was better than Bright. He abstained from opposition on the Collieries Bill, and gave positive support on the Calico Print-Works Bill. Gladstone is on a level with the rest; he gave no support to the Ten Hours' Bill; he voted with Sir R. Peel to rescind the famous division in favour of it. He was the only member who endeavoured to delay the Bill which delivered women and children from mines and pits; and never did he say a word on behalf of the factory children until, *when defending slavery in the West Indies*, he taunted Buxton with indifference to the slavery in England." [2]

The earlier attitude of Bright and Gladstone to the philanthropic reforms of Lord Shaftesbury might well seem incredible to modern readers. Yet the

1. Quoted, Dicey, "Law and Opinion in England," 415-6.
2. Quoted, Dicey, "Law and Opinion in England," 234.

explanation is simple. The Liberal statesmen looked behind them rather than around them. They saw that a policy of *laissez faire* in relation to industry had served useful purposes in the past; but they did not see that the validity of that doctrine was being destroyed by the very economic movement that had been responsible, in a large measure, for its general acceptance. We might search the pages of history without finding a more striking illustration of the power of an inadequate theory to turn men of genius and rectitude from the path of justice. Happily, Lord Shaftesbury and the policy of State intervention triumphed over Liberal statesmen and the doctrine of *laissez faire*. The demand for State intervention grew ever stronger. If we look at the legislation of the later part of the nineteenth century we find its general character typified in Workmen's Compensation Acts, Acts restricting the labour of women in factories, Acts for ensuring the education of the masses, Public Health Acts, and Acts for the Housing of the Working Classes.

I now turn to consider the significance of the rejection of industrial *laissez faire* in relation to the legislative ideals of the period. Undoubtedly, the rejection involved the necessity for a fresh interpretation of the democratic spirit. From very ancient times men had argued that liberty, in the sense of immunity from legislative tyranny, was the goal of democracy. Freedom, said the great Hellenic philosopher, is at once the peril and chiefest glory of the democratic State. Even

"the horses and asses have a way of marching along with all the rights and dignities of freemen; and they will run at anybody whom they meet in the street if he does not leave the road clear for them: and all things are just ready to burst with liberty." [1]

But experience has demonstrated that freedom, as

1. "Republic," viii. 563, in Jowett's translation.

here interpreted, is neither the glory nor the peril of modern democracy. If anywhere, one would have looked to England for a realisation of the Platonic prophecy. The Englishman is by nature an individualist; his reserve, his sense of self-completeness, and his exceeding anxiety to do as he pleases give distinction to his character. Yet even in England, as we have seen, the Platonic prophecy has been completely falsified. The demand for authoritative regulation has increased with each decade. If we except a few philosophers who are out of touch with social tendencies, and the individuals in whom the prejudices of self-interest beget an economic and political "liberalism," the whole tendency of modern feeling is towards the conviction that the liberty praised by our forefathers has done its chief work. Men no longer hope for salvation through "the free play of individual interests," and "freedom of contract" between employer and employee. They have less fear of being tyrannised over by their rulers than of being exploited by the plutocrat; and they are apt to identify the cause of liberty with a policy of social injustice. I am not immediately concerned to defend such views. I simply note them as deserving to be considered by every one who would understand the nature of the ideal towards which democracies are tending as they work out their destiny, not in Utopia, but on earth; not in times simple and stationary, but in times complex and progressive; not untrammelled and unperplexed, but encumbered by the changing problems and difficulties of modern civilised life.

It is one thing to admit that the prophets of the past have failed to give an enduring interpretation of the democratic spirit: it is quite another to assert the existence of a radical change in that spirit as it is expressed in the legislation of the nineteenth century. Such an assertion, however, would be in accord with the opinions of some of the most eminent writers of our time.

"Liberty," wrote Seeley, "is the spirit by, and the principles according to, which government is resisted . . . . Liberty is primarily the absence of restraint or the opposite of government; but in a secondary sense, which is also convenient, it is the absence of excessive restraint or the opposite of over government." [1]

Lecky, in his "Democracy and Liberty," endeavoured to demonstrate the logical opposition between liberty and the growing enthusiasm for authoritative regulation. Herbert Spencer, referring to the increased taxation that has been a corollary of increased State activity, declared:

"The implied address accompanying every additional exaction is—'Hitherto you have been free to spend this portion of your earnings in any way which pleased you; hereafter you shall not be free so to spend it, but we will spend it for the general benefit.' Thus, either directly or indirectly, and in most cases both at once, the citizen is at each further stage in the growth of this compulsory legislation deprived of some liberty which he previously had." [2]

Dicey, in his work on "Law and Opinion in England" writes:

"In accordance with the profound Spanish proverb, 'The more there is of the more—the less there is of the less,' the greater the intervention of the Government, the less becomes the freedom of each individual citizen." [3]

Notwithstanding the eminence of the writers just quoted and the plausibility of the opinions to which they have given expression, the more advanced thought of our time tends to take another, and as it seems to me a truer, view of the course of events. Democratic

1. "Introduction to Political Science," 120.
2. "The Man *versus* the State," 13.
3. "Law and Opinion in England," 309.

institutions and the legislative theory of *laissez faire* certainly involve theories about liberty. But these theories cannot be regarded, either singly or in combination, as final. They bring into clear relief, and indeed attach an exaggerated emphasis to, certain means essential to liberty. It is conceivable, however, that the extension of the sphere of State action in the later part of the nineteenth century was no more than a recognition of the need to adopt further means to the same end. Liberal statesmen of a past generation, and even some eminent thinkers of our own time, have failed to recognise that the real test of liberty is to be found, less in the form of government or in the number of the laws that control the action of the citizen, than in the extent to which government and the law enable men to develop inherent potentialities for good. Seeley was right when he affirmed that over-government and excessive regulation are hostile to freedom; but he does less than justice to the fact that under-government or inadequate regulation may also be hostile to freedom. They may permit individuals or classes to take advantage of existing law in such a way as to exploit the many. Seeley makes capital out of Shelley's affirmation that a man who is starving is not free. But the worker whose whole energies are spent in keeping the wolf from the door is in a true and deep sense a bondsman. The position of Lecky is equally open to attack. The "growing enthusiasm for authoritative regulation" proves nothing one way or the other as to the relation of the popular mind toward liberty. We must examine the precise forms in which the enthusiasm in question finds expression. Regulation may cramp human activities, or it may be the means of their emancipation. Herbert Spencer's dictum is manifestly absurd. A man who joins a golf club sacrifices his freedom to spend his subscription in other ways. In return, he secures a freedom to enjoy himself in ways which the isolated millionaire might envy. The taxes which the citizen pays are a form of subscription for which he receives in return new opportunities for self-expression. Doubtless, taxes may be exorbitant or unjust; but that is not in question. My point is that the mere fact that a tax is imposed does not of itself necessarily limit the self-development of the taxpayer. Dicey's application of the Spanish proverb suggests the naïve view that liberty is a substance from which every diminution means a net loss. It sounds curiously malapropos in an age when the inapplicability of mechanical analogies in social life is so generally recognised.

Broadly speaking, as society grows larger, as the economic structure becomes more complex, and as the possibilities of collective human action increase, the more elaborate must be the system of legal regulation if the liberty of the individual is not to be endangered. If it were true that the liberty of each individual was in inverse proportion to the amount of State regulation, the savage would be freer than the modern citizen. Further, the question whether any particular law involving a restriction upon the individual's desire to do as he likes is in derogation of his liberty cannot be answered merely by reference to the fact that a restriction is involved. It is only through the existence of such restriction that he has any liberty at all beyond "the desolate freedom of the wild ass." To determine whether a law of the State is really in derogation of liberty we must consider that law in its relation to the social and industrial conditions of the time. At one stage in English history the liberty of the subject came to be specially associated with the idea of protection from baronial tyranny. In the seventeenth, eighteenth and early nineteenth centuries, it came to be associated with the idea of protection from the government. In the later nineteenth century, the achievements of industrial progress gave a new direction to the demand for freedom. When the fear of governmental autocracy was succeeded by the fear of an economic plutocracy, men once again invoked the State to action.

The way was thus prepared for a completer theory of liberty. "Political liberty," said John Austin, "is fostered by that very restraint from which the devotees of the idol liberty are so fearfully and blindly averse."[1] The negative aspect of liberty as immunity from governmental interference has its roots in the positive element of governmental regulation. That thinkers of our own day, who would be the first to admit that the regulation of the feudal lord by government was a phase of liberty, should maintain that the regulation of the modern capitalist by government implies a necessary departure from liberty, must surely be regarded as a curious example of the limitations of the human intellect. The mistake of such thinkers is to confuse liberty in its concrete and abstract senses. "Is not the liberty to do mischief, liberty?" queries Bentham. "All laws creative of liberty are abrogative of liberty."[2] It would have been more rational to say that liberty is only possible through the diminution of liberties.

The relation of State regulation to liberty may be illustrated by four propositions. In the first place, such regulation may impose restrictions upon each citizen in the interests of the liberty of all citizens. The criminal code is an illustration. Men are not less free but more free because murder and robbery are prohibited. What they lose of the power of free self-determination in one way is more than made up by increased power of self-determination in other ways. Many laws for the promotion of public health rest on the same ground. The purveyor of microbes may be more hostile to freedom than the burglar. True, the burglar commits an intentional wrong, whereas the infected citizen injures through negligence; but both are a menace to the free self-development of the citizens in general.

In the second place, State regulation may impose

1. Jethro Brown, "The Austinian Theory of Law," 177.
2. "Works," ii. 503-4.

restrictions on the actions of the few in order to promote the liberty of the many. Grant Allen has told a story of some Martian citizens who had inaugurated a Liberty and Property Defence League. A delegate from London, invited for the purpose of assisting their deliberations, was amazed to find that the liberty which the Martian society sought to defend was the liberty of every member of the red-haired caste to consume in each year a dozen of the black-haired majority. We are entitled to assume that the delegate in question had little acquaintance with European history.

"What the Polish Lords called liberty," exclaimed Lord Acton, "was the right of each of them to veto the acts of the Diet, and to persecute the peasants on his estates."

What the opponents of factory legislation called liberty was the privilege of the manufacturer to exploit his workpeople. To-day, it is no longer necessary to argue that the factory legislation increased the freedom of the community. In improving the conditions of labour, it improved the health of the worker; in controlling the employment of children, it helped to protect the youth of the nation; in controlling the employment of women, it tended to safeguard the home; in restricting the hours of labour, it provided new opportunities for culture, recreation or indulgence. In a word, restraints were imposed upon the manufacturers as a means to the promotion of conditions essential to the free self-development of the working population. The Alkali Act of 1874, in limiting the amount of muriatic acid emitted from the chimneys of alkali works, imposed on manufacturers restrictions that were found to be not hostile to the manufacturing interests, while at the same time they saved the country immediately surrounding such works from devastation.

In the third place, State regulation may impose restrictions on the many in the interests of the liberty of the few. Some writers go so far as to declare that the recognition of the claims of minorities is the true test of liberty. We can admit, without assenting to this view, that laws protecting unpopular sects, or controlling the action of subordinate social groups in such a way as to protect the minority from the majority ought not to be regarded as necessarily hostile to liberty.

Finally, the liberty of an individual may be promoted by restrictions that the State imposes upon him in his own interests. In a later chapter, I shall refer to the *abuse* of this proposition. At present, I wish to illustrate the truth of the expressive paradox of Rousseau that a man may be *forced* to be free. In a humble sphere, the municipal legislation of our time affords some familiar examples. A by-law prescribes a penalty for boarding a tram which is already full. A would-be passenger, compelled to wait in the rain until the next car passes, may be tempted to complain that his liberty is thereby infringed. If, however, he will employ the interval in profitable reflection, he may learn to take a saner view. While the by-law prevents him from riding in one car, it ensures that he shall be free from being sat upon in the next car, and possibly from being deposited in the mud as the result of a breakdown. More important still, the by-law serves to protect him from being exploited in the interests of a tramway company that would like to run one car where it ought to run two. We have all heard of the suburban strap-hangers of New York; and we do not envy their freedom to pass a not inconsiderable portion of their lives in clinging to a strap.[1]

Municipal by-laws of the kind just considered illustrate my first proposition as well as my fourth, for one of their motives may be a regard to the interests of the general public. A more distinctive application

1. The passage in the text was adversely criticised by Mr. E. V. Abbot in his review of the first edition of this work, v. 12, "Columbia Law Review," 478 *et seq.* My rejoinder appears in 12, "Columbia Law Review," 613 *et seq.*

of the principle of forcing a man to be free may be found where the will of the citizen has become hopelessly enfeebled by vicious habits. A dipsomaniac is freer in an asylum than out of it. Self-discipline is better than discipline by an external authority; but the latter, if wisely exercised, may under particular circumstances promote the former. When it does so, it makes man more free, not less so. When opponents of certain temperance legislation declared they would rather see England free than England sober, they begged the question at issue.

"We ask the citizens of England," retorted T. H. Green, "to limit, or even altogether to give up, the not very precious liberty of buying and selling alcohol, in order that they may become more free to exercise the faculties, and improve the talents, which God has given them." [1]

A less controversial illustration may be found in the control of the unemployable. While it may be pleasant to live in idleness, I incline to the opinion that the stern discipline of the "work-shy," though it may restrict his power to do as he likes, is calculated to make a freer man of him. In these and a multitude of like cases, we can see exemplified the truth of the paradox that men may be forced to be free. "The convicts in the galleys at Geneva," said Rousseau, "have liberty stamped upon their chains." "The fetters of the bad self," comments Bosanquet, "are the symbols of freedom."

My discussion of the various ways in which State regulation may promote the liberty of the citizen has been parenthetic. I wished to show that the rejection of a legislative policy of *laissez faire* is not inconsistent with an ideal of liberty, but should rather be considered as a transition to a more adequate understanding both of the nature of liberty and of the means of its realisa-

1. "Works," iii. 386.

tion. I shall now indicate briefly the more important differences involved in this transition.

1. The conflict of law and liberty is seen to be accidental, not essential. It may arise when the machinery of government has been captured by a class, or when social and economic conditions have outgrown the traditional system of State regulation. In either case, liberty presents a positive as well as a negative aspect, although the negative aspect may at first be more apparent. If old laws have to be repealed, new laws have also to be enacted. Hence, in a truly progressive society, law and liberty grow together.

2. Liberty is catholic. It seeks freedom, not for some men only, but for *all* men. The supreme achievement of our time is to be found in the emphasis now laid upon the freedom that is another's, as distinct from the freedom that is one's own. While *laissez faire* proclaimed an era of equal freedom for all men, it failed to recognise that such freedom was impossible under economic conditions that made for the perpetuation of a proletariate. In the later ideal, the State is charged with the sacred responsibility of ensuring conditions that will enable every citizen to prove his manhood.

"The law of God," wrote Mazzini, "has not two weights and two measures: Christ came for all: He spoke to all: He died for all. . . . We cannot wish the brow that is raised to Heaven to fall prostrate in the dust before any created being: the soul that should aspire to Heaven, to rot in ignorance of its rights, its powers, and its noble origin, while on earth. . . . We protest, then, against all inequality, against all oppression, wheresoever it is practised. . . . This forms the essence of what men have agreed to call the Democratic movement: and if anything ever profoundly surprised me, it is that so many persons have hitherto been blind to the eminently religious character of that movement, which is sooner or later destined to be recognised."[1]

1. Mazzini, "Thoughts upon Democracy in Europe."

3. The liberty that the legislation of our day seeks to promote is less the power to do as one likes than the power to do as one ought. This does not mean that the State is justified in prohibiting all conduct that is morally wrong—a view which is sometimes urged, and to which I shall refer in a later chapter. But it does involve a wide departure from *laissez faire*. It agrees with *laissez faire* in defining freedom in terms of self-realisation; but it implies a distinctive view of the nature of the self to be realised. The true self, it holds, is not the momentary wayward self, the creature of wanton impulse, but the self Shakespeare had in mind when he wrote:

> ". . . . To thine own self be true;
> And it must follow, as the night the day,
> Thou canst not then be false to any man."

"The nature of a thing," said Aristotle, "is what it will be when its growth is complete." And again: "The State was formed that men might live; but exists that they may live nobly."

Huxley expressed, not merely a personal inclination but a nascent national ideal, when he said: "The only freedom I care about is freedom to do right." The ideal implies a qualitative as distinct from a purely quantitative view of liberty. It implies that we should consider not merely how many things a man may do at his will, but also the kind of things he may do. It implies as the object of legislation, not the removal of restraints upon individual inclination, but the substitution of rational for irrational restraints; the removal of hindrances which stand in the way of the attainment by human beings of the greatest of all goods, a life well lived. "The further development of the State," writes Mr. Hobhouse, "lies in such an extension of public control as makes for fuller liberty of the life of the mind."[1]

1. "Social Evolution and Political Theory," 203.

IV.—Review.

While the newer interpretation of liberty differs from the doctrine of *laissez faire*, the difference should not blind us to the continuity of political idealism in the nineteenth century. The rejection of *laissez faire* was due to the fact that it gave to the spirit of liberty a merely partial expression dictated by provisional necessities. Statesmen and thinkers, in seeking to give expression to national aspiration, mistook the part for the whole. Their mistake must not be taken to indicate a lack of continuity in our political development. If we turn from formulated theory to the course of events, we shall realise that the general trend of national thought and feeling has been persistently in the direction of assuring the true liberty of the citizen. Acts abolishing an archaic system of State regulation, and Acts imposing a new system of State regulation adapted to the changed conditions of modern industry, are alike expressions of a will to maintain the conditions of free self-development. Acts repealing the old Combination Laws and the Statute of Apprentices, for example, are no more and no less a proof of a desire for freedom than Workmen's Compensation Acts, Acts restricting the labour of women in factories, Acts for ensuring the education of the masses, Public Health Acts, and Acts for the Housing of the Working Classes.

It must be admitted that the particular means of promoting liberty have varied from time to time. Protection has been sought at one time from the tyranny of government and at another time from the tyranny of economic conditions or the exploitation of private individuals. It must also be admitted that, both in the past and in the present, means are apt to be mistaken for ends. If the past worshipped the fetich of self-help, our own time is not without portents of a coming fetichism of State regulation. It must be admitted, further, that the pursuit of liberty has at all times been marred by inconsistencies and extravagances that indicate a vague and uncertain grasp of the end in view. But the spirit of liberty is the same, although the forms in which it has found expression have been determined by immediate necessities, and although the limitations of statesmen and thinkers have led them into the error of mistaking means for ends, or the part for the whole. Our own opportunity of looking back upon the course of legislation in the last century enables us to recognise an essential unity of development where contemporaries saw only conflict. We can detect throughout that century a persistent progress towards the appreciation of an ideal whose complete nature has been, and is being, gradually realised. "Christianity," said Amiel, "can only triumph over Pantheism by absorbing it." So the newer ideal of liberty can only triumph over the old by embracing it. When this has once been realised, it will be seen that, although the spirit of freedom may seem to have followed diverse courses in the attempt to meet the special needs of particular generations, there has been a real and coherent movement towards a completer ideal, which is not something different from its particular manifestations but is inclusive of them. I shall endeavour in later chapters to give a greater definiteness to the ideal by considering its relation to the development of national life and thought, its underlying principles, and its bearing upon some problems of the past and present.

NOTE TO CHAPTER I.

Some Recent Books.

Since the publication of the first edition of this work, Mr. Hilaire Belloc, in "The Servile State," has expressed another and quite different view from that suggested above as to the goal towards which the national life is travelling. He characterises that goal as one which involves the servitude of the great mass of the citizens. In effect, he maintains that the ownership and control of the means of production has passed into the hands of a capitalistic class which is virtually parasitic; and that the deeper if unconscious purpose of recent ameliorative legislation is, not to establish freedom, but to supply such palliatives as will make the continuance of a parasitic class possible. In other words, the great body of the citizens, "the proletariat," has forfeited, or is about to forfeit, its birthright of freedom for a mess of pottage in the form of such a security of subsistence as may be afforded by Employers' Liability Acts, Social Insurance Acts, and the establishment of a minimum wage with its corollary of compulsory labour. Although the legislation to which Mr. Belloc refers belongs to the twentieth century rather than the nineteenth, that legislation is so directly related to the economic and legislative tendency in the nineteenth century that the author's argument involves a challenge of the views which I have expressed in the foregoing chapter.

For the sake of discussion, I shall assume in this note that capital has passed increasingly into the hands of the few, and that the minimum wage and compulsory labour for the many are inevitable. I cannot concede, however, that a man's status is necessarily servile either because he does not receive his fair share of the national dividend, or because the law ensures him a living wage, or even because he is compelled by law to labour. Compulsion to labour is the normal lot of men. Whether it derives from the fear of the laws or from the fear of starvation, it does not preclude the possibility of his being free. The really vital questions are, What are the conditions of labour? Are those conditions such as to make free self-development impossible? Has the labourer at his disposal the means to remedy real grievances? Mr. Belloc would describe a labourer as non-servile in a socialistic State simply because *all* men would be called upon to labour, even though it should be proved that the socialistic citizen worked under worse conditions than in a State where a capitalistic class took its toll. Mr. Belloc would describe as non-servile a mediæval peasant whose whole energies might be devoted to the struggle of keeping the wolf from the door, *provided he owned his holding*. Is there not in such views a fetichism of certain means to, or elements in, freedom? The fact that a class in a community live on the toil of others, may be deplorable. It does not of itself turn those others into slaves. The fact that the mass of the community are employees of a parasitic class does not of itself justify the application of the term servile to that mass unless we are to be guilty of distorting language. Of course the word servile may be used in different senses. But in all these senses, in so far as they are at all in accordance with the fair meaning of words, there is implicit an element of degradation, and a strictly limited power of self-development.

The distinguished author appears to me to labour under two fundamental misconceptions: one, the identification of freedom with ownership of the means of production; the other, the disregard of the gulf which separates a slave class, which does not possess the franchise, from a labouring class which does. As regards the first of these misconceptions, whether the ownership of the means of production by a small class must of necessity prove tyrannical depends upon the nature of the control which is exercised by the State over those owners. The modern State has shown, and shows in an increasing degree, a disposition to regulate the extent of the toll which a capitalistic class may levy upon the community in general. And this brings me to the second misconception. The modern State is democratic; and Mr. Belloc's veiled prediction that the State will continue to sanction a social or economic order which permits a few to live in luxury and indolence while the great mass of citizens are reduced to a condition bordering on mere subsistence, appears to me to be quite illusory. No doubt such a condition of things might come about if the activity of democratic legislatures stopped at the point where Mr. Belloc appears to suppose that they will stop. But no adequate ground for this supposition can be suggested. Mr. Belloc maintains in effect that the practicable alternative to the servile State is confiscation in some form or other; and he appears to be of the opinion that the vast majority of citizens would prefer servitude rather than confiscation because they have not the courage to carry out a policy of confiscation. *Assuming for the sake of argument that confiscation should prove to be the alternative to the servitude of the many,* I can see no reason for supposing that confiscation would not follow.

The foregoing remarks take me beyond the scope of the foregoing chapter. But Mr. Belloc's argument seems to me to illustrate just that fallacious identification of freedom with some particular forms of, or means to, freedom which has led so many eminent writers astray. The ownership of property and freedom of contract have been means to liberty in the past. It does not follow that they are indispensable to liberty for all time. To determine whether the multitude is less free to-day than at some previous epoch we have to take a much more comprehensive view than Mr. Belloc attempts. We have to consider the whole life of the citizen, his training, his opportunities, his conditions of labour, his leisure, and his place in the political as well as the economic structure. On the last point alone, the enfranchised citizen of the twentieth century is differentiated from the slave of ancient society in ways so fundamental as to make the application of the term servile to the workers as a class a travesty.

Mr. Belloc represents a type of economic fatalism. But a community which mitigates the operation of natural selection is also capable of controlling the economic structure of society. Concentration of control is in many industries, a condition of efficiency:

concentration of ownership is not. But if it were, the distribution of the national dividend would still be a subject over which a legislative control may be regarded as at once practicable and inevitable. Extensions of the sphere of public ownership, the public control of prices, the progressive taxation of incomes and bequests; these, and a number of other devices, are means which may be employed with a view to ensuring a more equitable distribution of the results of the national production.

If the reader were to regard the foregoing remarks as a review of Mr. Belloc's book, he would do less than justice to myself and far less than justice to Mr. Belloc. If the reader is not already acquainted with the work under consideration, its careful perusal is recommended. He may find in it much which looks like special pleading. He will scarcely fail to find much food for reflection—a stimulating and arresting statement of the great problem of securing the subordination of the power of capitalism to the freedom of the citizen.

M. Faguet, in "The Cult of Incompetence," takes a pessimistic view of the future for reasons which offer an interesting contrast to the argument of Mr. Belloc. While the latter author regards the franchise as almost valueless unless the elector has economic resources, M. Faguet represents modern democracy as the apotheosis of incompetence. The people "encroaches first upon the executive and then upon the administrative authorities, and reduces them to subjection by means of its delegates, the legislators, whom it chooses in its own image, that is to say, because they are incompetent and governed by passion." (p. 66.) The validity of this view will receive some consideration in a later chapter.[1] I refer to it here because of its bearing upon the thesis of Mr. Belloc. According to Mr. Belloc the average man is, or is becoming, a prey to plutocratic exploitation. According to M. Faguet he is, or is becoming, omnipotent. Either one or the

1. Chapter VIII, the remarks on The Right to Self-Government.

other of these writers is wrong. In my own opinion they are both wrong. They are both obsessed by particular facts to the exclusion of other facts. In consequence, they both present a distorted view of the social trend.

Mr. Philip Snowden, in his "Socialism and Syndicalism," while less original and suggestive than the authors previously mentioned, appears to me to get nearer to realities. But even his work may seem to challenge some of the conclusions to which I have given expression in the above chapter. He contends that there is a strongly marked tendency for wealth to become more highly concentrated, for the share of the national income which goes in the form of rent and profit to increase in amount and in proportion, and for the wages of the manual workers to remain practically stationary, while the cost of living moves steadily upwards. The author, however, is avowedly generalising from the years since 1900. He urges that at the end of the nineteenth century we enter upon a new cycle of tendencies marked by an increasing concentration of the forces of capitalism and an increasing helplessness of the multitude. It would be impossible to discuss the various steps in the author's argument without anticipating what I have to say in later chapters. No one, however, will dispute that the existing tendency towards the concentration of the control of capital in the hands of the few is a menace to the liberty of the many. The lesson to be taken to heart is that the price of liberty is eternal vigilance. We dare not rest content with past achievement, not only because that achievement is in itself imperfect but also because changes in the economic structure of society present new problems which call for new remedies if we are to be loyal to the ideals to which progress in the past testifies. As I view the march of events to-day I cannot help feeling that a complacent optimism or a fatalistic pessimism are alike unjustifiable. Both illustrate that lack in the sense of proportion which comes from a limited outlook.

CHAPTER II.

NATIONAL LIFE AND THOUGHT IN THE NINETEENTH CENTURY.

"'I want to know whether ideas are ever realised in fact? Is not speech more than action, and must not the actual, whatever a man may think, fall short of the truth? What do you say?'

"'I agree'

"'Then you must not insist on my proving that the actual State will in every respect coincide with the ideal; if we are only able to discover how a city may be governed nearly as we proposed, you will admit that we have discovered the possibility which you demand; and will be contented. I am sure that I should be contented—will not you?'"

—"The Republic," v. 473 (from Jowett's translation).

"THE history of institutions," remarked the late Lord Acton in his essay on "Freedom in Antiquity," "is often a history of deception and illusions; for their virtue depends on the ideas that produce and on the spirit that preserves them, and the form may remain unaltered when the substance has passed away. . . . The burden of my argument will lie outside the domain of legislation. . . . We are not so much concerned with the dead letter of edicts and of statutes as with the living thoughts of men." [1]

The justice of these remarks, when they are read in relation to the immense range of the subject discussed by their author, will not be called in question. Even in an epoch of legislative activity, such as the nineteenth century, when the letter of the law serves to express "the living thoughts of men," the meaning of that letter can only be discovered by the enquirer who pursues investigations far beyond the statute-book. The previous chapter discussed the industrial

1. "History of Freedom and other Essays," 2-3.

conditions in the nineteenth century. I now propose to follow in outline the development of the social life and thought of the period. I hope in this way to show that a broad view of the nation's progress tends to confirm the conclusions previously affirmed with respect to the trend of legislative idealism. The following subjects are selected for special treatment:

I. The Consciousness of the Claims of Human Weakness.
II. Social Equality.
III. Ideals of Womanhood.
IV. Religious Thought.
V. Review.

I.—The Consciousness of the Claims of Human Weakness.

If an ideal of liberty be catholic in sympathy, and if the self for which realisation is claimed be the social self, the presence of the ideal at any particular epoch should reveal a deepening sense of individual and corporate responsibility towards the weak. Is such an expectation fulfilled in the records of social progress in the nineteenth century? Some writers have answered this question in the negative. It has been urged, and with justice, that much of the apparent progress in moral ideas is a purely intellectual process—the result of realising that the neglect of certain classes increases taxation and imperils the health of the community. It has also been urged that the multiplication of various agencies of philanthropic service is no more than a consequence of those increased means of intercommunication which have brought men together into closer relationships, and for which they are indebted to the progress of scientific invention or discovery. It is further contended that an increase in nervous sensibility or irritability impels men to relieve suffering in others, not because they regard others as ends in themselves, but because they desire to be spared the contemplation of the disagreeable.

Such explanations, however, are quite inadequate to account for the social progress of the period. The greater publicity of modern life, for example, has meant much; but if the vision be blurred, the light of all the suns in the universe will not bring the soul into touch with reality. The study of social life in the past often suggests, not so much the permission of cruelties and injustice through ignorance of their existence, as an easy tolerance of injustice and, at times, a positive pleasure in cruelty. The contrast between past and present may be illustrated most vividly by concrete cases.

The Slave.—Christendom no longer traffics in human flesh, and nations fight to destroy a trade they once laboured to promote. To read the story of the emancipation of slaves in the last century is to gain a new faith in the possibilities of the human race.

The Criminal.—Within a hundred years, the crimes punishable in England by death were reduced from two hundred to four. At the dawn of the last century a man might have been hanged for pretending to be a Greenwich pensioner, or for stealing from the person of another an article of the value of thirteen pence, or for cutting down a tree. The felon who escaped hanging was crowded with other prisoners, often in some subterranean dungeon where the food was inadequate, the air poisoned, and the ventilation stopped in order to escape the window tax. Crowded with other prisoners, without distinction as to their guilt, their age, or their sex! In some prisons the unhappy victims lay with their backs on the floor, a spiked iron collar about their necks, and a heavy iron bar over their legs. In others, periods of cruel repression alternated with longer periods of license unrestrained and unashamed. Hanging in chains, and the pillory, were still in force. Women might be whipped!

The Insane.—As late as 1828, the lunatics in Bedlam were left from Saturday to Monday without attendance, chained to their beds like a dog in its kennel, and with no food within reach but bread and water. Private lunatic asylums were under no control at all.

The Poor.—While the problem of poverty still remains unsolved, the growing sense of responsibility in relation to it has expressed itself in an unprecedented activity of private and public philanthropy. Hospitals, Settlements, Charities and People's Palaces have multiplied indefinitely; and the dawn of the twentieth century presents the spectacle of the organised community attempting, through various forms of Social Insurance, to render the means of subsistence secure for all classes. Old Age Pensions, the Invalidity Pension, and Insurance against Unemployment represent the culmination of a movement whose inspiring principle is the doctrine "that all classes belonging to the community should be protected against the incidents of misfortune by the strength of the community as a whole." [1]

The Labourer.—In many ways the position of the labourer has altered for the worse. The change from hand to machine industry broke the old familiar relation between master and apprentice, and substituted the less intimate and less responsible relation of employer and employed. But this change, which was economic, must not blind us to the progress in moral ideas. In the course of the nineteenth century a marked improvement took place in the sense of corporate responsibility for the condition of the working classes. This is especially apparent in the legislation of the period.

"Most of the important legislation of the nineteenth century," declares Mr. Ruegg, "has been devised with the object of ameliorating the condition of the working classes, either directly, as in the case of legislation having for its object the cheapening of

1. Knibbs, "Social Insurance," 1.

food, the improvement of dwellings, the providing cheap locomotion, or indirectly by means of enfranchising laws, enabling these classes to work out their own salvation." [1]

The justice of this statement may be emphasised by a few illustrations. At the beginning of the last century, the man who combined with his fellow-labourer for the purpose of securing a just wage was guilty of a crime. If he broke his contract with his master he was liable to be imprisoned and flogged. Nor must we imagine that we have here to deal with the dead letter of the law. The records of the period supply abundant testimony to the contrary. In 1834, to take but one example, six Dorsetshire labourers, three of whom were Methodist local preachers, were tried for "mutiny and conspiracy" on the ground that they were members of a trade union. One of them said in his defence:

"We have injured no man's reputation, character, person, or property; we were meeting together to preserve ourselves, our wives, and our children from utter degradation and starvation."

Notwithstanding that they were admitted to be good labourers and that no charge was made against their character, they were condemned to seven years' transportation, and were sent to Botany Bay.

The Child.—The factory movement, which destroyed the quasi-family relation between master and apprentice, also created a new demand for child labour. This demand ultimately led, to quote from the report of the Factories Inquiry Commission of 1833, to "a tacit conspiracy between parents and employers." At first the demand for child labour was met in part by procuring children from workhouses. Pauper children were "apprenticed" up to the age of twenty-one—*children of both sexes, and from the age*

1. "A Century of Law Reform," 242.

of five! As the supply from this source proved inadequate, "children jobbers" traversed the country in order to buy children from parents and sell them at a profit to the factory owners. The apprentice system passed away; but not the conspiracy between parents and employers against those whom Southey called "our little white slaves."

"The Reports of the Children's Employment Commission of 1840 show that the age at which children began working in factories and in coal mines was sometimes four, was often five, and generally seven or eight; that in ironstone and copper and lead mines it was usually twelve; and that in almost every case they worked as long as adults, or from sixteen to eighteen hours a day. More than *one-sixth* of the whole number of persons employed in factories and about *one-third* of those employed in coal mines throughout the kingdom were under thirteen years of age, females working as early and for the same periods as males. In many coal mines the children never saw the light for weeks together in winter except on Sundays and very rare holidays." [1]

Needless to say, under such conditions, education was at a discount. According to the Report of the Education Commissioners of 1858, only one-fourth of the children of the poor were then receiving education of any kind.

The nineteenth century might thus appear to be distinguished from its predecessors less by its care for the child than by its exploitation of him. But here, as elsewhere, new economic conditions served to stimulate the sense of corporate responsibility. Despite these conditions and the misery they involved, the general trend of the period is nowhere more clearly shown than in the increased regard for child life. While the problem of child labour, like that of poverty, still remains with us, factory laws and the action of

1. "The State in Loco Parentis," *London Quarterly Review*, 75, 260.

public and private agencies have mitigated its incidents, and the general position of the child has undergone a radical transformation. At the dawn of the last century, the cruelty of parents was virtually unrestrained by law. While the father possessed what almost amounted to a right of life and death over his offspring, he was under no obligation at Common Law to maintain them. The right of supervision claimed by Chancery seems to have been rarely exercised save in the interests of a very limited class. These things have ceased to be; and, most momentous fact of all, various statutes have placed elementary education within the reach of every child.[1]

Nothing would be more easy, in contrasting past and present, than to exaggerate the advance that has been made. Lest I should be thought guilty of such exaggeration, I shall quote the opinion of a writer whose knowledge of English life in the eighteenth century was unrivalled, and whose distrust of the democratic movement of our time was sufficiently pronounced to guard him against the danger of oevr-estimating the social amelioration that has accompanied that movement.

"I think it is impossible," wrote Lecky, "to trace the history of crime, of the treatment of criminals, of the treatment of debtors, and of the maintenance of order, without acknowledging the enormous improvement which has in these fields, at least, been effected in England, as in most other countries, since the eighteenth century. The tone of life and manners has become indisputably gentler and more humane, and men recoil with a new energy of repulsion from brutality, violence, and wrong. It is difficult to measure the change that must have passed over the public mind since the days when the lunatics in Bedlam were constantly spoken of as one of the sights

1. For a review of recent legislation with respect to the child, the reader may be referred to Alden's "Democratic England," Chap. "The Child and the State."

of London; when the maintenance of the African slave trade was a foremost object of English commercial policy; when men and women were publicly whipped through the streets; when skulls lined the top of Temple Bar, and rotting corpses hung on gibbets along the Edgware Road; when prisoners exposed in the pillory not unfrequently died through the ill-usage of the mob; and when the procession every six weeks of condemned criminals to Tyburn was one of the great festivals of London."[1]

II.—Social Equality.

Liberty and equality, though united in the revolutionary banner of 1793, often appear in irreconcilable antagonism. If, however, liberty be understood in the sense adopted in my last chapter, and if equality be limited to social relationships, the two ideals are not inconsistent. Indeed, the extent to which equality is recognised affords some indication of the extent to which liberty is desired. The man to whom social precedence represents the thing in life most worth striving for may have a genuine zeal for liberty as comprehended by the school of *laissez faire*, but his zeal for liberty in any deeper sense may well be doubted. He may desire to do as he likes; he may even desire that others should have the same privilege; but the spirit that seeks the conditions of self-realisation for all men implies a sense of the dignity and potentialities of human life—a consciousness of kinship with others which is alien to the spirit of caste, and impels a respect for men and women as such, irrespective of their station in life.

Does the trend of English life in the nineteenth century indicate any substantial advance towards equality as thus understood? At a first view, we may be tempted to answer the question in the negative. In new lands, free from the despotism of an inherited environment, the Englishman will accept and appre-

1. "History of England in the Eighteenth Century," vii. 343.

ciate a measure of equality in his social relations. At home, social superiority and inferiority are still commonly accepted as a part of the order of nature.

"The second charm of American life," writes Mr. Bryce, "is one which some Europeans will smile at. It is social equality. To many Europeans the word has an odious sound. It suggests a dirty fellow in a blouse elbowing his betters in a crowd, or an ill-conditioned villager shaking his fist at the parson and the squire." [1]

"Inequality," exclaims the hero of a latter-day romance, "is our religion, as a great man has so finely said. Our humblest grocer likes, in his way, to have an eldest son; and even sometimes, in modest imitation of his superiors, a youngest daughter." [2]

The English attitude towards equality has been the subject of philosophic investigation by M. Boutmy.

"Inequalities," argues that eminent writer, "are established in England as the result of the severity of the struggle for existence. Once established, the citizen regards them with complacency for several reasons. (1) Their existence does not prevent him from realising his ruling ambition *to do something*. (2) He is too conservative in disposition and habits to desire much change in his social environment. (3) More disposed to act than to think or reflect, his analysis of the elements of the national life is arrested half way, so that Society appears to him nothing more than an aggregate of classes and corporations. His intellectual deficiencies prevent him from reaching a conception of society as made up of individuals between each of whom, in the last analysis, equality must be assumed as a working basis." [3]

1. "The American Commonwealth," 1910 edition, ii. 872.
2. Richard Whiteing, "The Island," 149.
3. "Psychologie politique du Peuple Anglais," 188–197, 268–270. The translation is free, but serves to indicate the general argument of the author.

The non-existence of social equality in England is, however, quite consistent with progress *in the direction of social equality*. It is impossible to imagine any Member of Parliament to-day employing the argument used by Mr. Buxton in his famous speech on the Thellusson Act.

"It is necessary that the bulk of the people should be very poor in order to render them laborious; and that the lower ranks should have little prosperity, in order to excite industry." [1]

Nor can we easily imagine a member of the aristocracy of our time emulating the language of the Duchess of Buckingham who, in refusing the Countess of Huntingdon's invitation to accompany her to a sermon of Whitefield's, concluded her indictment of Methodist preachers as follows:

"It is monstrous to be told you have a heart as sinful as the commonest wretches that crawl on the earth; and I cannot but wonder that your ladyship should relish any sentiments so much at variance with high rank and good breeding." [2]

Nor, again, can we imagine a reformer of our time following in the footsteps of Mrs. Hannah More, the celebrated pioneer of elementary education, who explained that she confined the curriculum to the Bible, the catechism, "and such coarse works as may fit the children for servants." "I allow," she added, "of no writing for the poor." [3] Nor can we imagine an economist and clergyman of our time approaching the problem of poverty with the reasoned optimism of the Rev. Joseph Townshend. The poor multiply rapidly in order

"that there may always be some to fulfil the most servile, the most sordid, and the most ignoble offices

1. *Parliamentary Register*, 20th June, 1800, xii. 140.
2. G. W. E. Russell, "Collections and Recollections," 94.
3. *Ibid.* 119.

in the community. The stock of human happiness is thereby much increased; whilst the more delicate are not only relieved from drudgery, but are left without interruption to pursue those callings which are suited to their various dispositions." [1]

In truth, the movement towards political equality has inevitably involved an advance towards social equality. The advance is slow; but its reality is shown in the change that has taken place in the conception of class. Class was once defined by the fact of birth; it is now coming to be defined by the character of the function which it serves. It was formerly *self-justified;* it must now prove itself of service to the social whole, or stand condemned by the social conscience. The modern community has no place for a class that is not serving a useful function. It appreciates the justice of Abraham Lincoln's famous retort to the statement that in England no gentleman blacks his own boots: "Whose boots does he black then?" On the other hand, it is intolerant, and justly intolerant, of an attitude of condescension on the part of one class towards another simply because the forms of social service may be different. The same spirit that demands service of all invests all who serve with a new dignity. There has been, undoubtedly, a levelling down; but the process in its most essential aspects is a levelling up. The fact is reflected in the art and literature of our time. The people, the life they live, the thought that stirs within them, their hopes, joys, and sufferings are coming to be regarded as worthy subjects of art—no longer to be set aside by the artist who selects his material with a constant regard to the fastidious sense, but to be welcomed as inherently noble in the estimation of him who has the soul to interpret. The new tendency was well described by John Addington Symonds in an eloquent passage in his Essay on Walt Whitman.

1. Quoted, Marx, "Capital," i. 602-3.

"Heroism steps forth from the tent of Achilles; chivalry descends from the arm-gaunt charger of the knight; loyalty is seen to be no mere devotion to a dynasty. None of these high virtues are lost to us. On the contrary, we find them everywhere. They are brought within reach, instead of being relegated to some remote region in the past, or deemed the special property of privileged classes. The engine-driver steering his train at night over perilous viaducts, the life-boat man, the member of a fire-brigade assailing houses toppling to their ruin among flames; these are found to be no less heroic than Theseus grappling the Minotaur in Cretan labyrinths. And so it is with the chivalrous respect for womanhood and weakness, with loyal self-dedication to a principle or cause, with comradeship uniting men in brotherhood, with passion fit for tragedy, with beauty shedding light from heaven on human habitations. They were thought to dwell far off in antique fable or dim mediæval legend. They appeared to our fancy clad in glittering armour, plumed and spurred, surrounded with the aureole of noble birth. We now behold them at our house-doors, in the streets and fields around us. . . . This extended recognition of the noble and the lovely qualities in human life, the qualities upon which pure art must seize, is due partially to what we call democracy. But it implies something more than that word is commonly supposed to denote—a new and more deeply religious way of looking at mankind, a gradual triumph after so many centuries of the spirit which is Christ's, an enlarged faculty for piercing below externals and appearances to the truth and essence of things." [1]

III.—Ideals of Womanhood.

An ideal of liberty that is catholic in spirit can scarcely leave women out of consideration. If we look askance at the ancient knight whose courtly homage to the fair was found to be consistent with the

1. "Essays Speculative and Suggestive," 263-4.

exercise of occasional chastisement, we may also view with suspicion the idealism of a modern citizen who is not deeply interested in the economic conditions, the intellectual and moral development, of womankind. What progress in this respect is revealed in the course of the nineteenth century?

The question takes us back to the views prevalent in the eighteenth century. Rousseau, who often differed from other men less in the originality of his views than in the candour with which he expressed them, probably voiced the popular opinion of his time when he urged that the education of women should always be relative to men, since to please men was the supreme object of their existence. It must be conceded that Rousseau, though the modern apostle of the Gospel of equality, laboured under the double disadvantage of being a pagan and a Frenchman. But Dr. James Fordyce, the British divine, illustrated a similar point of view when he enforced his argument in favour of religious exercises by reference to the fact "that a pious woman never strikes more deeply than when composed in pious recollection."[1] Dr. Johnson, though perhaps insensible to the fact just quoted, thought a studious wife would be very troublesome, and even condemned portrait painting as indelicate for females, since it involved staring into men's faces.[2] Dr. John Gregory, who possessed exceptional claims to rank as an exponent of feminine idealism of the period, laid it down as a maxim that a woman should be cautious in displaying good sense, and should conceal any learning she might have, lest men should regard her with a jealous and malignant eye.[3] If we pass from the eighteenth century to the early nineteenth, and from the moralists who advised women to

1. "Sermons to Young Women" (1765), often reprinted. I quote from Mary Wollstonecraft, "Vindication of the Rights of Woman," 1891 ed., 150.

2. The authorities are not quite clear upon Dr. Johnson's views as to conditions of domestic felicity; but *see* Hill's edition of "Boswell," ii. 76, and note.

3. "A Father's Legacy to his Daughters" (1774), several editions published. *Cf.* "Rights of Woman," 154-5.

the novelist who portrayed them, we find ample proof in the consummate art of Jane Austen that the ideal of womanhood was subordinated to the tyranny of sex conditions. Marriage was the one object of woman's existence. For this she was educated, dressed, and launched in society. Woeful was her lot if unsuccessful in her quest, for the old maid was a legitimate subject upon which the dullest wit might venture to distinguish itself with impunity.

The eighteenth-century view of woman, with its merits and demerits, stands or falls with the feudal conceptions of which it was clearly a survival. If we look beneath the surface of things, we find the mediæval ideal of woman curiously deficient and self-contradictory. With all the ceremonial deference and with all the petty consolations of a nominal precedence, there co-existed a tacit acceptance of woman's mental inferiority which degraded her to the level of a child while it professed to exalt her as an angel. Women were treated with *gallantry*, but not with *respect*. It is well known that, on more than one occasion in the Middle Ages, divines gravely discussed the question whether woman had a soul. It is perhaps not so well known that on the most famous of these occasions, the Council of Macon II., the question received a favourable answer on the authority of certain biblical extracts: "Male and female created He them." Clearly, nothing but divine revelation could be conclusive in such a doubtful matter!

"The Beatrice of Dante and the Madonna di San Sisto of Raphael," writes Flint, "are probably the highest and purest ideals of woman ever conceived by the human heart, and expressed by human art; yet the general tone of thought and feeling as to woman, as manifested, for example, even in the writings of the clergy and theologians of the times of Dante and Raphael, was coarse and base. The institutions of the middle ages which contributed most to the cause of female emancipation and improvement, affected chiefly women of wealth and rank, and did comparatively little for the poor and humbly born. The age of chivalry, as described in this reference by many historians, is scarcely less mythical than the age of gold. It can neither be dated nor located; in every country and century in which we are told it existed, the general state of womankind can be shown to have been one of enslavement and endurance of wrong, and one which knights and troubadours did much more to aggravate than to alleviate."[1]

There appears to me to have been more real progress towards the emancipation of woman during the nineteenth century than in the six preceding centuries. That woman is an end as well as a means, that she has duties to herself as well as to others, and that such duties involve the free exercise of all her faculties—these ideas have germinated and developed, invading the statute-book, shattering the pre-existing conditions of sex tyranny, and transforming woman's sense of her mission and purpose in life. No doubt, extravagant claims have been put forward; no doubt, in the transition from the old to the new there have been some losses; no doubt women, like men, are slow to realise that emancipation brings new responsibilities. Such things have accompanied every progressive movement. But the trend, on the whole, has been towards freedom in a wide and deep sense. We hear much to-day about the unsexing of women. The fear has an obvious origin. During long ages of repression, women had gained certain characteristics which must necessarily disappear in a freer condition of society. Mary Wollstonecraft speaks of the women of her time as confined in cages like the feathered race with nothing to do but plume themselves and stalk with mock majesty from perch to perch, provided with the necessaries of life at the price of liberty and virtue.[2]

1. "Philosophy of History," 131.
2. "Vindication of the Rights of Woman," 1891 ed., 98.

Still more candidly Schopenhauer asserted that Nature had destined women to be the weaker sex and therefore dependent, not on strength, but on cunning. Hence she had become instinctively crafty and deceitful. To quote his own words:

"As lions are furnished with claws and teeth, elephants with tusks, boars with fangs, bulls with horns, and the cuttlefish with its dark inky fluid, so Nature has provided woman, for her protection and defence, with the faculty of dissimulation."

All this savours of the ethics of the long age of repression. In the new conditions, many of the characteristics that women have developed in the past —characteristics often non-moral rather than immoral, often highly agreeable to the vanity and conducive to the meaner pleasures of the other sex—must necessarily disappear. Some observers, in watching this process, declare in alarm that women are ceasing to be women. Their remark may be true in a sense; but it is more than probable that their understanding of what women should be needs enlightening. Common sense to-day, at any rate, looks with some degree of confidence upon the changes that are taking place. It holds to the dictum of Aristotle that the nature of a subject is what it will be when its growth is completed; and that woman will be most truly woman when all the latent possibilities of her nature—physical, mental, and moral—have been fully developed. No doubt there are still to be found some who look upon homage to woman as a tribute to her weakness. The view is not essentially ignoble; it begets in man's relation to woman a certain tenderness which has exercised for ages a powerful influence for good. But it is surely not the highest view. It is not even the view that is like to have the best reactive influence upon man himself. There is something better than the reverence for weakness. It is the reverence for strength. When the claim of woman to the full development of all her faculties has been fully and freely admitted, the relation of the sexes may be less tender; but I cannot doubt that woman will be more worthy of man's reverence. Nor do I doubt that the change will be reflected in the development of a new and higher chivalry than can be found, or could have existed, under the social and economic conditions revealed to us in the records of the past.

The position of woman to-day has improved and is improving. A new chivalry is slowly developing amongst us. With all its failures and extravagances, the movement towards the emancipation of woman is one of the most striking features in the history of the nineteenth century. To what has its success been due? The clue to the answer to this question has been given with admirable brevity by Mrs. Fawcett:

"The idea that women are created simply to be ministers to the amusement, enjoyment, and gratification of men, was closely allied to the idea that peasants and workmen exist solely for the satisfaction of the wants and pleasures of the aristocratic classes."

To the plea for political liberty which found expression in the doctrines of the rights of man there succeeded, by inevitable sequence, the movement for the rights of woman. To the success of that movement many causes contributed. Many noble women spent their lives in this crusade. But the success of the movement was due, supremely, to the fact that the great wave of democratic and humanitarian feeling that passed over English life in the nineteenth century had left the minds of men prepared to receive the message which was being declared to them. Liberty, Equality, and Fraternity! These were great ideas, which no ingenious logic could limit to one sex. The words of a Mary Wollstonecraft, the lives of an Elizabeth Fry or a Florence Nightingale, the genius of a George Eliot—these would have been powerless to overcome the inertia, the great forces of prejudice, superstition, and a blind self-interest, if the ears of men had not already been attuned to receive the message of freedom for womankind.

"Democracy," exclaimed Walt Whitman in a characteristic passage, "in silence, biding its time, ponders its own ideals, not of literature and art only—not of men only, but of women. The idea of the women of America (extricated from this daze, this fossil and unhealthy air which hangs about the word *lady*), developed, raised to become the robust equals, workers, and, it may be, even practical and political deciders with the men—greater than man, we may admit, through their divine maternity, always their towering, emblematical attribute—but great, at any rate, as man, in all departments; or, rather capable of being so, soon as they realise it, and can bring themselves to give up toys and fictions, and launch forth, as men do, amid real, independent, stormy life."[1]

IV.—Religious Thought.

"Benthamism and Evangelicalism," writes Dicey, "represented the development in widely different spheres of the same fundamental principle, namely, the principle of individualism. The appeal of the Evangelicals to personal religion corresponds with the appeal of Benthamite Liberals to individual energy. The theology which insisted upon personal responsibility, and treated each man as himself bound to work out his own salvation, had an obvious affinity to the political philosophy which regards men almost exclusively as separate individuals, and made it the aim of law to secure for every person freedom to work out his own happiness."[2]

On the other hand,

"The Church movements, which from one side or

1. "Democratic Vistas," 35.
2. "Law and Opinion in England," 400-1.

another have attacked and undermined the power of Evangelicalism, have, as the assailants of individualism, been in the social or political sphere the conscious or unconscious allies of collectivism. Any movement which emphasises the importance of the Church as a society of Christians must, in the long run, direct men's thoughts towards the importance of the State as the great political and moral organism of which individual citizens are members. The High Church movement of 1834 was at its origin guided by Tories who supported authority in the State as well as in the Church." [1]

The remarks of Professor Dicey illustrate the general position of this chapter that the progress of political idealism finds a parallel in many departments of national life and thought. Further illustrations are suggested by the change that has taken place in two of the fundamental conceptions of theology. I speak with hesitation, but, so far as I understand the popular religious thought of the early nineteenth century, God was worshipped as the Supreme Ruler and Law-Giver, to whom reverent and unquestioning submission was due, and in whose presence man was but dust. So stern a conception of the Divine could not live in an atmosphere of enthusiasm for human solidarity, and men turned from the new discovery of their fellows to a new interpretation of their God.

"There is no fraternity without a common father," said Maurice. "No man can say sincerely, 'Our brothers who are on earth,' who has not said previously, 'Our Father which art in Heaven.'"

While the older religious thought threw the emphasis on Divine Sovereignty, the religious thought of to-day throws it on Divine Fatherhood. Thus, a principle that in the sphere of politics had made the king a servant to his people invaded religion, with the result of developing a conception

1. "Law and Opinion in England," 404-5.

of God as One who desires men's worship, not that He may be glorified, but that they may become like Him.[1]

Comparable to the change in the conception of God is the change in the conception of the just man. The thought of our day is intolerant of the individual whose supreme concern is the salvation of his own soul. Carlyle expressed this intolerance with characteristic vigour:

"Methodism with its eye forever turned on its own navel; asking itself with torturing anxiety of Hope and Fear, 'Am I right? Am I wrong? Shall I be saved? Shall I not be damned?'—what is this, at bottom, but a new phasis of *Egoism*, stretched out into the Infinite; not always the heavenlier for its infinitude! Brother, as soon as possible, endeavour to rise above all that. 'Thou *art* wrong; thou art like to be damned'; consider that as the fact, reconcile thyself even to that, if thou be a man." [2]

Our age has witnessed a real advance towards the recognition of the truth that he who seeks to save his soul shall lose it. The old test of saintliness was to have done nothing that one would wish to forget. The new test is to have done something that one would wish to remember. The sinner of to-day is he who has striven for himself; the saint is he who has striven for others. Sins, exclaims a latter-day prophet, are obstacles to the manifestation of Love.

The later point of view is further evidenced by the increased sense of responsibility to the heathen. An observer of modern life might think it strange that, at a time when many minds are concluding that Christianity is not good enough for Christendom, other minds should be influenced by an increasing conviction that it is an excellent thing for the heathen. He might also deem it strange that Christian England should have

1. Since writing the above, I have seen an article to which I refer the reader: "The Democratic conception of God," *Hibbert Journal*, January 1913.

2. "Past and Present," 101.

been apathetic towards missions in the eighteenth century when the eternal perdition of the heathen was generally assumed, but should display an unprecedented zeal for missions in the nineteenth century when men were increasingly disposed to doubt if the heathen were to be damned after all. The explanation of these anomalies is on the surface. The change in the conception of God to which reference has been made, and the increased recognition of the imperishable potentialities of human life, account at once for the repudiation of the notion that the heathen are to be damned, and for the growing zeal in missionary enterprise. The nineteenth century has been called, not undeservedly, the Age of Foreign Missions; and, whatever may be said in criticism of missionary methods, the fact is of the utmost significance for the historian of the period.

V.—Review.

The purpose of the present chapter has been to show that my interpretation of legislative idealism in the nineteenth century is confirmed by a wider view of the progress of national life and thought. The increased sense of responsibility to the weak, the advance towards social equality, the development of higher ideals of womanhood, and the progress of religious thought serve to reveal, in various ways and in different fields, the ideas already suggested by a review of the trend of legislation. It has not been necessary to my general argument, and it would certainly have been impossible, to show that the progress of the nineteenth century has proceeded with mathematical regularity. Advance has been more marked in some departments of national life and thought than in others; it has been more rapid at some periods than at others; and the complications of international politics, the rapid increase of wealth, and the multiplication of pleasures have exercised in various ways a disturbing influence upon the general course of development. Nor has it been necessary for me to prove that the millennium is close at hand. An ideal may be real, though not actualised. It may be deeply rooted in the national life, although it stands for something that far transcends the achievements in which it is reflected. When these limitations upon the scope of my argument are borne in mind, it will be conceded, I think, that the evidences to which I have referred tend to confirm the conclusions of my first chapter. Other evidences might easily be discovered, sometimes where the casual observer might least expect to find them. Imperialism, for example, though often regarded as a mere form of megalomania, testifies to the operation of the same spirit that is found in the sphere of legislative policy. Whatever extravagances may have accompanied the imperialistic movement, it owes much of its vitality to the growth of the sense of solidarity and to the widening of the area within which that sense operates. It owes something, too, to a growing sense of responsibility to inferior races. The "white man's burden" is often looked upon as a sort of afterthought invented to justify a policy of aggression. The significant fact is that the need for such a justification is felt, and is felt in an increasing degree. It reveals once again that the national life does not exist in water-tight compartments; it shows how ideals which are operative in the history of domestic legislation also assert themselves in the trend of external policy.

In my concluding chapter, I shall endeavour to show how imperfect have been the achievements recalled in the present and preceding chapters. The fact upon which I wish now to lay supreme emphasis is that, while modern progress has not abolished ancient ills, it displays an ever-growing consciousness of those ills and a more active resolution to cope with them. The questions thoughtful men are asking themselves to-day assuredly suggest the development of a new social conscience. Men want to know whether poverty, ignorance, stupidity, and crime are not avoidable. They look at the sweater's den, the woman in the streets, the criminal in the dock, the narrow outlook of the toiler in the fields, with a new and disturbing sense of personal responsibility. Not a few men only, but many, wish to know if it is right that some people should pass their lives in affluence while others toil in penury. They want to know whether the distribution of the good things of life cannot be made to depend upon the principles of justice rather than the accidents of fortune. They even want to know whether superior ability itself is any good title to unlimited abundance, and whether there is no higher conception of the claims of human service than payment according to results. Such questions as these are not confined to speculative dreamers; they are asked by men and women of every class. They evidence a divine discontent, which, while it has its dangers and is apt to blind the vision to the immense value of the victories already gained, is a proof of the enduring power of the ideas inherited by the twentieth century from the nineteenth.

CHAPTER III.

FUNDAMENTAL PRINCIPLES.

THE argument of the preceding chapters may seem to excuse, if not to justify, a confident optimism. Modern legislation reveals the attempt of men to give expression to an ideal which makes its appeal to higher types of motive and can be shown to be a power in national thought and life. But other ideals in the past have been exalted in their character and potent in their influence, yet the movements they inspired have ended in disillusionment and failure. The faith of the Crusader is an instructive example. We can still hear across the ages the echo of the exultant cry: "It is the will of God! It is the will of God!" We know, too, how powerful was that cry in its call to strange deeds of heroic adventure. For centuries, much of the best blood of Europe flowed eastward in strenuous endeavour to sweep the Moslem from the shrine of the Christian faith. The results we can fairly estimate. While civilisation derived some indirect gains, the flag of the infidel still guards the tomb of the murdered Christ; and the faith of the Crusader finds its place in the gloomy category of lost causes.

The history of Puritanism as a political movement is not less instructive. The conception of the end of the State as the realisation of God's Kingdom on earth was lofty; it was also, if only for a brief period, a power moving multitudes to a passion of heroic dedication which finds few parallels in the history of mankind. Yet the Puritan *régime* prepared the way for the orgies of the Restoration. Even the Puritans themselves could not hold for long the heights of self-surrender attained under the stimulus of the conflict of arms. When victory had crowned their endeavour on the field of battle, they relaxed their hold upon a stern creed which demanded of its votaries that they should live as ever in the "great Taskmaster's eye." Puritanism achieved much, yet the vision of a Puritan State takes its place amongst the splendid illusions of history.

The causes of such failures are various. Sometimes the faith of the idealist or reformer has been blended with baser elements which in the end have destroyed its power. Sometimes, as in the case of the Crusader, the object at which men have aimed has not been worthy of the effort required for its achievement. Sometimes, as in the case of the Puritan, the idealist has attempted too much in a world where limitations have to be lived down to. Perhaps, oftenest of all, the ideal to which men have clung in passionate devotion has been imperfectly apprehended; means have been confused with ends; the accidental has been mistaken for the essential; and the brilliance of early achievement has been dimmed by the blunders and excesses of those to whom the multitude has looked for guidance and inspiration. Such dangers beset every great movement; and they afford a reason for submitting the aspiration of the heart to the analysis of the intellect. If this course of action be followed with respect to the ideal of liberty, we shall be the better able to form an opinion upon the nature of that ideal, its value for the purposes of the statesman, and its destiny in times to come.

The ideal of liberty has two aspects. It affirms from one point of view the duty of the State to regard each citizen as an end in himself; from another, it affirms the right of the State to regard the citizen as a means to the general well-being. From these two aspects of the ideal are derived two fundamental principles—the Worth of Man and the Unity of Society.

1. *The Worth of Man.*—An ideal whose fulfilment demands the conditions of completest self-realisation for all men implies the admission of the claim of each man to be considered as an end in himself, be he wise or foolish, honest or criminal, poor or rich. Further, if each man is to be regarded as an end in himself, then each man must be assumed to have actual or potential worth. As a citizen, I cannot accept the consequences involved in the claim of my fellow-citizen to be treated as an end, until I have come to look upon him as worthy of being so treated, or at least as capable of becoming worthy.

"My chief motive in starting for Georgia," wrote John Wesley, "is the hope of saving my own soul. I hope to learn the true sense of the Gospel of Christ by preaching it to the heathen."

The confession suggests that Wesley thought more about saving his own soul than of helping the heathen. To take it in this sense, however, would probably be less than just to the priest who declared the whole world to be his parish. But if the confession be taken in its literal sense, then Wesley to that extent fell short of latter-day ideals. The willingness to go forth to foreign mission fields to-day, if I understand it aright, is not primarily an expression of an internal conviction as to ways and means for the salvation of the missionary. It expresses the awakenng of men to the consciousness of tragedy where human life runs to waste for want of light. In the sphere of politics, men have to deal with the life that more intimately concerns them—the life of the nation of which they are citizens. And with regard to their own attitude towards that life, they cannot fail to recognise the growth of a theory of social duty which makes a far-reaching and incessantly growing demand upon their faith in one another. They may deny, in thought or deed, the validity of that demand; but they cannot ignore the fact that it is being made.

2. *The Unity of Society.*—Granted, it may be said, that a man has worth, it does not follow that the State would be justified in controlling the actions of others in his interest. The ideal of liberty is a direct challenge to this negative conclusion. It affirms the right of the State to exercise over individuals a degree of control which, on whatever religious or moral grounds it can be defended, can only be defended from the point of view of political science on the ground that men as citizens are united in a common life where the gain of each is the gain of all and the loss of each is the loss of all—in a word, on the ground of the unity of the social life.

The ideal of liberty may be exalted and potent: it can only be shown to be rational by proving that the underlying principles just stated are fair generalisations from the world of actual facts.

I.—The Worth of Man.

The facts from which the principle of human worth is a generalisation belong to the commonplaces of morality. Like many other commonplaces, their nominal admission cannot be taken as an indication that men understand them, still less that men realise the practical consequences they involve. Before I attempt to state them, from the point of view of a student of politics, I wish to dwell for a moment upon two reasons why they are so imperfectly apprehended. The more obvious arises from the difficulty of appreciating worth in others when the individual's vision is obscured by an exaggerated sense of his own importance. Pride, the first of the seven deadly sins, concerns me in this connection solely as an obstacle to vision. Until a man has learnt the hard lesson of humility, not all the study and thought of a lifetime will enable him to see others as they are. That the lesson is seldom learnt will not be denied. For long centuries, the citizen of the Christian State has found diversion and solace in the parable of the Publican and the Pharisee—*thanking God in his heart that he is not a Pharisee!* "Finally, my boy, never forget that you are a Viscount," urged an anxious parent when sending his son to Cambridge. This final injunction, remarks a candid biographer, was the only part of the paternal advice that the noble youth acted upon. Bellamy, in his comparison of society to a prodigious coach to which the masses of humanity are harnessed, speaks of the

"singular hallucination which those on the top of the coach generally shared, that they were not exactly like their brothers and sisters who pulled at the rope, but of finer clay, in some way belonging to a higher order of beings who might justly expect to be drawn. This seems unaccountable; but, as I once rode on this very coach and shared that very hallucination, I ought to be believed. The strangest thing about the hallucination, was that those who had but just climbed up from the ground before they had outgrown the marks of the rope upon their hands, began to fall under its influence. As for those whose parents and grandparents before them had been so fortunate as to keep their seats on the top, the conviction they cherished of the essential difference between their sort of humanity and the common article was absolute."[1]

This is excellent so far as it goes; but it ignores the fact that the hallucination in question is shared in a greater or less degree by every class of society. "Thank God," exclaimed a coster, "there's always someone to look down on." If all men cannot pride themselves on their ancient lineage, they can at least pride themselves on some other grounds—preferably on the ground of their intellectual superiority.

"Such is the nature of men," remarked Hobbes, "that howsoever they may acknowledge many others

1. "Looking Backward," ch. i.

to be more witty, or more eloquent, or more learned; yet they will hardly believe there be many so wise as themselves; for *they see their own wit at hand, and other men's at a distance.*" [1]

Let anyone who doubts the truth of this censure reflect upon some everyday parallels—the boasting of the parvenu who would patronise every one with less dollars than himself; the vainglory of the youth who confuses learning with wisdom and despises the ignorant; the chant of the sectarian,

> "Of course you can never be like us,
> But be as like us as you're able to be."

"Nothing but a consciousness of our own weakness," said Fénelon, "can make us pitiful and indulgent to the weakness of others." Those who refuse to accept this serviceable hint will fail, not only to sympathise with others, but even to understand them. He who would estimate others must know himself; he who would know himself must have something more than that acquaintance with his own worth which, according to one eminent satirist, is apt to indicate the existence of very little worth with which to become acquainted. He must be able, in brief, to enter into the spirit of the Breton prayer: "Help me, O God, for my barque is so small and Thy ocean so vast."

But, after all, an unjust estimate of others is due less often to self-pride than to lack of imagination. A man fails to see the worth in others because he lacks the power to see things from any point of view but his own. Far from common is the saving grace of imagination which enables a man to appreciate the strength and honesty of purpose in those whom he rarely meets, or meets only in conflict. Differences of race or creed, of station or calling, of intellectual outlook or moral standards, create barriers which preclude sympathy because they obstruct the vision.

1. "Leviathan," part i. ch xiii.

"It is constantly said that human nature is heartless," writes Ruskin. "Do not believe it. Human nature is kind and generous; but it is narrow and blind; and can only with difficulty conceive anything but what it immediately sees and feels. People would instantly care for others as well as themselves if only they could *imagine* others as well as themselves. Let a child fall into the river before the roughest man's eyes;—he will usually do what he can to get it out, even at some risk to himself; and all the town will triumph in the saving of one little life. Let the same man be shown that hundreds of children are dying of fever for want of some sanitary measure which it will cost him trouble to urge, and he will make no effort; and probably all the town would resist him if he did."[1]

Men are apt, then, to think too little of others, either because they think too much of themselves or because they lack the power to escape from the thraldom of the outlook, standards, and opinion of the little world in which they live. These limitations do not prevent the formal admission of the validity of human worth as an abstract principle; but the results of attempts to apply that principle within the sphere of political practice reveal how inadequate is men's appreciation of the facts upon which the principle is based, and how imperative is the need for approaching their study with as open a mind as possible. Assuming the recognition of this need, the statement of the facts themselves is not a difficult matter. It demands no philosophical training; it does not presuppose a knowledge of history or of the natural sciences; it makes its appeal solely to the observation and experience of the life actually surrounding us.

First among the facts upon which the principle of human worth is based, I place the fact that all men respond, in a greater or less degree, to the appeal to

1. "Lectures on Art," ¶ 94.

their nobler impulses. It was said of a certain great man that he never entered a room without raising the tone of the thought and speech of those whom he met there. No finer thing could be said of a man; but it implies much more than praise of an individual. Deep answereth unto deep. Unless there were goodness within men making them responsive to the call of goodness in another, the call would be in vain. "The boys at Rugby could not tell Doctor Arnold a lie because he always took their word." The material upon which Arnold had to work was exceptional; but his principle can be applied in every class of society. No man is so degraded as to be wholly beyond an appeal to the finer feelings. "Beneath the wild waves of evil there are ever the eternal rocks of the good." Readers of "Les Misérables" will remember the scene where Jean Valjean, after being turned away from every inn and house because he is an ex-convict, at last seeks refuge at the house of the Bishop.

"'I have been nineteen years in the galleys,' he exclaims. 'At the inn they say "Get out." I am hungry. Can I stay?'

"'Madame Magloire,' said the Bishop, 'place another plate on the table.'

"'Stop,' exclaimed Valjean, 'not that! Did you not understand me? I am a galley slave. Can you give me something to eat and a place to sleep? Have you a stable?'

"'Madame Magloire,' said the Bishop, 'put some sheets on the bed in the alcove.'

"'Monsieur l'Curé,' said the amazed convict, 'you are good. You don't despise me. And I have not hid from you where I come from.'

"The Bishop touched his hand gently, and said, 'What need have I to know your name? Before you told me I knew it.'

"'You knew my name?'

"'Yes,' answered the Bishop, 'you are called my brother.'"

Those who have read this scene, which I have so imperfectly translated, will remember the sequel. At two o'clock in the morning Jean Valjean awakes. The powers for good in him, which the Bishop's kindness has awakened to new life, struggle for mastery with the powers for evil. Evil triumphs, and after an awful struggle the ex-convict rushes away into the night taking with him the Bishop's silver. Next day he is brought back by the *gendarmes*.

"'Ah, there you are,' said the Bishop, looking towards Valjean; 'I am glad to see you. Why did you not take the candlesticks, which I have also given you? They are silver like the rest.'

"'Monseigneur,' said the *gendarme*, 'then what this man said was true. He had this silver——'

"'And,' interrupted the Bishop, 'he told you that the silver had been given him by a good old priest with whom he had passed the night. I see it all. And you brought him back here? It is all a mistake.'

"'If that is so, we can let him go.'

"'Certainly,' replied the Bishop. Then, turning to Jean, 'Before you go away, here are your candlesticks. Take them.'"

Before this final proof of goodwill, the ex-convict is overwhelmed. For long dark years of wavering struggle towards the light, he hears still the voice, sees still the face, of the one who had trusted and forgiven. The Bishop had given two silver candlesticks. He had reclaimed a human soul. Such results would not always follow in actual life. I am not concerned to prove that they would, or to urge the Bishop's example for universal and undiscriminating imitation. The immediate results of an appeal to higher impulse depend upon the circumstances under which, and the mode in which, the appeal is made. What cannot be called in question is that no man is so mean as to be wholly beyond the reach of such appeals. That this is not blind optimism but common sense is conclusively shown by the history of certain reforms in our system of gaol discipline. Those reforms have achieved much; but what they have achieved is but an earnest of what they will achieve when our criminal code and our system of gaol discipline have been remodelled with a due regard to the reformation of the criminal as well as the prevention of crime in others.

Man's responsiveness to the call of good suggests another fact. The forms of the good are infinite in number. Man specialises in goodness no less than in knowledge, and classifies others as good or evil according to a narrow standard dictated to him by the nature of his own qualities. But the difference between men is not that some are good and others evil, for all men are both good and evil. What really distinguishes one man from another is the form in which good and evil manifest themselves.

"If anything is absolutely certain," writes Mr. Lilly, "it is that there is innate in every human being a propensity which renders him prone to evil and averse from good."

To which the retort is obvious that there is innate in every human being a power or influence that renders him prone to good and averse from evil. The code of honour among thieves is a fine thing, and no mere creation of fiction.

> "God be thanked, the meanest of his creatures
> Boasts two soul-sides, one to face the world with,
> One to show a woman when he loves her!"

"It was not strange I saw no good in man," laments Parcelsus; and he gives the reason why:

> "In my own heart love had not been made wise
> To trace love's faint beginnings in mankind,
> To know even hate is but a mask of love's,
> To see a good in evil, and a hope

In ill-success; to sympathize, be proud
Of their half-reasons, faint aspirings, dim
Struggles for truth, their poorest fallacies,
Their prejudices and fears and cares and doubts;
All with a touch of nobleness, despite
Their error, upward tending all though weak,
Like plants in mines which never saw the sun,
But dream of him, and guess where he may be,
And do their best to climb, and get to him."

I have known—who has not known?—of one who cheated his customers, yet could fight like a man for some one he held dear; of a rogue who preferred prison to the betrayal of his comrade; of a woman who defied the laws of God and man, yet starved in a garret that her child might live; of an anarchist who gave his life for a mistaken cause. "I have seen," exclaimed Heine, "women on whose cheeks red vice was painted, and in whose hearts dwelt heavenly purity!"

Of all the facts upon which the principle of human worth is based, the supreme fact is man's capacity for being born anew. The cynic may say that it is seldom evidenced in human experience. I am not speaking, however, of the commonness of re-birth, but of its existence as a possibility in men's lives which scepticism cannot challenge. To the least of men we cannot deny the hope of radical reform without denying the evidence of our senses. Around us every day men and women steeped in vice, pass under the spell of some new influence, in the presence of which hidden and unsuspected possibilities of character reveal themselves, sweeping the soul onwards towards the higher levels where old things have passed away and all things have become new.

For the purpose of politics, re-birth is a term of wide meaning. It is important, therefore, to refer to certain theories that unduly limit its range. In the first place, some have sought to limit re-birth to the instantaneous conversion which is a prominent feature of most religious revivals. The suggestion that it must be instantaneous is not in accordance with the convictions of Catholics, or with those of Protestants in general, or with the facts of human life.

In the second place, some writers have adopted what appears to me an equally untenable position, and declare the instantaneous conversion to be a sort of pious fraud. The position is defended on the ground of the hysterical excesses and speedy relapses so often connected with religious revivalism. For my own part, I am prepared to affirm the ethical value of the experience of conversion even where the results are transient. That a drunkard should be sober or a criminal honest, were it but for a month, is surely something. But there is a more conclusive answer to those who scoff at religious revivalism on the ground of its hysterical excesses and speedy relapses. Any one who has studied the religious revival, open-mindedly and at first hand, should know that both the hysteria and the relapse are the exception rather than the rule. It is, moreover, an historical fact that it was as a result of instantaneous change that some of the noblest of the world's saints entered upon the spiritual life.

In the third place, for the purposes of politics, re-birth is not necessarily dependent upon the acceptance of any particular creed. Although re-birth within a religious community is usually accompanied by an adoption of the creed of that community, many men have turned from the error of their ways without any theological profession or religious belief. If such spiritual regeneration should prove to be of less value for this world or the next than admission to a religious sect, it is at least sufficient in range and power to serve as a proof of the possibilities of human nature. Sometimes the love of one has made the whole world sacred. The faith-state of Tolstoy, writes William James, "was the sense come back that life was infinite in its moral significance." [1]

1. William James, "Varieties of Religious Experience," 247, note.

"It is a gross error," writes Professor Leuba, "to imagine that the chief practical value of the faith-state is its power to stamp with the seal of reality certain theological conceptions. On the contrary, its value lies solely in the fact that it is the psychic correlate of a biological growth reducing contending desires to one direction; a growth which expresses itself in new effective states and new reactions; in larger, nobler, more Christ-like activities. . . . . The ground of this specific assurance in religious dogmas is, then, an effective experience. The objects of faith may even be preposterous; the effective stream will float them along, and invest them with its unshakable certitude."[1]

I do not contend that all forms of re-birth are of equal value. I neither deny nor affirm the possibility of a special value attaching to the experience of conversion as defined by religious communities. Nor do I consider it a part of my duty, or necessary to my general argument, to venture any explanation of the seeming miracle of re-birth. That task I leave to the theologian and the philosopher. For me it is enough that re-birth is a fact. One person may say that already the Kingdom of Righteousness is within all men, and that re-birth is merely the control of all lower kingdoms by that Kingdom. Another may say that God Himself can appear to us in every man, and that He does so when man is born again. Whichever explanation is given, the scope and value of my present argument are unaffected. I am not concerned with the question of *how it happens*, but with *the good that comes of it*. That good is a possibility within the reach of all men. The fact that it is within the reach of all men is at once an incontestable proof of human worth, and an indictment of any social system that ignores the claim of the least.

In dwelling upon the facts from which the

1. *American Journal of Psychology*, vii. 346-7.

principle of human worth is a generalisation, I may be accused of stating moral truisms. Happily, the charge would not be without justification. What differentiates modern politics from the politics of preceding centuries, is not the discovery of something entirely new, but the growing recognition of the significance, for the purposes of political science, of truths that have long been recognised as fundamental in the more developed of the humanistic sciences. The student of politics, so far from denying his indebtedness, will do well to emphasise the fact that the ideas for which he seeks to find expression in his own science have been attested by the seers and the prophets of the ages. Even the prophets whose censure of men has been most bitter have attested by their very censure their faith in human possibilities. When they seek to awaken that divine discontent which drives men out of the snug harbour of self-complacency, their criticism of human shortcomings may seem at times to indicate a low estimate of human character. But the message of genius lies beyond the spoken word. The prophet may come to smite, yet the ardour of his faith would languish but for the power of the ever-present vision of man as he may be. He who has once seen that vision—and it comes not to prophets only—will view the sordid actualities of life—man's ignorance, superstition, prejudice, or malice—in a new and, I believe, truer perspective.

"I speak," said John Ruskin, "with a fixed conviction that human nature is a noble and beautiful thing; not a foul nor a base thing. All the sin of men I esteem as their disease, not their nature; as a folly which may be prevented, not a necessity which must be accepted. And my wonder, even when things are at their worst, is always at the height which this human nature can attain. Thinking it high, I find it always a higher thing than I thought it; while those who think it low, find it, and will find it, always, lower than they thought it; the fact being, that it is infinite and capable of infinite height and infinite fall; but the nature of it—and here is the faith which I would have you hold with me—the nature of it is in the nobleness, not in the catastrophe."

II.—The Unity of Society.

The demonstration of the unity of Society would be superfluous if men were angels. Under existing conditions, the demonstration may seem possible, only by trifling with language or by ignoring facts. An observer of modern life might urge, not without plausibility: "When I turn from dreams of the imaginable to an examination of reality, I find that the individuals of any existing State are very far from answering to the description implied in theories of human solidarity. If men obey common rules of life, their obedience is due to the pressure of Society through its manifold social, political, and legal institutions rather than to any desire to promote a common good. A wave of patriotism may obliterate for a moment the baser and more enduring characteristics of human association; but the nation in its normal temper is a union of individuals who are dominated by self-interest, and are held together in the main by force; a union justified, so far as it can be justified, as a mere instrument for the promotion of the well-being of the separate individuals composing it. Evidences of co-operation undoubtedly abound; but the dominant note of relationship between individual and individual is one of unceasing competition. The competition may vary in form from age to age; it may be mitigated by advancing ideas of justice and philanthropy; but it persists as a fundamental and determining characteristic of human as well as of infra-human association. Even where co-operation exists, it is often but a means to glorify competition. The egoism of the man-to-man struggle is replaced by the less restrained, the remorseless, egoism, of a group-to-group struggle, with 'the State as keeper of the lists.'"

There is sufficient truth in this indictment to account for scepticism as to the rationality of the principle of the unity of society in the sense assumed in the political idealism of our day. Yet that principle is a generalisation from facts. Whether the generalisation be reasonable must depend upon the nature, the range, and the significance of these facts. Before I attempt to state them, I may point out that our supposed censor has failed to do justice to the rôle that is played in human association by conflict and competition. In the conflict between two savages who are engaged in a life and death struggle we may be unable to discover anything but a display of brute force; but such conflicts have played an important part in early social development. The cohesion of the tribe was attained through the pressure of inter-tribal struggles, sustained through long ages, in the course of which the tribes distinguished by a relatively feeble organisation were gradually eliminated. If man has become increasingly a social animal, that achievement is largely due to the fact that he has been always a fighting animal. When we come to civilised society, the rôle of conflict as a means of promoting human association is not less conspicuous. It needs no argument to show how conflict between nation and nation tightens the bonds between citizen and citizen. "The nation finds itself through becoming aware of other nations." Further, the competition of citizen with citizen is something very different from the savage combat *à outrance*. It is carried on with an increasing regard for "the rules of the game"; and such rules imply some degree of unity between competing individuals. The competition finds a close analogy in the rivalry we find in the field of sports. If two men try conclusions in a game of golf, an observer may see at first nothing but conflict. On a closer view of the facts he will find co-operation. While each combatant seeks to defeat the other, they have united for a common purpose; and their game is conducted under rules which both agree to stand by.

Their rivalry may be hostile; each may be supremely conscious of the desire to defeat the other; but the conduct of the game presupposes a social code and imposes a discipline in co-operative effort. Not less does the competition of citizen with citizen imply a discipline in co-operative enterprise. As regards the tendency of our time to the multiplication of groups within the State, although that tendency may have an immediately disruptive influence upon the integral character of the State itself, and although the group-to-group struggle may be less restrained by conscientious scruple than the rivalry of individual with individual, at least the unity of the several groups is being promoted and men are thereby being disciplined for membership of the common life of the nation. The group interest is narrower than the national interest, but it is wider than self-interest. It evokes and strengthens the social spirit in the individual, and substitutes the instinct of group advancement for the instinct of self-advancement.

"The conviction," writes Professor Henry Jones, "is taking possession of the common mind that men, in pursuing their own ends, have to take account of one another. If at times they may be tempted to regard the peaceful gospel of the brotherhood of man as a noble but rather empty and impracticable sentiment, the ceaseless struggle in the industrial world teaches them very effectively that in order to live they must associate. The individual in his isolation and singularity has had his weakness laid bare. It has become altogether undeniable that the life of every man in civilized society is inextricably entangled with that of his fellows. In a word, the world has turned its back upon individualism in its commercial and industrial practice, and even its selfishness has been constrained to take upon itself a more or less social form." [1]

1. "The Working Faith of a Social Reformer," 232-3.

No doubt, conflict and competition are often disruptive forces; no doubt, also, human character would appear more admirable if those forces had played a less important part in the complex scheme of the causes responsible for the attainment of present results. All this can be admitted without losing sight of the fact that conflict and competition in human association, so far from proving the atomistic character of the social structure, have largely promoted such cohesion as that structure now exhibits.

I turn to state the facts from which the principle of the unity of the society is a generalisation. Although their significance is especially marked in the case of the State, they exist in all forms of human association. The first and most obvious is man's consciousness of likeness in others. This consciousness has sometimes found an exaggerated expression in dogmas of human equality; sometimes a more legitimate expression in the assertion of human potentialities. Never entirely absent, even in the oppression of governing classes or in the clash of economic interests, the consciousness of kind mitigates the severity of the fiercest conflict. The member of the most selfish class, or of the most apparently soulless corporation, is never entirely emancipate from its restraining influence.

"The Freemason or the friar, the capitalist or the union laborer, keeps a bit of his personality, even if he has cast in his lot with an aggressive association. When the demands of his group reach a certain pitch of exorbitance, he remembers he is, after all, a man and a citizen." [1]

Men are united not only by a consciousness of likeness in others but also by a consciousness of purposes in common. In every group—whether industrial, social, religious, or political—the nature of these purposes, while in part determined by the characters of the several individuals, reacts upon those

1. Ross, "Foundations of Sociology," 286.

characters, and tends to socialise the life of the individual. The consolidating influence of community of purpose is evidenced in varying degrees of intensity; it takes its beginning whenever two individuals act in a common undertaking. Each individual brings to every group with which he associates something of the group-spirit with which inheritance and environment have endowed him, and in proportion to the number and importance of the ends pursued in common is the solidarity of the social group intensified.[1]

The two facts to which I have referred as formative of social groups—the consciousness of kind and the consciousness of purposes in common—constitute the primary aspect of the process of civilisation. The operative force in the one case is sentiment; in the other case it is the perception of practical ends. One appeals to feeling; the other to reason. Their relative value varies in different stages of social evolution.

"Our connection with the race," said the late Lord Acton, "is merely natural or physical, whilst our duties to the political nation are ethical. One is a community of affections and instincts infinitely important and powerful in savage life, but pertaining more to the animal than to the civilised man; the other is an authority governing by laws, imposing obligations, and giving a moral sanction and character to the natural relations of society."[2]

The dependence of the individual upon the social life is the third of the facts from which the principle of the unity of society is a generalisation. This may seem to be involved in that community of purpose to which reference has been made. But the significance of community of purpose as a social bond is primarily subjective: men are united by the community in so far as they are, or become, conscious of it. The fact of dependence, on the other hand, serves to emphasize

1. *Cf.* Jethro Brown, "The Austinian Theory of Law," Excursus A.
2. "History of Freedom and other Essays," 292-3.

an objective condition. Whether the individual be conscious or unconscious of the purposes he shares in common with his fellows, his life is so dependent upon society that his social relationships should be regarded, not as an addendum to his personality, but as an integral part of it—not as something he can assume or discard at will, but as an essential part of himself and the very condition of his being.

"He is," as Mr. Bradley expresses it, "penetrated, infected, characterised by his relations with his fellows. . . . The soul within him is saturated, is filled up, is qualified by, it has assimilated, has built itself up from, it *is* one and the same life with, the universal life; and if he turns against this, he turns against himself; if he thrusts it from him, he tears his own vitals; if he attacks it, he sets the weapon against his own heart." [1]

The nature of this dependence of the individual may be illustrated by several propositions.

In the first place, man's life to-day, his thought, his ideals, his actions, are conditioned by the nature of a common inheritance which he owes to those who have gone before him. Does he enjoy freedom of thought and speech? Has he free political institutions? Is the world of Art, of Music, of Painting, of Sculpture, of Architecture, of Literature, in some measure open to him? Has he a State? A City? Laws? Schools? Homes? All these he owes to the thought and efforts of bygone generations. Every letter in the alphabet of childhood is a symbol of inherited achievement. If the lisping infant learns "to shape the wonder of a word," it is past ages that have given him the means of expression. If man reads, the wisdom of the ages ministers to his understanding. He cannot travel, toil, learn, or pray, save by availing himself of the heritage of a long past of human efforts, strivings, failure, and attainment. With each age that heritage grows richer. Of all the

1. Quoted, Henry Jones, "Working Faith of a Social Reformer," 132.

generations that have been in the long history of the world, none is so great a debtor as our own. In our power over nature and in our accumulated stores of knowledge we are in advance of all the generations that have gone before us. Each and all of us are debtors to those generations. The wider the range of the activities of the individual and the higher the altitudes he may attain, the more use he makes, or can make, of past achievement, and the greater, therefore, is his debt. In order that the genius of a Shakespeare might realise itself in immortal art, man must have stammered slowly towards articulate speech through long aeons of progress. The magic music of Chopin and of Wagner could never have taken form in the minds of those great artists but for the slow perfecting of musical instruments by generations of toilers whose names have been long forgotten. From whatever point of view we regard the matter, the past is not dead, but lives in us. The individual may protest against this or that institution or idea; but the contribution of the most gifted mind sinks to insignificance in comparison with the riches that he has received and that make his own achievement possible.

In the second place, man is dependent, not only upon a structure of inherited ideas and institutions, but also upon the active and hourly co-operation of those by whose aid this structure is maintained. A man's existence, his culture of body, mind and soul, the completion of his development,—all are conditioned by the social environment in which he lives.

"If," wrote Sir Leslie Stephen, "I can devote myself to write an ethical treatise, it is because thousands of people all over the world are working to provide me with food and clothes, and a variety of intellectual and material products. If another man lives by putting one brick on another, it is because he can trust the discharge of other essential functions to the numerous classes who are contributing more or less directly to his support, protection, and instruction."[1]

1. "Science of Ethics," 109.

The full significance of the form of dependence just referred to can only be realised when it is distinguished from the dependence existing throughout the totality of nature. The earth in its orbit, the stars in their courses, pursue no independent path, but realise the conception of Law as the harmony of the Universe. Within our own world, existence displays—not in human life only, not in animal life only, but throughout all life—an unceasing and far-reaching interdependence. In return for the shelter it receives, the crab, guest of the mussel and a more effectual procurer of food than its host, gives of the superabundance of the food it has gathered. The humble violet, nestling in the shelter of some ampler growth, serves to maintain by its presence the conditions of soil moisture that are essential alike to its own development and to that of its protector. The bee, stopped in its swift flight by the lure of some wayside flower, fructifies the plant from which it takes its burden of honey. As Kerner remarks when speaking of such social communities as the lichens:

"The reciprocity here implied is at bottom but a copy of the complementary interaction of plants and animals which takes place on a grand scale in the organic world."[1]

Such analogies from the vegetable and animal kingdom, while they reveal an interdependence, fall far short of that degree of interdependence which we find in human society. In the instances quoted, the individual or the species pursues its own self-interest: in human society, other factors are present—*love and the sense of justice*. The attempt has often been made to represent human society as simply based on the pursuit by each of his own private gain. But such a representation will never explain the loving care of parents, the deeds of friendship, the sacrifices to the Fatherland, or the myriad self-denials of everyday life. In the story Tolstoy tells in "What Men Live

1. "The Natural History of Plants."

By," the exile angel learns on earth a truth that most men never learn—*how much love counts for in life.*

"When I was a man," he confesses, "I remained alive not by the care I took of myself, but because there was love in the hearts of a stranger and his wife, and they pitied and loved me. The orphans remained alive, not by the thought they took of themselves, but because there was love in the heart of a strange woman, and she pitied and loved them. And all men live, not by the care they take of themselves, but by the love that is in men. I have learned that it only seems to men that they live by care for themselves; but in truth they live only by love."

Is this fable? Some would have us think so. Pseudo-realists in fiction suggest by their art that human nature is essentially bestial. Man's weakness, greed, excesses, and lust are represented as normal; whilst his service, his self-denial, his sense of fair play, and his wavering struggle towards the right are represented as abnormal. "St. Simeon," says the Pilgrim's Scrip, "saw the Hog in Nature, and took Nature for the Hog." We shall not learn from such false prophets the real secrets of the human heart, or the nature and meaning of human association. If the world were as they picture it to be, the fabric of society must swiftly crumble. The indisputable fact is that in the home, in the streets, in our business relations, in every step of life, we act in reliance upon the honesty, good faith, and good will of others. That reliance is sometimes misplaced, but in the long run it is justified; and the fact is the greatest of all reasons why life appeals to us as a thing to be cherished or desired.

One aspect of man's dependence, although suggested by what has been said, calls for special emphasis. Man *gives* to others as well as *receives* from them; and it is only through such acts of service that he can attain to the full stature of his being. He is so constituted that service to his fellows, from one point of view his duty, is from another point of view his privilege. Hence the answer to those who may consider, rightly or wrongly, that they have a grievance against society because they have not received equally of the advantages that the race has accumulated for all. It is not necessary to retort that a man does not pay his debt by proving some other person to be a greater debtor than himself: it is sufficient to dwell upon the fact that, apart from a man's duty to society, he is impelled to the service of his fellows by the duty he owes to himself. If he sins against society, he not only sins against an order whose interests are inextricably interwoven with his own, but he becomes, as Cicero would say, an exile from himself. For the impulse to service is as natural to man as any other impulse he may have; and all attempts he may make to stifle it are really a denial of the higher self within him. Such denial is common enough; but so also is it common for a man to prefer a momentary gratification to an enduring personal gain. As Butler remarked, *men as often contradict that part of their nature which they regard as leading to their own private good and happiness, as they contradict that part of it which leads to the public good.* The philanthropists of a past generation, who regarded the poor as a divine institution for the spiritual salvation of the rich, were doubtless guilty of bad theology; but they were only giving a narrow and perverse interpretation to the truth that "others," rich or poor, are the material out of which each man fashions himself—for good or for ill according as he is dominated by the impulses of love or hate, of service or of exploitation.

The power of these facts—man's consciousness of likeness in others, his possession of purposes in common with others, and the manifold forms of his dependence upon others—is enhanced by social pressure. Whether the pressure is external to individuals or is only partly external (as in the democratic State and in most private associations), it is at once an evidence and a cause of human solidarity. States have sometimes been distinguished by reference to the extent to which they are upheld by force; and it is often assumed that progress implies the gradual elimination of force. The assumption is only justified if we use the term "force" in an unduly restricted sense. Progress has consisted, not in the gradual elimination of force, but in its socialisation. The socialisation is apparent if we regard communities either from the point of view of the functions which they exercise or from the point of view of the structure which they tend to adopt. Force has become more humane and moral; it is exercised more according to rule; and it is less external to individual wills. But it remains as a fundamental factor in social development. "Social pressure" is a term of wider meaning than "force." We see evidences of its existence, not only in the fine, the hangman, or the gaoler, but also in ostracism, the cold shoulder, and the discipline of civil, religious, and educational institutions. In all these forms social pressure is at work, moulding the human character in accordance with the requirements of associated life, and thereby consolidating the unity of the social groups in which men live.[1]

The argument immediately preceding has dealt with the facts of social life in general. The range and significance of those facts, however, necessarily vary according to the form of social life under examination. Legislative theory is primarily concerned with the form of social life we know as the State. It remains to be considered, therefore, how the facts to which reference has been made are affected when we regard men as citizens. In the political community the element of pressure is so manifest and important that some writers have seen nothing else. But each of the other elements mentioned is also present. Although men have long since passed

1. *Cf.* the valuable and suggestive works of Professor Ross on "Social Control," and "The Foundations of Sociology."

beyond the stage when philosophers could extol "the loyal and heartfelt hatred of the foreigner," no one can deny that man's consciousness of likeness in others has a special basis in reality when "others" are members of the same State. The crimson thread of kinship is no fiction of the imagination.

"The people of to-day are in a body the children of the people of ancient times. The inheritance has been completely diffused and intermingled; so that, going back some centuries, it would be much harder to find a man who was not our ancestor than one who was."[1]

Further, the purposes common to members of one State, though perhaps less apparent to the sense than those uniting smaller groups such as the family and the social club, touch the life of the citizen at every point. Finally, the manifold forms of man's dependence upon others find their supreme illustration in the relations of citizenship. It is through the State, more than through any other social group, that the gifts of the past and the services of the present are secured to men. The more the citizen reflects upon his daily life, the more he will realise how completely dependent he is, in living that life, upon the support of the State of which he is a member. If he should attempt a profit-and-loss account of his relations to the State he would find that, when all allowance has been made for defects in legislation or in the administration of justice, he receives far more than he gives. As a member of an ordinary social group, his own contribution to the group good is slight in comparison with the benefits he receives; but in the case of the State, more than of any other social group, the extent of his indebtedness exceeds the utmost that he can do in return. If he is injured in his person, reputation, or property, he must look to the State for redress. If his life is endangered by the adulteration of food or the spread of disease,

1. "The Principles of Heredity," *Edinburgh Review*, January 1911, 84.

he must look to the State for prevention. If his home is threatened by invasion, he must look to the State for protection.

"The individual life and conduct," says Archdeacon Cunningham, "are permeated and penetrated by State enactments; the individual is what he is, and has what he has, chiefly because the State has conferred on him the privileges he possesses."[1]

"The State," writes Professor Henry Jones, "is the stable background of the individual's welfare, and just as truly the indispensable condition of his rational well-being as are the earth and air of his physical life."[2]

Some writers of to-day, impressed by the growth of international organisations, speak of the State as if it were a transient expression of man's social nature. But if we are to learn the true significance of the tendency towards the internationalisation of labour, we must take into consideration the justification for that tendency which is found in the danger that modern militarism and international competition in industry may retard domestic reform. The internationalisation of labour is but a means to an end. That end is the collectivist State. The immediate effect of the pursuit of this end may be to emphasise a class war within each State. The alternate effect aimed at is the reconstruction of social and economic institutions within each State in a form which would imply a greater cohesion than exists in the State as we see it to-day.

This is not the place to discuss the merits or demerits of the collectivist State; but the ideal of such a State is more open to criticism on the ground of demanding for its fulfilment a despotic control over the life of the individual than on the ground of denying the unity of the State or of challenging the value of laws and institutions which shall express and promote that unity.

1. "Politics and Economics," 137.
2. "The Working Faith of a Social Reformer," 244.

CHAPTER IV.

THEORETICAL FORMULATIONS OF THE SOCIAL UNITY.

THE most sanguine observer of social life to-day must admit how inadequate is men's appreciation of the facts from which the unity of society is a generalisation. Men do not realise that, in performing their daily tasks, they "have been strengthening the structure of the State and serving purposes which far outspan their own." Nor do they realise the immensity of their debt to, and the extent of their dependence upon, the social and political institutions that make life possible for them. The very magnitude of the modern State, while it multiplies indefinitely the opportunities of individual development, is apt to make the State itself appear a remote abstraction. Too often the lesser loyalties of the individual—those which he recognises as due to his family, his class, his party, or his local community—occupy the whole range of vision. Although the consciousness of national unity asserts itself in the presence of a national calamity, as soon as the crisis is past the more immediate and apparent claims of everyday life resume a despotic control. The Nation is no longer enthroned in the consciousness of its citizens.

The inadequacy of men's appreciation of the unity of society is traceable in part to intellectual causes. No great truth can become a part of the popular consciousness until it has been expressed in ways capable of appealing to men. It is one of the functions of political philosophy to perform this service. Men build better than they know; but they would build better still if they had a clearer vision of the truths of which they are but half conscious. It seems to me, therefore, that the attempts of the political philosophy of our time to formulate the principle of social unity deserve a careful examination. Such attempts will be the subject of the present chapter.

The problem with which political philosophy has to deal in the endeavour to formulate a theory of social unity is only one aspect of a problem confronting the student in every department of thought. A molecule is a society of atoms; a chemical substance is a society of elements: the solar system is a society of celestial bodies; a plant or an animal is a society of cells; the thought of a man is a society of ideas. Thinkers who have concentrated their attention upon human society have endeavoured to explain it in terms suggested by one or other of the types just mentioned. More often than not, the explanation has been far from successful; it has been shown, sooner or later, to be quite inadequate, if not positively misleading. The human material has stubbornly refused to run into the moulds fashioned by thinkers whose thought has been inspired by the undoubted analogies which exist between human societies and molecular, mechanical, or chemical combinations. But the theories of the State as an organism and as a person stand upon a different footing. They represent a great advance in constructive analysis upon other doctrines; and they have entered largely into the popular phraseology of our time. We imply a social organism when we use such expressions as "State growth," or "the body politic," or when we speak of Parliament as "the organ of public opinion." We imply a social personality when we talk of "the popular will," "the social conscience," or "the soul of a people." The theories of the State as an organism or as a person represent attempts to justify the use of such terms and to give them a scientific precision and value.

I.—The State as an Organism.

The theory of the State as an organism may be illustrated by three propositions:—the members of a State are related to the State as the cells of an organism to the organism; the advance of the State from age to age is a process that is essentially of the nature of organic growth; and, finally, the individuals through whom the State performs official acts are related to the State as organs to an organism.

In the first place, the relation of the State to the citizens who compose it finds its parallel, not in the inorganic world, or in the world of machinery, but in the world of living substance. If a stone be taken from a heap of stones, the nature of the stone is not affected. It remains what it was before. In ceasing to be part of the heap it has neither gained nor lost. If a wheel be taken from a steam engine, the engine may run off the track, but the nature of the wheel is unaffected. But if a leaf be taken from a plant, it withers and dies. Its relation to the whole of which it is a part is a relation so intimate and so essential that the leaf itself now ceases to be what it was. So, too, with regard to the individual and society. In society as in the plant, we have to recognise a whole whose existence is bound up with the existence of its parts; a whole throughout which there beats the pulse of a common life; a whole upon which each part is dependent, and to the well-being of which each part contributes.

"It is as true that man is dependent upon his fellows," wrote Sir Leslie Stephen, "as that a limb is dependent upon the body. It would be as absurd to ask what would be the properties of a man who was not a product of the race, as to ask what would be the properties of a leg not belonging to an animal; or to ask what would be the best type of man without considering his place in society, as to ask what would be the best kind of leg without asking whether it belonged to a hare or a tortoise. And, in the next place, it is true that the properties of a society cannot be deduced from the independent properties of its members in the same sense as it is true that the properties of any living body cannot be deduced from the mechanical and chemical properties of the elements of which it is composed. Destroy the life in either case, and the remaining properties of the dead materials do not enable us to assign their properties when forming an associated whole. We cannot infer the properties of a society by supposing it to be an aggregate of beings independent of society, because such beings are mere nonentities." [1]

In the second place, the advance of the State from age to age is a growth, not a manufacture; an organic, not a mechanical process. The life of a people is not enriched or enlarged in the same way as additions are made to its territory. Such additions are expressible in arithmetical symbols. The development of the nation, on the other hand, is from within, not from without. We may increase the height of a wall by the simple process of putting on more bricks. We may patch a cloak, or may add to it, but we cannot make it grow; the patches or additions remain unchanged; they enter into no vital relation with that to which they become related. With the nation, as with the organism, change is a process of development in the course of which that which comes from without is *assimilated*. Nowhere is this indicated more clearly than in legal development—whether it be slow or rapid, irregular or systematic, unconscious or conscious, the work of democratic assemblies or of an autocratic legislator. On a superficial view, legislation may be distinguished from the "spontaneous" generation of usage and declared to be mere manufacture. But, to begin with, the form and content of a legislative act are conditioned by a nation's past. The most despotic of legislators cannot think or act without availing himself

1. "The Science of Ethics," 110–11.

of the spirit of his race and time. His most despotic laws reveal the influence and potency of that spirit. Further, when a law has once been promulgated, it has to be interpreted and administered; in the process of interpretation and administration the spirit of the legal system as a whole will reassert itself at every stage; and, accordingly, if we are to describe the change in the legal system, we must call it a *growth*—not in the mechanical sense conceived by some writers who mean by growth nothing more than slow and unsystematic manufacture, but in the living sense in which we employ the term when describing the processes characteristic of organic nature.[1]

Finally, the relation between the State and the persons who express its will in external action is a relation aptly described by saying that they are the organs through which the community acts. The older theory of sovereignty, according to which Kings and Parliaments ruled subjects as a father rules a family or as God rules the world, has become increasingly untenable. Loyalty to rulers is felt, not as loyalty to persons, but as loyalty to the State for which those rulers act. The making of laws by the legislature and their interpretation by the courts, as well as all the administrative actions of government, are effected by individuals who possess no inherent authority but derive their right to exercise their functions, mediately or immediately, from the community of which they, like the humblest citizen, are a part. They are the "organs" of the social organism. To realise how apt is this expression it is only necessary to attempt to find a substitute for it. The term "agent" is condemned by the mere fact that an agent acts for a principal who himself wills and acts independently. The term "representative" is not so palpably inadequate. Rulers may be said to derive their authority from the fact that they represent their subjects, just as in law a guardian acts for certain purposes as representing his

1. *Cf.* Jethro Brown, "The Austinian Theory of Law," 347-8.

ward. But the guardian and the ward are two entirely distinct persons, not parts of a common whole. A more intimate term is needed to express the character of the persons who, in acting for the State, are acting for a whole of which they are themselves parts. That more intimate term is found in the word "organ."[1]

Sufficient has been said by way of illustrating the meaning of the theory of the State as an organism. What objections may be urged against the theory? One objection is suggested by progress in biological research. While political theorists have experienced an increasing satisfaction in the conviction that society finds its truest analogy in organic as distinct from mechanical or chemical aggregates of matter, many thinkers in a wider field have been occupied in the endeavour to show that the organic aggregate is only a form of mechanical or chemical combination. There are two reasons that prevent me from attaching much importance to this fact. In the first place, the belief that the mystery of life may be explained in terms of non-living matter is at present no more than a speculative hypothesis. While no one questions the existence of chemical transformations within the living organism, or the analogies that exist between organs and the parts of a machine, the results of scientific research in these fields by no means justify "the sanguine optimism of the seventies of the last century." The phenomena of growth, of repair, and of reproduction, "the rhythm of rest and regeneration," so characteristic of the organism, have still to be explained, if they can be explained, in terms of non-living matter. Certainly, no chemist has succeeded in the analysis of the living protoplasm.[2]

In the second place, even if the natural organism should prove to be explainable in terms of chemistry or mechanism, the discovery would not affect the validity of the several categories for the purposes of

1. *Cf.* Jethro Brown, "The Austinian Theory of Law" 258-9, 265-6.
2. *Cf.* Duclaux, "La Chimie de la Matière Vivante." Also, Marcus Hartog, "Mechanism and Life," in the *Contemporary Review*, April, 1908.

thought, although it might necessitate a new nomenclature. Categories may have a practical value though proved not to be ultimate. If "the mechanical theory of life" were to be established beyond all question, life would still display special characteristics of its own, including those to which reference has been made in expounding the organic theory of society. The nature of the relations of reciprocal service between the organism and its cells, many of the qualities of the organs, and the phenomena of growth, though they might be ultimately explainable in terms of mechanism, would still distinguish the natural organism from other aggregates of matter, and would serve as a valid basis for the existing categories of thought. If the physical organism be a machine, it is indubitably a machine of a very special character.

A second objection to the theory of the State as an organism is more plausible.

> "It may be legitimate," writes Sir Roland Wilson, "to describe society as an organism, but if so it must be identified with something either greater or smaller than the State . . . whereas the cells of the human body are wholly bound up with that body, the citizen of an independent State may have closer relations with individual members of other States than with most of his fellow citizens or with his own government." [1]

The argument, however, goes to show, not that the State is not an organism, but that it is only one of many organisms, and that the same individual may be a cell in several. The argument is a refutation of an exact parallelism between one State and a physical organism; but to admit that a group within the State, or an international society is an organism is destructive of the author's main contention. If any group is an organism, the State is.

A more serious objection to the theory of the State as an organism was stated by Herbert Spencer. "The

1. "The Province of the State," 223.

parts of an animal form a concrete whole; but the parts of a society form a whole which is discrete."[1] While some of the inferences drawn by Spencer from this distinction are highly questionable, the distinction itself is important. By identifying the position of the individual in society with that of the cell in the natural organism, the conception of the social organism may be employed to justify a specious despotism. In reality, while the State and the individual, no less than the organism and its cells, are united by relations of mutual service, the individual is an end in himself in a sense that finds no complete analogy in the case of the organic cell. Not only is he an end in himself as well as a means to society; he reproduces in himself the life of society in ways to which no parallel exists in the physical organism. In particular, the end a nation sets before itself is one in whose attainment the individuals themselves may consciously share.

More and more the thought of our time has come to recognise the inadequacy of the interpretation of society in terms of biology.[2] Men live by love as well as by appetite, by intelligence as well as by instinct. Their union in a society is an expression of factors of which the most significant are mental rather than physical. "As in the individual, so in the society, the natural and the unconscious is but the basis of the conscious and rational."[3] Social unity, in a word, is a psychological rather than a biological fact.

"The organisation which is effected in social life," writes Professor Baldwin, "is in all its forms a *psychological organisation.* Its materials are psychological materials; thoughts, with all their issue in desires, impulses, sanctions, consciences, sentiments. These things are incapable of any organisation but that which finds its analogy in the actual growth of

1. "Principles of Sociology," i. 445-9.

2. *See*, however, J. A. Hobson, "The Crisis of Liberalism" (1910), 73. "I think the view of Society as a physical organism is justified, and will obtain more and more acceptance."

3. Montague, "The Limits of Individual Liberty," 89.

living minds. Where in the analogy from an organism will we place the influence of ethical and religious sentiment? Social progress is essentially, in its method, a reproduction of the growth of the individual; and the individual grows up in the social circle just because it is so akin to him that he is able to reproduce it in himself." [1]

The inadequacy of biological interpretations of the State is seen most clearly when the attempt is made to explain the nature of social progress. The growth of an organism is spontaneous; the growth of mind is relatively purposive, the result of the pursuit of ends consciously recognised as good or desirable. Further, the operation of environmental influences is less limited in the case of the mind than in the case of a physical organism. While in the mind, as in the case of the physical organism, an environment can only work upon latent potentialities, the influence exerted by that environment in the case of mental development may continue indefinitely. The body attains its full stature when maturity is reached, but the mind may continue to develop as long as the individual lives. To sum up, while physical growth is relatively spontaneous and limited, the growth of mind is relatively purposive and illimitable. When we turn from individual to national development, we find that, in both these respects, social progress can only be explained in terms of mind.

The failure to appreciate the fact just stated has been a prolific source of political fallacy in the past. In expounding the theory of the State as an organism, I remarked that mechanical interpretations of national development persisted long after their nominal rejection. Growth was conceived to mean little more than slow and unsystematic manufacture; and the ruler continued to be regarded as a kind of mechanic, dealing with material which, if stubborn and reluctant in the hands of the timid or incompetent, could be

1. "Social and Ethical Interpretations in Mental Development," 522-3.

shaped at will by the courageous and enlightened. When it was realised that social progress was growth in a very real sense of the term, thinkers not infrequently fell into the opposite error of supposing that the process was purely spontaneous. Scientific writers, in particular, sought to explain the whole phenomena of social development in terms of natural selection. Hence a certain fatalism in political speculation; a disposition to hold that the less the part played in politics by conscious agency the better, since the more unfettered would be the operation of those natural laws by which alone any real progress was held to be possible. In other words, the conception of organic growth in sociology, while it served to emancipate men from the thraldom of a mechanical superstition, gave plausibility to the doctrine of *laissez faire*. A theory of social progress, if it is to be true to the facts of social life, must recognise that national growth, being a mental rather than a physical fact, must be interpreted in terms of psychology rather than biology. It is a development in accordance with reflective adaptations to ends conceived to be good or desirable. Society, like man, is impelled

> ". . . not to make, but grow,
> Yet forced to try and make, else fail to grow."

As a result, while the wisest and most beneficent government is powerless to do more than develop the latent possibilities of the individual life, no limit can be set to the good it is capable of effecting within this sphere through the operation of environmental influences. The State, indeed, might be described as a device to escape from the thraldom of the laws which, according to Darwin, determined the course of biological evolution. Natural selection must necessarily continue to operate in human life; but its rigours may be mitigated without interfering with racial progress by conscious agency expressing itself in an improved environment, and if necessary through artificial selection.

"Social organisms," says Ritchie, "differ from other organisms in having the remarkable property of making themselves; and the more developed they are, the more consciously do they make themselves."[1]

The distinction between mechanical, organic, and psychological interpretations of social phenomena is strikingly illustrated in the history of theories of legal development. The mechanical interpretation was ill adapted to explain the evolution of legal rules during an epoch of customary law. The activity of the modern legislator, however, while it stimulated the demand for a theory of some sort, gave a plausibility to the mechanical view of law as the mere expression of the will of rulers who imposed *ab extra* their rule of life upon a subject community. Long before this doctrine received an implicit sanction in the "Jurisprudence" of John Austin, its inadequacy had been demonstrated by the genius of Savigny. Savigny, upholding the organic theory of legal development, represented law as a product of the national life. So far from being the mere fiat of an arbitrary legislator, law was the spontaneous and unconscious expression of the juridic sentiment of a people. In other words, while he proved once and for all that law was growth in a very real sense, he committed the fatal error of underestimating the importance of the element of conscious direction in legal evolution. Juridic sentiment, wrote Jhering, in criticism of Savignian theory, has not created the law: it is law that has created the juridic sentiment. Nature has not made herself the directress of man. She has given him wants and the intelligence to meet them. The history of law is that of human thought directed towards the practical realisation of the conditions of collective human life. In this sense, all law on earth has been made. If it appears as spontaneous it is only because we cannot

1. "Principles of State Interference," 49. *Cf.* the remarks in chapter vi. *infra*, on the rejection of the biological argument in support of *laissez faire*. *Cf.* also Chap. ix. *infra*, the remarks on the Problem of the Child.

discover the successive phases of its origin.[1] This may seem at first to be a reversion to the theory of manufacture. But Jhering adopted the view of Savigny that law was a product of national life. In so doing he was, of course, impelled to recognise that legal development is only a phase of social development in general, and is therefore, like it, a growth. But he corrects and completes the theory of Savigny by showing that law is a growth of a very special kind which can only be interpreted in terms of mind.

The foregoing criticism of the theory of the State as an organism will be seen to involve the theory of the State as a person. While the latter theory is a far more exact and serviceable instrument of thought, its adoption is quite consistent with a due recognition of the value of the earlier doctrine. If society is something more than an organism, it yet exhibits some of the characteristics of the organism. (1) The conception of the ruler as an organ of the community is an enduring contribution to political thought. (2) The State, if not an organism, is an organic unity. Although in strict logic the adjective "organic" should correlate to the substantive "organism," the term "organic unity" has long stood for a type which, if suggested by analogies to be found in the non-rational world, has been refined and adapted for the purpose of representing any totality of which all the parts are reciprocally means and ends to one another and the whole. In this, the Kantian, sense, the term organic unity has served to describe, not merely a most important feature of human association, but also such diverse unities as may be found in a system of thought, a work of art, or a code of laws. (3) Any attempt to give scientific precision to the theory of the State as a person must reckon with the fact that psychology itself is frequently compelled, for lack of a vocabulary of its own, to employ biological terms. If mental development is different from physical, it nevertheless

1. "Histoire du Développement du Droit Romain."

displays, as I have already shown, characteristics for which no adequate expression can be found but that of *growth.* For the purposes of political thought, the general result can be expressed by saying that the theory of the State as a person, instead of standing in direct opposition to the theory of the State as an organism, is inclusive of it. The older theory is not superseded, but is corrected and completed, by the new.

II.—The State as a Person.

Such expressions as "the popular will," "the social conscience," "the national honour," and "the soul of a people," imply the personification of the State. Is this personification adopted for purposes of brevity, or imposed by practical necessities? Is the personality of the State a serviceable fiction or a reality? In speaking of the will of the community, do we mean a mere arithmetical sum of individual wills, or something more? The answer to these questions has been anticipated in my exposition of the State as an organism. If the State is an organic unity, it must be something more than the mere sum total of its parts. The conclusion is not affected by the fact that the term "organic unity" is employed to express mental facts. Those who advocate the theory of the State as a person are not in search of convenient fictions. Nor are they symbolists. They are realists who seek to express in language what they find in the world of fact.

I am not, of course, contending that the State is a "natural person." Some writers have so regarded it, and have drawn inferences that belong to the curiosities of literature.

"Diseases of the body politic," said Cusanus, "should be treated by the Emperor in accordance with the counsel of books and of experienced state-physicians. He should himself test the medicine by taste, smell, and sight, that it may suit time and place, and then bring it to the teeth (privy council), stomach (grand council), and liver (judicial tribunal), for digestion and distribution. If preservative measures fail, then in the last resort he must proceed to amputation, but this will be *cum dolore compassionis*." [1]

The fascination exercised over some writers by anthropomorphic interpretations of social life has been illustrated with engaging felicity in the works of King James. When that author expounds his views of kingly privilege, he concludes the matter by putting a searching question:

"And for the similitude of the head and the body, it may well fall out that the head will be forced to garre cut off some rotten member to keep the rest of the body in integritie; but what state can the body be in if the head for any infirmitie that can fall to it be cut off, I leave it to the reader's judgment."

The fantastic anthropomorphism of Cusanus and King James might be paralleled by extracts from authors of higher repute and of more recent date. It is important, therefore, to distinguish clearly between the natural or physical person and the real person. A natural person is a human being. A real person, whether natural or not, is a being endowed with the attributes of mind and will. The theologian who speaks of God as a person does not impute to the omnipresent Deity the limitations of human nature. He implies only that men conceive of God as a Being endowed with the elements that constitute the essence of personality—supremely, the elements of mind and will. The mind may be omniscient and the will all-powerful; but they are still facts that can only be expressed in terms of personality. The theory of the State as a person implies the recognition of a third type of personality, not natural or Divine, but social. In the remainder of the present chapter I shall endeavour to explain the meaning of this theory, and to illus-

1. Quoted, Gierke, "Political Theories of the Middle Age," 132.

trate its value, by reference to the conception of the social will.

Two types of social union require to be distinguished. They are illustrated in the world of sport. Two lacrosse teams are engaged in a game. In one team, each player desires only to amuse or distinguish himself; in the other team, every one seeks to win a victory for his side. In one team, the player takes possession of the ball as often as he can and retains it as long as he can: in the other team, the player subordinates his inclination to amuse or distinguish himself to the requirements of effective combination. In popular parlance, one team has not, the other has, *esprit de corps*. In both teams there is a union of wills, since the members of each are working towards the same goal; but one team has not, while the other has, a *unity of will*. In the language of Rousseau, one has a mere will of all; the other has a general will.

Whether we accept this terminology or reject it as fanciful, it stands for differences of real importance for which some terminology must be found. I shall endeavour to show that the terminology suggested is appropriate. Some writers have contended that a union of individual wills, however highly socialised they may be, can never result in a true unity of will. "Whether the will of the individual be socialised or self-seeking, it is still an individual will." [1] The conclusion is suggested that the supposed general will is only a sum of particular wills of a particular type. However plausible this view may be, its illusory character can be readily demonstrated by analogy. There is a real unity in a statue: a symphony is something more than a mere concurrence of sounds; and a cathedral is no mere aggregate of stone and mortar. In each of these cases a unity results from the subordination of the parts to a common plan. If a statue be destroyed, the pre-existing unity disappears, and there remains a mere aggregate of molecules. If we

1. Combothecra, "Conception Juridique de l'Etat," 60-1.

re-form the statue we have still the aggregate; but we have something more—the unity of a work of art. Each grain of sand finds its place in an ordered system which is something more than a mere aggregate because its parts have acquired a new meaning from their relation to the whole. The analogy to social organisation will be evident. A union of self-seeking wills produces nothing more than a mere aggregate—a "will of all." A union of socialised wills results in a true unity of will, because each separate will realises itself in serving the whole. It is true to say that the will of the individual, whether self-seeking or socialised, is still an individual will. But it is altogether false to say that the union of social wills is nothing more than the sum total of those wills, because the very meaning and essence of their being socialised implies that subordination to a common principle or plan which constitutes in any aggregate whatsoever a new unity.

The foregoing argument from analogy is in one respect imperfect. The unity of a work of art exists only for the artist, or for his sympathetic interpreter. It is like the beauty of the primrose. But those who see, in the highly-developed social group, a mere coincidence of wills without a unity of will, a mere aggregate of purposes without a community of purpose, are guilty of something more than the obtuseness of the man of whom it was said:

> "A primrose by a river's brim
> A yellow primrose was to him,
> And it was nothing more."

As Professor Mackenzie observes:

"The necessity of being regarded as a unity may have various degrees, and even various kinds, of cogency. A house must be regarded as a whole; but the necessity which compels us so to regard it arises from the fact that it has reference to an end apart from which it has no significance. This end, however, lies outside of itself : it lies in the nature of man. . . . A Greek play is not a necessary unity for the mere philologist or grammarian, but only for one who recreates its passion and thought. . . . The house has no self, but is a whole for another self : the work of art has a self (*i.e.*, a self-reference), but it also has a self only for another self. With an organic being the case is different. Such a being is a necessary unity apart from any other finite self to which it refers. The elements of which it is composed cannot be understood except in relation to the whole to which they belong; and in referring them to that whole, we do not directly refer them to anything which lies beyond it." [1]

The unity of will in society belongs to the type of unity last mentioned. Society is a whole in a deeper sense than is a house, or even a work of art.

Before I discuss the practical value of the conception of the social will in politics, I may be permitted to indicate an important consequence of the preceding argument. Since the social will results from a union of rational beings, its admission involves the acceptance of the theory of the State as a person. If we must conceive of the will of a group as something more than the mere sum total of individual wills, and if this will derives its reality from a unity of conscious purpose, then the something more is necessarily a reality which we can only interpret in terms of personality. Dr. Salmond, who regards the conception of a social person as a fiction, remarks that men who combine for a particular purpose no more become one than several horses become one simply from the fact of their being harnessed to the same coach.[2] But the union here suggested is just the type of union Rousseau had in mind when speaking of a will of all. Each horse pursues its own end, seeking perhaps to exercise its limbs, to escape the whip, or to get back to the

1. "Introduction to Social Philosophy," 180-1.
2. "Jurisprudence," 2nd ed., 288.

stables as speedily as possible. There may even be a coincidence of ends; but there can be no community of purpose. Whatever unity may exist in the team as a whole is the result of external pressure in the form of the harness or the whip. The nearest analogy that can be suggested in human groups is that of a number of slaves under the control of a master; or a truly imperialistic State, if such could be found, where the rights and duties of the subject were determined by external authority and maintained by its coercive force.

The value of the conception of the social will within the sphere of politics requires examination from several points of view. The conception may be regarded as an ideal, as a representation of actualities, or as affording a useful indication of the functions and structure of the legislature. Its value as a political ideal is too evident to admit of controversy. Writers who admit the possibility of a unity of will in some highly developed social groups, but question the existence of such unity in the case of the State as at present constituted, will not deny the importance of the social will as an ideal toward whose realisation the activity of the statesman and the citizen should be directed. A community where each individual desires to promote the common good is a much higher and more efficient type of social union than a community where popular decisions represent the mere coincidence of a multitude of particular wills, each of which is bent upon some private gain. Even if, therefore, the idea of a social will were visionary, it would still have value as an ideal. By the proclamation and reiteration of such ideals, the world of actualities has been transformed in the past and will be transformed in the future.

The value of the conception of the social will as a representation of actualities varies with differing conditions of time and race. One statement may be made with confidence. Although the social will is not the only force finding expression in the organs of civic action, it is actual in political communities, in the sense that it exercises a real influence both in maintaining and in revising the system of rights and duties defined by law. While in any particular community, at a particular period, questions of more immediate interest may be decided by the voice of those in whom the social will is relatively feeble, no State is likely to endure for any length of time unless its citizens desire its continuance and to some extent identify its interests with their own. Certainly, in the modern community, the citizens are neither devoid of a consciousness of interests in common, nor lacking in the will to maintain those interests. Law in its totality, is an expression of the popular will, not merely in the sense that it is supported by popular opinion, but also in the deeper sense that it stands for what the members of a State maintain in their corporate capacity and for the common good.

Two objections may be urged in criticism of the conclusion just stated. In the first place, it is sometimes contended that democratic government is a system where the really operative will is that of the majority for the time being. This objection overlooks two facts of importance; one, *that the matters in which majorities and minorities may differ are trifling in comparison with those in which they are in accord;* the other, that the community itself wills that the majority shall prevail when differences of opinion arise as to the revision of the established system of rights and duties. This understanding is not a fiction, but a working agreement imposed by practical necessities. Few things in practical politics are more significant or instructive than the facility with which a minority of yesterday, which has become a majority of to-day, adapts and administrates legislation which it had previously declared to be monstrous and impracticable. Political parties, like rival advocates in the Courts of Justice, are a means of ensuring that various sides of a question shall be considered when unsolved problems call for solution. All parties of any political importance stand for law and order; they acknowledge the sovereign claims of the common good and the right of the electorate to decide in what that good consists. Each elector of whatever party finds some place in his scheme of things for the common good. He desires to promote that good; and whether his desire be feeble or strong, it is present, and the conflicting views with respect to the means for promoting a common good are no more a denial of a unity in the social will than is the conflict and inconsistency in the conduct of an individual a denial of the unity of the individual will.

M. Duguit, the eminent French jurist, attacks the conception of the social will on other grounds than those just considered. He sees in popular majorities and party organisations a means of expressing the will of the strong.

"The State," he writes, "has always been a society where the strong rule the weak. Between the precarious authority of the savage chieftain and the power of a modern government there is merely a difference of degree. The collective will is a mere fiction which only serves to veil the brutal reality of facts." [1]

The savage chieftain would soon cease to be a chief if he set himself in opposition to the tribal code. That code has been slowly evolved through the agency of tribal usage and opinion; and the extent to which the life of the savage is controlled by the commands of the chief is relatively slight as compared with the extent to which it is controlled by the established code. In other words, the collective will is actual even in the savage community. When we come to civilised society, the difference consists, not in the presence of the collective will, but in the discovery of more effective means for its expression, the extension of its sphere

1. "Le Droit Objectif et la Loi Positive" (1901), 255, abbreviated.

beyond the limits of a real or assumed kinship of blood, and the recognition of its intrinsic authority. Alike in savage and in civilised society, a collectve will is operative. If the strong rule, they do not do so as God may rule the world, or as a master rules his slaves. They are themselves products of a social life which they can only control by interpreting. A statesman or an ambitious ruler may achieve much; in particular, as Bagehot pointed out, he may determine to some extent what questions shall be most before the public mind at a given moment; but he can only retain his hold over a people by identifying himself in some way with them. "A party leader," it has been well said, "must follow his party or he cannot remain their leader."

"With all his (Napoleon's) egotism," wrote T. H. Green, "his individuality was so far governed by the action of the national spirit in and upon him that he could only glorify himself in the greatness of France; and though the national spirit expressed itself in an effort after greatness which was in many ways of a mischievous and delusive kind, yet it again had so much of what may be called the spirit of humanity in it, that it required satisfaction in the belief that it was serving mankind. Hence the aggrandisement of France, in which Napoleon's passion for glory satisfied itself, had to take at least the semblance of a deliverance of oppressed peoples, and in taking the semblance it to a great extent performed the reality; at any rate in western Germany and northern Italy, wherever the Code Napoléon was introduced. . . . The idiosyncrasy, then, of the men who have been most conspicuous in the production of great changes in the condition of mankind, though it has been an essential element in their production, has been so only so far as it has been overborne by influences and directed to ends, which were indeed not external to the men in question—which on the contrary helped to make them inwardly and spiritually what they really were—but which formed no part of their distinguishing idiosyncrasy. If that idiosyncrasy was conspicuously selfish, it was still not through their selfishness that such men contributed to mould the institutions by which nations have been civilised and developed, but through their fitness to act as organs of impulses and ideas which had previously gained a hold on some society of men, and for the realisation of which the means and conditions had been preparing quite apart from the action of those who became the most noticeable instruments of their realisation." [1]

The social will is not only operative in social and political life; it is operative in an increasing degree. The individual retains his will; but that will is more and more a socialised will—something which is conditioned by social relations and expresses a community of purpose. Such a statement might be questioned in view of the activity of sectional interests. But (1) those interests, while often hostile to the welfare of the political community as a whole, imply at least a developing social spirit within the limits of a particular class. (2) As I have already suggested, sectional hostility to the common welfare is neither avowed nor conscious. The apologist of vested interests and the advocate of the claims of labour, however much they may differ as to the best means of promoting the common good, defend their views by reference to that good, and generally believe they are promoting it. (3) There are forces which lie deeper than the antagonisms of parties and in comparison with which such antagonisms are negligible quantities—very much in evidence, but also very misleading. I have already referred to the facility with which a majority in power adopts and administrates the legislation of its predecessors. I may add that popular government is not government by majority, but government by

1. Philosophical Works," ii. 440-1.

successive majorities whose accession to power is very largely the result of the fact that in every party electorate there are a large number in whom the social will is operative in a special degree, and who in cases of conflict will prefer the public good to the party programme. Parties have sometimes gained access to power by the easy device of bribing a section of the electorate; but Time brings its own revenges. Even 'the average elector' has a will to be just. If for a time he may be lured into what is in a true sense a form of self-betrayal, that is more from want of head than want of heart; and Time, whether or not "on the side of the angels," is on the side of Truth.

If we reflect upon the facts to which I referred in my last chapter we must realise that they are not static but dynamic. Any one who is sceptical as to the quality of modern progress should ask himself such questions as the following:—Is it not true that men have to-day a deeper consciousness of kind than in the times immediately preceding our own? Is it not true that the interests men have in common have grown indefinitely with the increasing complexity of modern social structure? Is it not true that our common inheritance becomes richer with each generation, and that man's dependence upon others has increased with the progress of the mechanical and scientific discoveries that bring men together in more numerous and more intimate relationships? Is it not true that the increasing interdependence of men makes the realisation of self more than ever a realisation in and through others? Is it not true that, with the widening of the sphere of State activity, man's dependence upon the State has become at once more extensive and more apparent? Is it not true that in all these ways we can detect great forces at work which not merely explain, but render inevitable, the tendency to attach a supreme importance to the conception of a social will? When I reflect upon the answers our judgment must give to these questions, I am impressed, less by the occasional extravagances of the optimist, than by the tardiness with which men recognise truths that for so long have been living and working in the world of fact.

The conception of the social will, apart from its value as a political ideal and as a representation of progressive actualities, has a peculiar value for the theory of legislation, since it enables us to realise more clearly the function of the legislature. It would be unnecessary, at the present stage, to discuss the ancient notion of a ruling class delegated by God, or privileged by Nature, to prescribe the rules of life to a community of passive subjects. The notion of the legislature as a mere mechanism for recording the opinions of the majority of the moment is more worthy of examination. That notion, however, stands for a policy of despair which can only be justified on the ground that the legislature is unrepresentative or corrupt. Clearly, if the social will exists in a community, the primary function of the legislature is to interpret that will in terms of law. In order to discharge this function efficiently, the legislature must submit the verdict of popular majorities to a process of critical interpretation, not only in order to give the best *form* to the expression of the social will but also to discover what that will really is. Just as the action of an individual at a given moment may imperfectly represent, or even conflict with, what he really desires, so the community may express its will in ways which, if translated into legislation, would defeat the deeper purposes which it is the function of the legislature to express. As Professor Bernard Bosanquet remarks:

"The criticism or interpretation which elicits the general will or actual social spirit, by removal of contradictions, and embodiment in permanent form, is essentially one with the work which Rousseau ascribes to the legislator. . . . The legislator is merely one of the organs of the social spirit itself, as it carries out its self-criticism and self-interpretation, in part by trial and error, and in part by conscious insight and adjustment." [1]

While the consciousness of community of interest is the primary element in the social will, that will must be understood, for the purpose of defining the legislative function, in the sense of the "real will" as distinct from the "actual will." It reflects an abiding purpose not that mere wayward mood of the moment. "Surely," says Dr. Mckecknie, "The people know best themselves what they really want." The people *think* they know what they want. The legislator has to carry on this thinking one stage nearer to reality.

Finally, the conception of the social will, in indicating the nature of the legislative function, enables us to realise the deeper issues involved in the problem of the constitution of the legislative organ.

"Mere government by majority," says Mr. J. H. B. Masterman, "is an extraordinarily unsatisfactory and clumsy way of reaching this general will. . . . I have not the least doubt that Queen Elizabeth expressed the general will of the English people a good deal better than some of her Parliaments."

The author proceeds to quote Dr. Bright's eulogy of Gladstone:

"He possessed in an extraordinary degree the power of returning to his audience, elaborated and beautified, their own idea. The immature and formless will of the people found in him an exponent of unequalled power, and received from his genius and earnestness the form and life that was necessary for its realisation." [2]

While I agree that the general will may be interpreted more effectively by a statesman of enlightened judgment and catholic sympathy than by the verdicts of a popular majority, the value of such verdicts cannot

1. "The Philosophical Theory of the State," 122-3.
2. "Parliament and the People," 45-6.

be tested by reference to this point of view alone. A political institution must be judged both by its efficiency as an instrument of expressing the general will and by its value as an educational institution in strengthening and developing that will. While the government of a popularly-constituted autocrat might prove efficient, its value as an educational factor would be incomparably less than that of democratic institutions even in their present form. The problem of strengthening the general will is just as important as that of interpreting it; and, if the will is to be strengthened, means must be provided for its active expression. The more the people are called upon to do, and the graver the responsibilities they are called upon to share, the greater will be the opportunities of evolving a will worthy of expression. The conspicuous merit of representative government is that it is at once efficient and educative. Though it may be less efficient than the government of an enlightened despot, and less educative than a direct democracy, it is on the whole incomparably superior to either if it is representative in fact as well as idea. It is sometimes urged that representative government has had its day. I believe the attitude of hostility towards it, which prevails in certain quarters and finds expression in a plea for direct democracy, has its origin in the fact that existing Parliamentary institutions are so inadequately representative. A restricted franchise, archaic methods of conducting elections, and the abuse of power by Upper Houses, are debited to representative government, although they defeat rather than express it. While we cannot claim for the members of Parliament to-day the complete freedom which Burke claimed, they are still capable of doing much; and, if we would increase their utility, we should provide more adequate means of ensuring that they should be truly representative.[1]

The importance of keeping in view the dual aspect of the problem of the constitution of the legislative

1. *Cf. infra,* in Chap. viii. "The Right to Self-government."

organ may be illustrated by reference to the referendum and the bicameral legislature. In Australia, the referendum is compulsory in the case of all amendments of the Federal Constitution, and it is occasionally employed by State legislatures in matters where public opinion needs to be ascertained as a condition of effective legislation; *e.g.*, the control of the liquor traffic. While its value for such purposes is indisputable, I believe that a frequent use of this expedient would be a calamity. The more completely it invaded the domain of everyday politics, the greater would be the power of momentary majorities, the less honourable and responsible would be the status of the Parliamentary representative, and the more restricted would be the power of the legislature to perform that work of critical interpretation upon the importance of which all impartial thinkers are agreed. Most of the arguments in favour of the frequent reference of political issues to the decision of the electorate derive their importance from the survival of an archaic method of conducting elections. When some system of proportional representation has been adopted, and the legislature is in consequence more adequately representative, we shall hear less about the referendum.[1] The subject has been recently discussed in Great Britain with special reference to the problem of settling disputes between the two Houses of Parliament; and the Imperial Government invited the opinion of members of the Australian Federal Ministry as to the working of the referendum in Australia. Several reflections suggest themselves. (1) Deadlocks are generally settled in Australia in accordance with the representative idea. There is a double dissolution, a general election, a further Parliamentary deliberation, and, if necessary, a joint sitting of both Houses. Only in the State of Queensland is the referendum employed

1. *Cf.* Jethro Brown, "The New Democracy," chapters on "The Referendum" and "The Hare System," where the relative merits of these proposals are discussed at length.

for the purpose of settling deadlocks.[1] (2) Even if we were to suppose that the referendum ought to be employed for the purpose of settling deadlocks, it is extremely important not to lose sight of the dangers involved in its frequent use. Under the stimulus of party conflict or momentary exigencies, grave constitutional changes are apt to be advocated without regard to deeper issues. People who want a thing badly are too often prepared to welcome any means of obtaining it that are not apparently dishonourable, without stopping to enquire whether those means may not involve changes of a revolutionary and even disastrous character. (3) As the supporters of the referendum in Great Britain are at present mainly found in the ranks of the Conservative party, it may not be out of place to question the validity of the prevailing opinion that this method would prove in practice a check upon hasty legislation. That opinion is based upon a generalisation from conditions of which some, at least, are passing away. In proportion as the electorate is effectively organised on party lines, a momentary majority in the legislature will find it easier to command a momentary majority of the electorate, and so to secure the passing of laws it would not have ventured to pass on its own initiative and responsibility. Already, in Australia, the Labour Party in Parliament is being constantly attacked by the Labour Party in the electorate for its tardiness in carrying out its platform. It is even accused of flagrant disloyalty. The real explanation of the tardiness in question is that a Labour leader who is elected to Parliament, and is compelled to face the criticism of a deliberative assembly and to grapple with the practical difficulties of translating a policy into terms of law, learns much—learns, among other things, the wisdom of looking all round a question before rushing into legislation. (4) One argument in favour of the use of the referendum

1. Harrison Moore and Ernest Scott, "The Referendum in Australia," *Quarterly Review*, April, 1911, 534.

in Australia, though not directly connected with the problem of deadlocks, deserves mention. It is urged that "the tyranny of the caucus" is brought to bear upon the Labour representative in such a way as to turn him into a mere delegate of the caucus. While I believe that the accounts given of the Labour caucus by the organs of Conservative opinion have been greatly exaggerated for party purposes, I cannot but admit that, if such a tyranny actually existed and appeared destined to continue, the question of the referendum would enter upon a new phase. A legislature composed of persons who were the passive instruments of organisations external to Parliament would possess the advantages neither of representative government nor of a direct democracy.

The question of deadlocks is only one aspect of the more general problem of the bicameral legislature —a problem that involves issues of the highest importance and has evoked a bewildering conflict of passion and opinion. One conclusion may be asserted with confidence. An Upper House is justifiable as a means of ensuring that legislative proposals shall be more completely expressive of the social will; and if it fails to promote this end, and becomes a mere organ of class interests, it should be either abolished or reconstructed.

The problem, however, presents itself in different countries under curiously different aspects. Great Britain and Australia may be quoted in illustration. An author who has won a high and deserved reputation for clearness of thinking and cogency of argument, writes of the House of Lords as follows:—

"Take a list of the most representative acts of legislative reform relating to religious liberty, freedom of the press, purity of elections, improvements in municipal government; turn to the long array of reforms of our criminal and civil codes, the building up of our public system of education, the structure of

Factory and Workshop Acts and of other laws relating to the protection of workers, sanitary legislation, Irish legislation, and, in particular, laws attempting to repeal or modify the power of landlordism, and to secure to the people of Great Britain or Ireland a freer access to and fuller use of their native land—there will be found hardly a single important measure belonging to any of these orders which in its endeavour to express the popular will that gave it birth has not suffered death or mutilation at the hands of the House of Lords."[1]

At the very moment of the appearance of Mr. Hobson's indictment of the House of Lords, an Australian Senator was engaged, in the pages of the *Contemporary Review*, in attacking the Commonwealth Senate on very different grounds.

"The Senate, as a revising or a redeliberative separate House, might as well be closed up. . . . The Labour Socialists have a majority of eight in a House of thirty-six, and that majority is pledged, every man of it, (*a*) to support the platform of the party, and (*b*) on matters affecting that platform to vote as a majority of the party at a duly constituted caucus shall determine. . . . To send a measure up to the Senate is now a useless formality."[2]

Mr. Hobson has his own remedy to suggest with regard to the House of Lords. That House, reconstituted on an elective basis, is to be entrusted with a power of submitting to the referendum any measure which, though passed by the House of Commons, is adjudged not to have received the sanction of the people. In order to secure substantial equality between Liberal and Conservative Governments, the author suggests that the power to call for a referendum shall also be vested in a minority of the House of

1. J. A. Hobson, "The Crisis of Liberalism," 18-9.
2. "The Australian Federal Election," *Contemporary Review*, July, 1910, 19.

Commons (say two hundred members). Senator St. Ledger is more reticent. There are, indeed, obvious difficulties in the way of suggesting a remedy for the ills he diagnoses. Neither a reconstruction of the Federal Senate nor a substantial alteration of its franchise appears to be within the sphere of practical politics. Nor would any delimitation of Senatorial powers meet the difficulties of the situation, as viewed by Mr. St. Ledger, for the point of attack is not that the Senate is dangerous, but that it is useless. Nor, again, would the problem be satisfactorily solved by allowing a minority of either House to compel a referendum. Apart from other objections, a party that controls a majority in two Houses elected on an adult suffrage is likely to command a majority for the time being in the electorate.[1]

With regard to Mr. Hobson's indictment of the House of Lords and his proposals for reform, I shall not venture to express an opinion. But, as one who has had some opportunity of observing the trend of recent legislation in Australia, I may be permitted to make two remarks with regard to the charges of Mr. St. Ledger against the Federal State. In the first place, I am inclined to think that he overstates his case. I do not believe the Senate is at present so docile an instrument in the hands of the Labour Party as Mr. St. Ledger suggests. But, even if it were, it could still do useful work as a chamber of revision. It certainly brings an entirely different body of men to the discussion of the legislative measures submitted to it. Even if its majority be controlled by the same powers as control the majority in the House of Representatives, their control is limited to general policy

1. Not always, as is shown by the rejection of the proposals submitted by referendum in 1911. One result of that rejection, however, has been to give a new impetus to the movement towards electoral organisation. I may add that, since the appearance of Mr. St. Ledger's article, there has been in 1913 a re-submission of the proposals of 1911 in a modified form. While the proposals were again rejected, the hostile majorities were much smaller. I incline to the opinion that the proposals would have been carried but for the fact that the Labour Party had lost prestige owing to strikes and other causes.

rather than to questions of detail; and any one who is at all acquainted with the history of statutory legislation will realise how important is the function that can be discharged in this way.[1]

In the second place, although, as I have already indicated, the question of finding means for increasing the utility of the Federal Senate is a difficult one, a partial remedy could be found in an improved method of conducting elections. The adoption of some system of proportional representation would make the Senate more representative, and would improve its *personnel*. Under the Commonwealth Electoral Acts, each State is a single constituency in elections for the Senate; each elector must vote for the full number of candidates to be elected; and the candidates receiving the greatest number of votes are thereby elected.[2] Hence an organised majority of voters in any State may secure the whole of the representation for that State. A system of proportional representation would provide against this unfortunate result; and it would specially protect those classes which, from the variety of their interests, are less easily organised in a combined vote than the party that is directly representative of labour.

III.—Review.

From this digression into the region of practical politics I return to the general subject of this chapter. It has been my object to review the efforts of thinkers to formulate a theory of social unity. I have endeavoured to show the sense in which society can be described as organic, and to illustrate the theory of State personality by reference to the conception of the social will. In conclusion, I may remark that the

1. Mr. St. Ledger wrote his article in 1910. At the Federal elections in 1913, while the Labour Party maintained its control over the Senate, the Liberal Party secured a majority of one in the House of Representatives. Hence that concurrence of opinion between the two Chambers, which is the foundation of Mr. St. Ledger's indictment, has ceased to exist.

2. *Cf.* Moore, "The Constitution of the Commonwealth of Australia," 2nd ed., 115.

conception of the social will is only one of many elements in the theory it illustrates. Professor Hugo Münsterberg has been twitted for his recent explanation of the mental state that leads the rich American to cheat the customs. The eminent psychologist had affirmed that, while the wealthy citizens of America may be scrupulously honest, they are

"unable to personify the United States, and therefore do not hesitate to try to defraud it. Because they regard it as impersonal, they are likely to regard smuggling as a game of chance."

I venture to endorse Professor Münsterberg's conclusion. The theory of the State's personality, in addition to the services it renders to the theory of legislation, gives new meaning and emphasis to the citizen's responsiblity to the State. In proportion as men recognise the realities of which this theory is an expression, they will realise that, in defrauding the State, they are not defrauding a merely impersonal abstraction, such as exists in the imagination of the speculator who makes his profits "off the market," but are engaged in an act of treason towards a Being whose honour and welfare are indissolubly bound up with their own. Some other questions, too, will appear in a new light. It will not be so readily supposed, in the sphere of international relations, that a community can be aggressive, unscruplous, and false, without besmirching its own honour and degrading the character of its own citizens. A "social conscience" which exists only in relation to domestic affairs, and has no existence for external relations, is of course conceivable; but only as a type of conscience in an early and unreflecting stage of development.

PART II.

THE PRINCIPLES IN APPLICATION.

INTRODUCTORY NOTE.

In Part I., I have stated two principles that appear to me to underlie modern legislation. I now propose to illustrate the application of these principles by discussing two doctrines that have exercised, and still exercise, a wide influence in the arena of political debate. I allude to the doctrines of *laissez faire* and natural rights. Whenever a political question is under discussion, these doctrines, though possibly in a disguised or qualified form, are certain to be invoked by one party or another according to the exigencies of the moment. Both contain important elements of truth, though alloyed with much that involves a disregard or distortion of the principles already affirmed. While in general tendency one doctrine is conservative and the other is revolutionary, both imply views as to the limits within which the action of the State is legitimate. For this reason alone, if for no other, they appear to me to deserve a careful examination in an age especially distinguished by the rapidity of the movement towards collective control.

In the course of my discussion I shall especially consider the attitude of the State to the enforcement of morality, the function of competition in civilised society, "the living wage," and "the right to work."

CHAPTER V.

THE TRUTH IN *LAISSEZ FAIRE* (1)

"Statesmen, instead of exploding general prejudices, employ their sagacity to discover the latent wisdom which prevails in them."—BURKE.

PARENTAL GOVERNMENT AND CLASS LEGISLATION.

MR. J. A. HOBSON, in a recent work, exposes "the Tactics of Conservatism." These tactics are alleged to consist in the elaboration of an informal sociology designed to degrade the moral and intellectual forces of democracy. According to the author, biology has contributed to this sociology a doctrine of racial salvation through natural selection; political economy has contributed a theory of the beneficence of competition as a means of industrial efficiency; psychology and ethics have contributed a theory of social reform which, professing to concern itself with the development of character, deprecates any dependence upon legislative aids as calculated to sap the self-reliance of the individual; and religion has proved an invaluable ally, either in the crude form which teaches or implies that man should concern himself about the salvation of his immortal soul rather than about the safety of the Commonwealth, or else in the more refined forms offered by Hegelian dogma or by the later determinism distilled out of evolutionary science.[1]

"No sooner are we approaching such large issues of social policy as are involved in taxation of land values,

1. "The Crisis of Liberalism," 177–87.

pensions, unemployed relief, the House of Lords, than everywhere the atmosphere is kept abuzz with whispers about 'sanctity of contract,' confiscation, pauperisation, and those hints of popular indifference which take the heart out of reformers."[1]

The work just referred to has a militant purpose. Its author may be excused, therefore, for not insisting upon the fact that the enemy has something worth saying for himself. To the impartial student, however, the "informal sociology" that has excited Mr. Hobson's derision must appear to contain much that is true, although not novel; much that the reformer would do well to bear in mind if he is to win for his cause something more than a momentary triumph. Mr. Hobson is all for a policy of plucking up the wheat with the tares in the field of tradition. True progress consists less in making a clean sweep of ancient doctrine than in effecting a revision and re-statement of ancient doctrine in accordance with new conditions, advancing knowledge, and higher ideals of social justice. The attitude of some reformers to-day reminds one of the proposal of the librarian who has urged that the more accessible shelves in a public library should be reserved for books published after 1900!

The arguments that Mr. Hobson would relegate to the museum of political antiquities have an obvious parentage in the doctrine of *laissez faire*. But that doctrine, even in the extreme form of "the less law the more liberty," was no more absurd than a later doctrine, which might be summarised with equal justice in the formula, "The more law the more liberty." While both doctrines might claim a measure of justification in time conditions, one doctrine made a fetich of non-intervention, whilst the other makes a fetich of State regulation. If, as seems more than probable, the right path lies between these extremes, the very existence of the present trend towards collectivism is a reason for

1. "The Crisis of Liberalism," 92.

endeavouring to discover how far, or with what qualifications, the *laissez faire* doctrine possesses enduring value. The more the State controls in some directions the actions of its citizens, the more imperative must be the need of recognising the importance of free self-determination in general. *Laissez faire* undoubtedly taught non-intervention; but it did much more. It not only attacked certain types of legislative interference, but it also gave reasons for its hostility. Most of those reasons remain valid to-day, though with qualifications imposed by the progress of thought or by changes in economic conditions. Such reasons and qualifications will be the subject of the present and following chapters. I shall endeavour to show that they are not inconsistent with the legislative principles stated in previous chapters, but, on the contrary, are the corollary of those principles in their negative application.

At the outset, however, I shall venture to insist upon a truth which seems to me of cardinal importance. An examination of an important doctrine, if it is to be truly critical, should be sympathetic. I shall illustrate, therefore, the dangers of collective control—dangers which formed the staple of *laissez faire* argument—by reference to two historical examples of despotisms which are especially suggestive since they were enforced with the intention of promoting a social and individual good. My first example is the State of classic times.

"The ancients," wrote the late Lord Acton, "understood the regulation of power better than the regulation of liberty. They concentrated so many prerogatives in the State as to leave no footing from which a man could deny its jurisdiction or assign bounds to its activity. . . . Individuals and families, associations and dependencies, were so much material that the sovereign power consumed for its own purposes. What the slave was in the hands of his master, the citizen was in the hands of the community. The most sacred obligations vanished before the public advantage. The passengers existed for the sake of the ship." [1]

No one at all acquainted with Greek thought can suppose that Greek philosophers or statesmen were unfamiliar with the idea that the State exists for the individual as much as the individual exists for the State: but that idea received a very inadequate recognition in Greek laws and institutions.

My second example is taken from more modern times. Puritanism, though in origin an affirmation of the rights of the individual, became "a grinding social tyranny." The Puritan rebel had fought for religious and political freedom. The Puritan ruler displayed a narrow and fanatical intolerance. With the best of intentions, he showed a distrust of human gaiety which went far to justify the suggestion of Macaulay that he "hated bear-baiting, not because it gave pain to the bear, but because it gave pleasure to the spectators." There was to be no more dancing round the maypole; no more cakes and ale; no more mince pies. Such frivolities were to be repressed in order that the Puritan might realise his vision of God's Kingdom on earth. But he failed. Because he attempted too much, he achieved less than he might. It is true that his thought was of the individual soul rather than of the collective good; but his conception of what individual salvation meant was narrow; and, in the extent to which he was prepared to go in enforcing that conception upon others, he was more despotic than the royalist tyranny he had overthrown.

The Hebraism of the Puritan and the Hellenism of the Greek have often been contrasted. We find in the Puritan a strength of will, an integrity of character, and a moral earnestness of view. We find in the Greek an urbanity, a breadth of vision, and an incom-

1. "History of Freedom and other Essays," 16-7

parable sense of beauty. But alike with the Puritan and the Greek, though in very different ways, a beneficence of aim did not preclude a despotism in fact. It is perhaps in this respect that our times may learn most from Puritan and Hellenic polities. The increasing magnitude of the modern State, the ever-growing complexity of modern industry with its tendency to turn human beings into mere specialists, the multiplication of agencies for the expression and strengthening of public opinion, and the growing tendency to embody public opinion in legislative enactment—these are facts of the present which, no less than the history of the past, serve to warn us of the possibility that with the best of intentions government may be used as an engine of despotism. To assert so much is to assert that a *prima facie* case exists for a sympathetic examination of a doctrine that endeavoured to work out a theory of the legitimate limits of State control.

In its origin *laissez faire* stood for the policy of allowing every one to make whatever he chooses, and was distinguished from *laissez aller*, or the policy of allowing every one to take his labour and send his goods to whatever market he pleases.[1] But in later times the term *laissez faire* has been employed in a wide sense to express an attitude of hostility to certain types of governmental action which may be described as parental government, class legislation, and the regulation of industrial competition. I propose to consider these types in the order indicated. For the purposes of discussion, I shall deal with parental government under the two heads of maternalism and paternalism.

(*a*) *Governmental Maternalism.*

By governmental maternalism I mean the type of polity which, in a spirit of maternal solicitude, treats the citizen as if he were an infant. The normal mother is anxious to do as much for the child as possible. She

1. Marshall, "Principles of Economics," 567 note.

punishes him lightly or not at all for his misdeeds, and is supremely concerned to remove all difficulties from his path. In the governance of the citizen the maternal legislature emulates this type of domestic polity. It is more anxious about the citizen's comfort than about the strength of his character, and prizes security above liberty. Or perhaps I should say that it makes security an end, instead of regarding security as a means to the realisation of liberty. The citizen is to have things done for him that he should do for himself; he is to be shielded from temptation; and he is generally to be treated as if he were incapable of looking after his own interests.

No one would defend governmental maternalism as thus defined. It is an obvious violation of the principle of human worth, since it underestimates the potentialities of human character. In its exceeding anxiety to care for the citizen, it assumes his total inability to care for himself. "The individual," says Dr. Mckechnie, "has only to get himself born: the State will do the rest." But *laissez faire* teaching on this subject requires to be qualified if it is to be of practical value. I submit with diffidence, and with a full consciousness of entering upon highly controversial topics, the following qualification. *A government is not necessarily precluded from doing things which the citizens ought to do for themselves, if, as a matter of fact, there is no reasonable probability that the citizen will do these things, and if the ends to be gained are of great importance.*[1] An exaggerated emphasis used to be laid by the individualist upon the argument that, since temptation is necessary to strengthen character, the State should never legislate with the object of limiting the sphere of temptation. But if

1. The qualification suggested in the text appears to me to be in substantial accord with a more recent formula of Mr. Hobhouse, who defines the general function of social control as that of ensuring the best conditions for the common life (*a*) so far as these are best obtained by the use of public resources and governmental machinery, (*b*) so far as such conditions are only obtainable by the use of compulsion. "Social Evolution and Political Theory," 200.

experience proves that a particular form of temptation is undermining the morality of the community, the argument from the discipline to character falls to the ground. Temptation may be a good thing; but a man may have more of it than is good for him. Again, no one now condemns the factory legislation of the nineteenth century, although at the time of its enactment there were many who thought it an unwise effort on the part of the State to do for individuals what they should do for themselves. Even if the operatives of a factory had been *able* to combine effectively for their own protection, there was no reasonable probability of their doing so.

"While," writes Jevons, with reference to more recent legislation, "it is a fact that people live in badly-drained houses, drink sewage water, purchase bad meat or adulterated groceries, it is of no use urging that their interests would lead them not to do so. The fact demolishes any amount of presumption and argument." [1]

My insistence upon the necessity of qualifying the *laissez faire* doctrine with respect to governmental maternalism might appear to lend countenance to the belief that the conception itself has a merely academic value. Some justification for such a belief may be found in the fact that English legislation in the past has seldom erred on the side of maternalism. Indeed, were this not so, Lord Acton could not have written: It is

"the native qualities of perseverance, moderation, individuality, and the manly sense of duty, which give to the English race its supremacy in the stern art of labour, which has enabled it to thrive as no other can on inhospitable shores, and which (although no great people has less of the bloodthirsty craving for glory)

1. "The State in Relation to Labour," 43.

caused Napoleon to exclaim, as he rode away from Waterloo, 'It has always been the same since Crécy.' "[1]

But the suggestion that the conception of governmental maternalism has a merely academic value overlooks two important facts. In the first place, the humanitarian movement of our time, admirable though it is, has its attendant dangers. In the second place, instances may be found, even in the past, of misguided philanthropy on the part of the legislator. The working of the old Poor Law, as it existed in the earlier part of the nineteenth century, is a classical example. In view of recent tendencies as displayed in the "Reports of the Poor Law Commission of 1909," a reference to the "Report of the Poor Law Commission of 1834" might seem belated. I do not think it would be so regarded by competent judges. While the recommendations of the earlier Commission, even if they had been carried into effect, would have proved inadequate to solve the many and changing problems of Poor Law administration, the evidence accumulated by that Commission has an enduring value. It shows how a misguided philanthropy may tend to degrade the national character. The system of indiscriminate out-door relief, the admission of an absolute right in the pauper to maintenance by the State, and the State endowment of motherhood, had sapped the habits of industry, and imperilled the family life, of whole classes of the community. The policy of the State gave an official sanction to the refrain:

> "Then drive away sorrow, and banish all care,
> For the State it is bound to maintain us."

Multitudes grew careless and apathetic as workers, shamelessly dependent as citizens, and callous as parents.

"The patriotic parent," writes Archdeacon Cun-

1. "History of Freedom and Other Essays," 60.

ningham, "was apt to feel that in providing children he had done his duty, and that a grateful country ought to provide for them." [1]

Children were even discouraged by their parents from seeking employment, lest the State allowance should be discontinued. At Thaxted, it was said, mothers and children would not nurse each other in sickness unless they were paid for it.[2] Cases were alleged where parents threatened to turn their sick children out of doors if an allowance were not forthcoming. In the homes, instead of thrift, economy, and a resolute desire to make the best of things, there were too commonly idleness, extravagance, and neglect.

"In the pauper's habitation," said one witness, "you will find a strained show of misery and wretchedness; and those little articles of furniture which might, by the least exertion imaginable, wear an appearance of comfort, are turned, as it were intentionally, the ugliest side outward; the children are dirty, and appear to be under no control; the clothes of both parents and children, in nine cases out of ten, are ragged, but evidently are so for the lack of the least attempt to make them otherwise; for I have very rarely found clothes of a pauper with a patch put or a seam made upon them since new." [3]

There is no need to enlarge on the burden such a system inflicted upon the ratepayer. But this was by no means the gravest of the resulting evils.

"A person," said Mr. Cowell, "must converse with paupers—must enter workhouses, and examine the inmates—must attend at the parish pay-table, before he can form a just conception of the moral debasement which is the offspring of the present system; he must hear the pauper threaten to abandon his wife and

1. "Politics and Economics," 90.
2. "Report of the Poor Law Commission, 1834," 96.
3. *Ibid.*, 89.

family unless more money is allowed him—threaten to abandon an aged bedridden mother, to turn her out of his house and lay her down at the overseer's door, unless he is paid for giving her shelter; he must hear parents threatening to follow the same course with regard to their sick children; he must see mothers coming to receive the reward of their daughters' ignominy, and witness women in cottages quietly pointing out, without even the question being asked, which are their children by their husband, and which by other men previous to marriage; and when he finds that he can scarcely step into a town or parish in any county without meeting with some instance or other of this character, he will no longer consider the pecuniary pressure on the ratepayer as the first in the class of evils which the Poor Laws have entailed upon the community." [1]

One would be strangely optimistic to suppose our own generation stands in no need of taking to heart the lessons that may be learnt from the misguided philanthropy of the older system of Poor Law. We suffer from the defects of our good qualities.

"If poor men," says Mr. Harold Cox, "are to be helped out of the public funds simply because they are poor, poverty will become by itself a title to pecuniary reward." [2]

"For some years," writes Sir John Collie, "the accident laws have revealed to the unscrupulous the infinite possibilities of fraud, and I feel confident that, unless the fact is recognised by those who will have the responsibility of working the Insurance Act, the moral currency of the working classes will be debased." [3]

The dangers of governmental maternalism have never been more real than to-day. The argument drawn

1. "Report of the Poor Law Commission, 1834," 97.
2. Quoted, McKecknie, "The New Democracy and the Constitution," 140.
3. Quoted from an article in the *Edinburgh Review*, July 1913, p. 30.

from these dangers should therefore neither be forgotten nor cheapened by an undiscriminating use. On the one hand, as Professor Bosanquet puts it, simply to *do* in every case what you desire to see *done*, is a policy which frustrates itself. On the other hand, to leave a thing undone because you think others ought to do it, without stopping to enquire whether they can or will do it, is to ignore realities. The question of old age pensions is in point. An attitude of uncompromising hostility to this form of social insurance gives plausibility to the view that the argument from governmental maternalism is merely a phase of "Conservative tactics." On the other hand those who have realised the dangers of maternalism must recognise the important differences in the merits of the various schemes that have been proposed or are in actual operation. While the suggestion to limit the pension to deserving applicants is impracticable, a great deal might be said in favour of other proposals not incorporated in the British scheme. Mr. Charles Booth has urged that the pension should be given to every person of the prescribed age who chooses to apply for it. Among the many advantages of such a scheme is the encouragement which it offers to thrift. The citizen is not made to feel that if he saves as a wage earner he may be penalised as a pensioner. While some would rely upon the pension absolutely, the great majority would seek to supplement it. The assurance of a minimum would stimulate the desire for more. That, as far as may be practicable, the pension should be contributory is even more important than that it should be universal. One of the problems before British statesmanship is to discover some method of engrafting upon the present scheme a system of contributions proportioned to the age and conditions of those who, in the years to come, will be applicants for the pension. One scheme, which appears to me to deserve careful consideration, has been sketched in broad outlines by Mr. Carson Roberts. He proposes that those who are now between twenty and sixty years of age shall have the option of joining in a new and improved contributory scheme or retaining their expectant rights under the old.[1] A non-contributory is to be converted into a contributory system by a proless of voluntary election in favour of a better offer.[2]

Is the British National Insurance Act an example of governmental maternalism? The question would be answered by many in the affirmative. The Act purports to provide for insurance against loss of life, and for the prevention and cure of sickness, and for insurance against unemployment. In an able article which appeared in the *Edinburgh Review* for July 1913, the writer refers to the evil results of the Act in the form of new nervous diseases, far slower recoveries, insurance hysteria, unnecessary or fraudulent claims, and open pride in successful dependence on the public purse. But against these results, in so far as they are actual, must be placed the alleviation of much suffering and poverty, and the degradation of character which in the past has accompanied the conditions of economic insecurity under which a large mass of the population have lived. The Act, moreover, is contributory. Its broad purpose is to assist the working population in meeting certain contingencies against which, of their own initiative, they have failed to protect themselves with any approach to adequacy. I submit that the Act comes within the qualification of *laissez faire* doctrine already stated. The ends to be gained are of great importance; experience has shown that those ends have not been adequately secured by voluntary association in the past; and there is no reason to believe that they will be in the future. That in some respects the Act should be amended, that the machinery for its administration admits of improvement, and that no conceivable amendment of the Act or improvement in its administration will entirely

1. "How to improve and extend our National Pension Scheme," *Nineteenth Century and After*, December 1910, 958.
2. *Ibid.*, 960.

eliminate all abuses must be conceded. But the line of true progress in the future appears to me to be, not in reversion to pure voluntaryism, but in minimising abuses and in safeguarding the integrity of existing voluntary agencies.[1] Two general conclusions may be expressed with confidence. (1) The most ingeniously devised social reform is sure to be accompanied by some disadvantages. (2) The practical value of the doctrine of *laissez faire* as here revised will be found to consist, not so much in affording a justification for non-intervention by the State, as in serving to indicate the ways in which State intervention can secure the most gain at the least sacrifice.

(*b*) *Governmental Paternalism.*

Governmental paternalism, in the sense adopted in the present chapter, is closely associated with the polity just considered. Both polities are despotic, in a broad sense, since they treat the citizen as a child. In both, the despotism is benevolent, since it aims at promoting an imagined good of the citizen. Many legislative Acts might be quoted which offered equally both polities. Yet there are between them certain differences which are important. The spirit of the one is typified by the mother who coddles the child; the spirit of the other by the father who "lays down the law." In one case, the despotism is fussy: in the other, it is repressive. While maternalism makes the State a nursery for hothouse plants, paternalism turns it into a bed of Procrustes. The former finds its typical expression in exaggerated State aid; the latter in excessive State regulation. While both profess to promote the good of the citizen, that good consists in

1. On several of the subjects involved in the above discussion, the reader will find a forcible presentation of useful data in the Alden's "Democratic England." See especially the chapters on "The Problem of the Unemployed," "State Insurance against Sickness," "The Problem of Old Age," and "The Problem of Housing the Poor." See also the article by Mr. Chiozza Money on National Insurance in the *Fortnightly Review* for October, 1913. I shall discuss the subject of Unemployment in a later chapter on "The Rights of the Individual."

the one case in "having a good time," in the other case in the conformity of character to a type determined *ab extra.* It follows from this conception of governmental paternalism that the term should be distinguished, not merely from governmental maternalism, but also from the State regulation of industrial competition—a subject to which I have referred when discussing legislative idealism in the nineteenth century, and to which I shall return in my next chapter. The *laissez faire* argument under immediate consideration might be summarised as a protest against attempts to make men moral by Act of Parliament or as an appeal for the legislative minimum in the sphere of individual conduct. It is important to bear this in mind because the whole doctrine of *laissez faire* has suffered in popular estimation as a result of its identification with the argument in favour of "free competion." It is one thing to contend that the competitive system should be controlled (or abolished) out of regard to the general interest; it is quite another to contend that the State should undertake the responsibility of enforcing rules of conduct upon individuals in their own interest. To some extent, no doubt, there is an overlapping of argument in the two cases; but they require to be considered apart.

Critics of *laissez faire* have pointed out that there is no such thing as a sphere of individual conduct, and that for all practical purposes every self-regarding duty has also a social significance. To any one who has realised the unity of society, the validity of this criticism does not call for demonstration. But although the purely self-regarding duty may be a fiction, a distinction can be drawn between duties according as their violation more especially affects the individual himself or other people. The distinction, though one of degree rather than of kind, and in practice often difficult to draw, is of real importance. It is one thing to insist that a man shall have his house connected with a system of deep drainage; it is quite another thing to insist that he shall practise calisthenics, or that he shall go to bed at a reasonable hour. It is one thing to punish drunkenness when accompanied by disorderly behaviour; it is quite another thing to punish drunkenness *per se*. Vaccination laws, though often defended as requisite for the well-being of the individuals with regard to whom compulsion is necessary, are essentially a means of protecting the general public from the dangers of infection. Sumptuary laws, on the other hand, except when simply the expression of class domination, may be assumed to have been inspired by a paternal desire to promote the good of the persons who were subjected to them Anti-gambling laws are more difficult to place. Whether they fall within the conception of paternalism must depend upon the extent to which they go and upon the conditions under which they are passed. If, however, in a particular community, the habit of gambling has become a national vice which is undermining the morals and industry of the people, no sane exponent of *laissez faire* would oppose legislative action. Of course it is not always easy to say when a particular vice has become a menace to the national well-being; but the question is one of fact. The important thing is to keep clearly in view the two distinct sets of considerations that are involved. A recent Act of Parliament of South Australia forbids the Sunday "*bona fide* traveller" to refresh himself by the way. The alleged justification for this legislation was the nuisance occasioned to the general public by Sunday drinking at suburban hotels. But the more ardent advocates of the change were really influenced, I believe, by the conviction that "refreshing" was bad for the individual.

The arguments against governmental paternalism are numerous and important. Several of them apply to excessive regulation whether in the general or in the individual interest. I shall indicate later the qualifications to which, in my opinion, they are subject. In the meantime, I wish to state these arguments as briefly and forcibly as I can. The first is the fallibility of rulers. I have already enlarged upon this topic in the Prologue to the present work. I shall only remark here that, while a governing body may be wiser than the individual, it is necessary to take into consideration the individual's special knowledge of his own circumstances and character, and the unique stimulus he possesses to discover in what his real interest consists. Even if we assume the existence of an ideally representative legislature, the opinion of that legislature may be wrong, and its enforcement by positive enactment may involve unjustifiable tyranny. True, the legislature exists to interpret popular opinion in terms of law. This fact, however, is quite consistent with the recognition both of the need of educating popular opinion to a due consciousness of its fallibility and of the wisdom of proceeding with the utmost caution in prescribing rules of conduct that are not imperatively demanded in the general interest. Such a statement is, of course, a truism; but a truism that is in danger of being overlooked in an age when "the fatalism of the multitude" threatens to become an accomplished fact. "The belief in the right of the majority," writes Mr. Bryce, "lies very near to the belief that the majority must be right."[1]

A more important argument than the fallibility of governments is to be found in the limitations of legal machinery. A government must legislate for men in the mass; it can only secure an external conformity to rule; and its sanction is one of punishment. Each of these limitations deserves consideration.

(1) *Government legislates for men in the mass.* As Sir Henry Maine remarked, although a minute discrimination between individual and individual was possible in the family groups of patriarchal society, the distance that divides the modern ruler from the bulk of his subjects compels him to deal with great

1. "The American Commonwealth," 1910 ed., ii. 350.

classes of acts, and with great classes of persons, rather than with isolated acts and particular individuals.[1] But if legal rules ignore in a greater or less degree the infinite variety of individual conditions and possibilities, their indefinite multiplication must tend to produce an artificial uniformity of character.

"We should think we had done wonders," wrote Mill, "if we had made ourselves all alike; forgetting that the unlikeness of one person to another is generally the first thing which draws the attention of either to the imperfection of his own type, and the superiority of another, or the possibility, by combining the advantages of both, of producing something better than either."[2]

A saner policy would recognise the justice of Prior's praise of his friend who denied to have his

"freeborn toe
Dragoon'd into a wooden shoe."

We hear much to-day of co-operation; and it often appears to be assumed that, in the name of co-operation, we are justified in any amount of dragooning. But, as Professor Hobhouse points out, co-operation has its negative as well as its positive aspect. If mutual aid is necessary to social life, mutual forbearance is no less necessary.

"In thinking of social life as a form of co-operation we must lay stress not only upon the activities which it cultivates in common, but on the idiosyncrasies which it tolerates, the privacy which it allows, the divergent developments of personality which it fosters."[3]

(2) *A Government can only enforce external actions.* The State may compel a man to do, or to forbear from, certain actions; but it cannot ensure that his doing so or forbearing shall proceed from the right

1. "Early History of Institutions," 293. *Cf.* Jethro Brown, "The Austinian Theory of the Law," 17 note.
2. "On Liberty," 105.
3. "Social Evolution and Political Theory," 186.

motives, since no machinery can be devised for enabling judicial tribunals to determine whether the motives were good or bad. The inner workings of a man's heart defy the scrutiny of the Courts of Justice.

"The thought of man," said Chief Justice Brian in the reign of Edward IV., "shall not be tried, for the devil himself knoweth not the thought of man."

This may be questionable theology, but it is sound law. While modern statutes and judicial decisions have shown a tendency in the direction of punishing an apparent moral culpability, the standard of culpability is determined by reference to what would be blameworthy in the average man; and, in the application of that standard, the Courts look to the external actions of the individual whose conduct is under adjudication. Dr. M'Kecknie has pointed out that the enforcement of a formal and outward habit of right living may ultimately lead to an inward and free morality. If this happy result could be generally relied upon, the argument that the State can only ensure an external conformity to rule would have little value. But I believe that the *laissez faire* scepticism on this point was justified. There is a fable of a lover whose consciousness of the defects in his personal appearance led him to wear a beautiful mask. At length, determined to profit no longer by the deceit, he discarded the mask, only to find his face transformed to the likeness of his ideal. The fable has been quoted by one writer in illustration of the view that a State-enforced morality must tend to become spontaneous. A strange misreading, surely! The lover of the fable was transformed in feature just because the mask was self-imposed in pursuance of an ideal that was self-determined. The difference between the re-active influence upon character of self-imposed law and law imposed *ab extra* is illustrated by a curious and instructive fact in the history of religion. The most intensely religious sects have not infrequently displayed hypocrisy in its most objectionable forms. The explanation is not difficult. An intensely religious sect is apt to be despotic; it prescribes, with a rigidity that admits of no exception and an emphasis that overwhelms revolt, the things a man must do, and the things he must not do. If the member of such a sect finds its teaching congenial to the spontaneous prompting of his will, he becomes a devotee; but if he is not so fortunate, and if he has not the strength of character to become an open rebel, he drifts into a conscious or unconscious hypocrisy as the line of least resistance. He professes dogmas that he does not sincerely hold, because he is constrained to do so by the force of the collective opinion around him. "You will admit," urged an apologist, "that compulsory religion is better than no religion." "I fail to see the distinction," was the reply.[1]

Political despotism, no less than religious, yields a harvest of deceit, evasions, and trickery. A recent controversy, upon a question of imperial policy, is in point. It has been urged that monogamy should be enforced upon subject communities even where polygamy is deeply ingrained in tribal habit. Now monogamy in the abstract is a good thing; but an Imperial State which enforces this good thing upon a community without any regard to historical circumstance may do no more than establish monogamy in form and immorality in fact.

(3) *The legal sanction is one of punishment.*—With respect to the means available for insuring conformity to rules of conduct, a legislature is less favourably situated than the father of a family. A father can teach by example as well as by precept. His precept may be sanctioned by punishing disobedience or by rewarding obedience. His reward may take the form of praise or gift. His gift may be promised in advance, or may be given without promise. The motives to good conduct which are thus provided

1. Bosanquet, "Philosophical Theory of the State," 193 note.

vary immensely in their ethical value. As between the sanction of reward and the sanction of punishment, for example, the former is preferable if it can be made efficient; it avoids the infliction of suffering and leaves more freedom of action. The child does not feel that he *must* do certain things, but that he will gain if he does them. The line between the sanction of reward and the sanction of punishment is not always easy to draw: what purports to be a sanction of reward may be one of punishment in disguise. But the distinction is important, and depends upon the extent to which the idea of compulsion is present. Punishment is the natural or normal sanction of a command. Reward is a means for inducing conformity to an appeal.

When we turn from the family to the State, we find that almost invariably, and from practical necessities, obedience to regulation is enforced by penalties.[1] "Law," said Reclus, "instead of appealing to man's better part, appeals to his worst; it rules by fear." Martineau remarks that the place of fear in the hierarchy of the springs of action cannot be definitely assigned, since it varies according to the nature of the thing feared.

"The egoist will have fears only for himself; the benevolent, largely for others; and the moral quality of these fears will be imported simply from the affections that inspire them."[2]

But, in the case of positive law, the object of fear is physical punishment together with any social stigma that may chance to be associated therewith. Hence, one of the gravest arguments against governmental paternalism consists in the fact that the State has not at its command the complex apparatus of motives that enables a wise parent to achieve desired results with no more employment of lower springs of action than may be necessary. It treats the adult in ways in which the judicious parent would not treat the child.

1. *Cf.* Jethro Brown, "The Austinian Theory of Law," 8 note.
2. "Types of Ethical Theory," part II., book I., chap. vi.

In the preceding statement of the arguments against governmental paternalism I have referred to the fallibility of rulers and to the various limitations of the machinery at the State's disposal. While the statement of these arguments cannot be dissociated from the question of the effects of paternalism upon the happiness and character of the citizen, the argument from this latter point of view calls for further consideration. *Laissez faire* regarded a law as *per se* an evil, and implied a conception of liberty as consisting in doing what one liked. While we no longer regard law as *per se* an evil, and have outgrown the related conception of liberty, we must not forget that a man's freedom to choose his own line of conduct is an important element in both his happiness and his character. From the point of view of happiness, the matter would scarcely call for mention but for the existence of an energetic school of reformers who find a peculiar satisfaction in framing codes of conduct for other men, and appear to attach no importance whatever to the fact that a man likes to frame his own code of conduct. In a recent story, purporting to be written in the twenty-fifth century, the author bemoans the ever-widening range of the criminal code. By that time it has become a statutory offence to sleep within closed windows, to lick a postage stamp, or to woo without the consent of the Matrimonial Department of the National Health Office. The hero of the story finds himself so beset with such restrictions that, in a fit of perversity, he proceeds to the Post Office and licks a postage stamp in the presence of a horrified staff of officials. He is promptly imprisoned for several months at the Depôt for Mental Diseases. When the term of his imprisonment expires, he is offered his freedom. He refuses. "It makes little difference," he protests, "whether I am in prison or not. The State takes so much care of me that I am a prisoner anywhere—a Prisoner of the State." The story cannot be regarded as altogether fanciful. I fear there are many people to whom liberty as a legislative end means no more than a right to do as they like and to prevent other people from doing what they like.[1] At a recent election in a certain part of his Majesty's dominions, the propaganda of one section of the voters was of such a nature as to provoke, not without reason, the following satirical travesty :—"Drinking is a sin! Smoking is a sin! Dancing is a sin! Gambling is a sin! Enjoying yourself is a sin! Everything's a sin!"

From the point of view of individual character, the argument against governmental paternalism is mainly based upon the danger of producing in the citizen the attitude of mind that looks to superior authority for its whole rule of life. As an acute economist has observed:

"By degrees inspectors will make their way into our houses to see that our drains are in good order, our rooms well ventilated, our kitchen boilers safe, our cisterns clean, our children at school. If this sort of thing is to progress, we shall be guided and tutored and inspected at every hour of the day."[2]

While the danger in this direction may be exaggerated by the apologist of the *status quo*, no one can doubt its reality. Over-regulation of the individual can only end in "substituting a dead legality for a living morality."

"In theological terms," writes Professor Flinders Petrie, with respect to the type of State action under consideration, "people are trying to overcome the Fall by abolishing Free Will: and they forget that compulsory virtue is no virtue at all, but merely incapacity. A free will which solely worked one way, and never let a man down, would be only a supreme prize-giving with no blanks, fit for plaster princesses in a world of sugar-plums. For living men and women, for endurance of the flesh and restraint of the blood, for

1 *Cf.* Faguet, "The Cult of Incompetence," 68.
2. Jevons, "The State in Relation to Labour," 41.

strength of will and force of action, for hardy courage and free affection, the more we are trained to carve our own destinies, and the more we suffer for our faults and triumph in our successes, the higher the result and the nobler the characters that will be produced."[1]

In actual practice, the foregoing statement of the arguments against governmental paternalism is subject to certain qualifications. The *laissez faire* doctrine, in so far as it is defensible, is really directed, less against paternalism *per se*, than against the expression of paternalism in the way of coercive regulation. But the State may exercise a controlling influence over the lives of its citizens in indirect ways to which the foregoing arguments are either inapplicable, or applicable in a very modified degree. Unhappily, exponents of *laissez faire* have seldom realised the importance of this distinction; and their attitude of hostility to State control as such has predisposed them to oppose Governmental paternalism in any form. There is, however, a vast difference between prohibiting men from doing certain things and providing conditions which shall predispose them to choose right action for themselves. It is one thing to make drunkenness a crime; it is quite another to ensure that the rising generation shall know something of the dangers of alcoholism. The State can emulate St. Louis, of whom Montesquieu said that he got rid of an evil by making patent the better way. On this subject I can do no better than quote from Professor Ross's admirable work on " Social Control."[2]

" What lifts the bristles in man is external pressure. He kicks against the pricks. Whipping makes him balk. Threat suggests resistance. Ostracism, prison, hell, provoke in certain natures defiance of God and man. If, now, society will lure him instead of drive him, he will cause no trouble. The moulding of his will by social suggestion, the shaping of his

1. *Hibbert Journal,* July 1908, 795.
2. " Social Control," 420.

ideas by education, the enlightenment of his judgment, the setting up of shining goals and black scarecrows in the field of life to influence his choices—these, if skilfully done, do not arouse the insurgent spirit."

Moreover, on the single ground of the economy of disciplinary agencies, a

"method that, once and for all, moulds character is superior to one that deals merely with conduct, which is but the index of character. A roundabout course of procedure, such as the instilling of social valuations, is more politic than a direct assault upon the individual will with threats and promises. A far-sighted policy, such as the training of the young, is preferable to the summary regulation of the adult. In the concrete, these maxims mean that the priest is often cheaper than the detective, that the free library costs less than the jail, and that what is spent on the Sunday School is saved at Botany Bay."[1]

One illustration of the possibilities of indirect control by the State is suggested by Sidgwick. While he protests against prohibiting the citizen from consulting a quack, he points out that Government may reduce the mischief of quackery in several ways: (1) by requiring an uncertified practitioner to abstain from concealing the absence of a certificate; (2) by giving damages or inflicting punishment for grossly unskilful treatment; and (3) by refusing to uncertificated practitioners the legal right of receiving fees from their patients. No one could object to the legal punishment of such a man as the enterprising person who advertised himself as M.B.—on the ground, as he explained to the Court, that he practised both in the city of Melbourne and in the suburb of Brunswick!

The qualification just considered has reference to the forms in which governmental paternalism finds expression. A second qualification relates to the

1. "Social Control," 428.

character of the individuals over whom a paternal control is exercised. Obviously, an act forbidding juvenile smoking may be justified on the ground that restraints which are inadmissible in the case of the adult may be necessary in the case of the child. But even the adult may be so weakened in will power, as a result of indulgence in vicious habits, that only drastic action can save him from complete degradation. He may be addicted to drink, to opium smoking, or to the luxury of living on the toil of others. The dipsomaniac, the opium smoker, and the unemployable may be regarded as types of a class with respect to which the *laissez faire* presumption in favour of freedom of action is rebutted by facts. It is futile to talk of the advantages of leaving a man to look after himself when the only use he makes of his opportunity is to go to the Devil as speedily as he can. The arguments against paternalism can only be maintained in the case of the normal adult; and where an adult exhibits an extraordinary degree of irrationality or of weakened will power, the State is justified in treating him as a child. Indeed, in such cases as I have indicated, the question is not so much one of the State's right as of the State's duty to act in the individual's own interest. The proper place for the dipsomaniac is an asylum; the proper place for the idler is in the prison colony. Such institutions, if wisely controlled for reformatory purposes, so far from being an invasion of the liberty of the subject, are to be regarded as means for the enlargement of liberty. They exemplify the legitimate application of the formula that a man may be "forced to be free."

A third qualification upon *laissez faire* doctrine is frequently suggested; but I do not think it can be defended.

"It is no disadvantage to the good citizen or to society at large," writes Professor Henry Jones, "that the legislature should more and more effectively block the paths that lead to wrong action. . . . The good citizen is thereby sustained in his attempt to do what is right. . . . *Even the immoral or unsocialised person is not really wronged by such regulation, nor deprived of any of his rights. . . . Liberty to do wrong is scarcely a right.*"[1]

The conclusion is suggested that the mere fact of certain conduct being morally wrong confers a right upon the State to prohibit that conduct by positive law.

The conclusion may appear to be in accord with the conception of the nature of self-realisation to which I referred in an earlier chapter. If the self to be realised is man's social self, it might seem that no injustice is done to the citizen by legislation prohibiting an act which, since it is immoral, may be fairly assumed to be anti-social. But this view of the matter ignores the practical difficulties and considerations that constitute the argument against paternal legislation. The modern ideal of liberty does, indeed, stand for the maintenance of conditions that will enable the citizen to realise his social self; but such conditions imply more room for the exercise of a free self-determination than could exist if the law of the State attempted to proscribe every immoral act. Professor Henry Jones appears to me to confuse the scope of liberty and right in Law, Ethics, and Politics respectively. Law defines legal rights; Ethics defines moral rights; Politics defines those moral rights that would be legally enforceable if law were what it ought to be. Each of these sciences has, for example, its own rules for determining whether a lie is wrongful. Except under special circumstances, a man is legally free to lie as often as he chooses. Politics, which is always in advance of law in progressive communities, may advocate the delimitation of the area within which a man shall be legally free to tell a lie. But no one would urge

1. "The Working Faith of a Social Reformer," 253-4. The present writer is responsible for italicising the concluding sentences.

that the State should punish lying in all cases where it is morally wrongful. The most perfect legal code that could be framed must concede the liberty (in the political or legal sense) to do wrong (in the moral sense). But if this be the case, liberty to act in certain ways which every one must agree to be immoral, is one of the political rights of the citizen. It is a right because its possession cannot be denied to the individual without making government an instrument of intolerable despotism. As Professor Hobhouse remarks, "Since personality consists in rational determination by clear-sighted purpose as against the rule of impulse on the one side or external compulsion on the other, it follows that liberty of choice is the condition of its development."[1]

Professor Henry Jones, however, may be safely assumed to be too sensible of practical realities to advocate that the State should embark upon the absurd project of making every moral wrong a legal offence. Possibly he means that a State has a right to prohibit moral wrongs, but that the right should be exercised with a due regard to consideration of expediency. If, however, this be his meaning, it invites the reflection that the rights of the State in relation to its individual members cannot be determined until considerations of expediency have been taken into account. Among such considerations are the various arguments against paternalism that have been already stated. The argument based upon the fallibility of rulers is of itself a strong reason against admitting the right of the State to punish conduct on the single ground that it is morally wrong. The *laissez faire* position is that a citizen has a right to be left alone so long as his action does not inflict grave and direct injury upon others; and it is surely an easier matter to determine whether such injury is inflicted than to determine whether the conduct is morally wrong. As a matter of historical fact, the

1. "Social Evolution and Political Theory," 199.

liability of the State to err in the determination of what is morally wrong has been too amply demonstrated by experience to call for comment. But apart from the fallibility of rulers, the other arguments to which I have referred in expounding the *laissez faire* position have to be taken into consideration. If law can only ensure an external conformity to rule, and makes its appeal to lower types of motive; and if the happiness and the character of the citizen are to be promoted, less by governing men than by enabling men to govern themselves—then there is on these grounds a conclusive reason for denying the right of the State to prohibit conduct merely because it is morally wrongful. The far-seeing legislator will always remember, not merely the immediate advantages to be gained, but also the price to be paid. In a particular case, the advantage of State regulation may seem so obvious, and the limitation of freedom so slight, that the reformer is apt to overlook the danger of an intolerable accumulation of limitations.

"If," exclaimed Milton in Areopagitica, "every action which is good or evil in man at ripe years were to be under pittance, prescription and compulsion, what were virtue but a name, what praise could then be due to well-doing, what gramercy to be sober, just, or continent?"

The wise State builds

> "Upon the *inward* victories of each
> Her hope of lasting glory for the whole."

(*c*) *Class Legislation.*

We should strangely misunderstand the doctrine of *laissez faire* if we attributed its distrust of State action solely to the fear of benevolent despotism. The intensity of that distrust was largely due to a conviction that State action meant class tyranny. The statute book, mediæval or modern, afforded some justification for this conviction.

"Esquires and gentlemen under the estate of a knight," declares a mediæval statute, "shall not wear cloth of a higher price than four and a half marks; they shall wear no cloth of gold nor silk nor silver, nor no manner of clothing embroidered, ring, button, nor brooch of gold nor of silver, nor nothing of stone, nor no manner of fur: and their wives and daughters shall be of the same condition as to their vesture and apparel, without any turning-up or purfle or apparel of gold, silver, nor of stone."[1]

While this statute *may* be regarded as a diverting example of paternalism, it *probably* expressed the spirit which dictated the ancient prayer,

"God bless the squire and his relations."
And keep us in our proper stations."

Certainly, that spirit is revealed in legislation of a more important character. According to Brentano, all Statutes of Labourers in the Middle Ages were framed with regard to the powers and wants of the feudal lords. The great Statute of Apprentices of the time of Queen Elizabeth, observes Jevons, aimed at establishing an industrial slavery. Every servant or artificer was to work in the trade to which he was brought up; any workman who left his city, town, or parish without a testimonial might be imprisoned until he procured one; and if he failed to do so within one-and-twenty days, he was liable to be whipped. The legal day's work was fixed approximately at twelve hours at the *least*. Unmarried women, of the age of twelve and under forty, might be ordered by the magistrate to serve for such wages and in such manner as the magistrate should think fit.[2] Although this statute was only partly carried into effect, it was not finally

1. "Law in a Free State," 76-7.
2. 5 Elizabeth, ch. iv. *Cf.* Jevons, "The State in Relation to Labour," 35-7.

repealed until the passing of the Conspiracy and Protection of Property Act of 1875. The Corn Laws, which were the subject of so much agitation in the early part of the nineteenth century, were maintained in the interest of the landlords. It was a memorable day in the history of England when, in the autumn of 1841, Cobden called to express his sympathy with Bright, who had just lost his wife. "I was in the depths of grief," said Bright in after days, "for the life and sunshine of my house had been extinguished." Cobden spoke his word of condolence, and delivered a sterner message. "There are thousands of homes in England at this moment where wives, mothers and children are dying of hunger. When the first paroxysm of your grief is past, come with me and we will never rest till the Corn Laws are repealed." Bright accepted the challenge, and won for himself a name which must last as long as English liberty endures.

To multiply such examples as I have just given would be superfluous. I have merely referred to them in order to illustrate the extent to which the *laissez faire* opposition to State action was stimulated by experience of State action of a particular type. The question remains whether, in view of the democratisation of political institutions, this type can be regarded as possessing more than a merely historical interest. It is not difficult, however, to find an answer. In the first place, a Parliamentary majority is often a mere conglomeration of groups whose wills find expression in legislation for reasons of party tactics. According to one eminent and impartial observer,

> "The bidding for support of whole classes of voters by legislation for their benefit presents probably the most serious menace to which British institutions are exposed."[1]

In the second place, legislation may be class legislation even though it be approved by a majority of

1. Lowell, "Government of England," ii. 535.

the people. While the sovereign claims of the common welfare are to-day admitted in form, the modern multitude, like the aristocracy it has displaced, is apt to assume that its own interest is necessarily *identical* with the common welfare. It threatens at times to pass under the domination of those who, in place of the old notion that the welfare of the majority should be subordinated to the interests of the minority, would substitute the doctrine that the interests of the majority need not be taken into account. A majority acting on this doctrine would sooner or later pay heavy penalties; but the operation of these penalties is seldom immediate, and may be far from obvious. The very fact that our political institutions confer supreme power upon a majority of citizens makes class legislation more plausible, if not more easy. Few impartial thinkers of our time will endorse Nietzsche's attack on democratic institutions, but the dangers to which he refers are far from imaginary. Democratic institutions offer an ideal means whereby mere numbers may establish, through the medium of the ballot-box, a political and economic system which will level down the few rather than upraise the many, and will so develop a race of invertebrates rather than a race of super-men. The dangers in this direction appear to me to be exemplified by certain proposals for social reconstruction to which I shall refer in the following chapter. Meanwhile, I desire to guard against a possible misinterpretation of my remarks on class government. I do not attack majority rule; on the contrary, I believe in it, even if a liberal price has to be paid for it in the shape of occasional tyranny or misgovernment. But I also believe in so framing political institutions as to impose a check upon the despotism of a momentary majority, and I believe still more in the possibilities of the political education of the electorate. A majority which exploits a minority is not a maintainer of right but an enforcer of wrong. It is not always easy to convince the elector of the fact, but that is only an illustration of the need for educating the electorate in the principles of wise legislative action. In proportion as those principles are understood, it will be realised that the true and lasting interests of majorities and minorities are too interrelated to admit of dissociation. The so-called "self-regarding majority" is only capable of planning its own destruction. On the other hand, the "rights of minorities," in so far as they are deserving of recognition, are claims in the enforcement of which the well-being of majorities as well as minorities is involved.

CHAPTER VI.

THE TRUTH IN *LAISSEZ FAIRE* (II).

Competition.

Few subjects of our time involve issues of more vital import, or have been more discussed, than Competition. Much of the discussion, however, has been of the unprofitable kind that results from mutual misunderstanding. I propose to begin the present chapter with a statement of certain propositions which appear to me to constitute a common ground upon which the "individualist" and the socialist may agree as a basis for argument. I shall then consider the bearing of these propositions upon some proposals for social reconstruction.

(1) *Competition in trade and industry must be subject to State regulation.* The form of such regulation is a matter of opinion; its necessity in some form will be universally conceded. Men no longer hope for salvation through "the free play of individual interests," or regard "freedom of contract" as an immutable article of faith. The change in modern opinion on these matters has been noted in an earlier chapter.[1] In the present place, in order to facilitate our enquiry into the extent to which the teaching of *laissez faire* in relation to competition remains valid, I wish to dwell briefly upon the fallacious character of two arguments to which that school attached importance.

The first of these arguments was economic. It was urged that free competition was for the good of all classes, since it tended to cheapen commodities, to

1. Ch i, "Legislative Idealism in the Nineteenth Century."

stimulate the production of wealth, and to secure a fair wage to the labourer as a result of the rivalry among employers in the labour market. That argument has been completely discredited by two facts. In the first place, experience in the nineteenth century demonstrated that "free competition" involved a prodigal waste, both in material resources and of human life. The waste in material resources, whether due to maladjustment of supply and demand or to the friction of industrial warfare, was at least partly counterbalanced by the tendency of competition to stimulate the rate of production. But the value of a high rate of production is largely conditional upon an equitable distribution of the results of production—a distribution which was conspicuously absent. The sacrifice of human life constituted an even more serious indictment. We have to reckon not merely with the statistics of mortality, though these were appalling enough, but with a condition of degradation which denied to masses of the population the life of the soul though it might not destroy the life of the body. In reality, what was called "free competition" was free in name only. Under the prevailing conditions competition could only be free by being regulated. But however this may be, it became increasingly clear, with the development of the factory system, that "the free play of individual self-interest" was *not* for the good of all classes.

"I am convinced," said Thorold Rogers, "that at no period of English history for which authentic records exist was the condition of manual labour worse than it was in the forty years from 1782 to 1821, the period in which manufacturers and merchants accumulated fortune rapidly, and in which the rent of agricultural land was doubled."[1]

In the second place, experiments in the way of State regulation, whatever their demerits, at least served to prove the possibilities of wise action on the

1. "Six Centuries of Work and Wages," 63.

part of the State in relation to industrial competition. No one now condemns the Factory Acts of Lord Shaftesbury. The irresistible logic of fact refuted even those economists whose objection to State regulation was based, not on the cheerful optimism which believed that the system of "natural liberty" was the shortest route to "natural justice," but on the ground that such regulation must do more harm in lessening the aggregate of production than it could do good in effecting a more equitable distribution. The industrial legislation of the nineteenth century, in improving the conditions of labour, served to promote the economic efficiency of the labourer as well as to secure good things for him. In this way it increased the aggregate of production.

"The English cotton manufacturer," writes Miss Black, "produces more cheaply and more profitably upon the whole, than any competitor" because "the good conditions enforced by law, and the comparatively high wage conferred by the trade unions, combine to create for him the most efficient body of cotton workers in the world. Once more, the facts of industrial history proclaim the truth that efficiency is not the cause but the product of fair wages, healthy surroundings and reasonable leisure."[1]

The case for "free competition" has been materially weakened in our own time by the intrusion of a new force in the arena of industrial conflict. The *laissez faire* economist, though not unaware of the existence of that inter-class struggle which is sometimes described as competition, held that the struggle was transformed into a harmony of interests by the operation of true, or intra-class, competition. The war between capital and labour, for example, was held to be checked, controlled, and corrected by the competition among employers for the labour necessary to production, and among wage-earners for the means of

1. "Sweated Industry," 226-7.

subsistence. To some extent this has always been true; but the consolidation of classes has revealed how little the check can be relied upon.

"The economist's traditional *apologia* for competition," writes Professor Lovejoy, "seems curiously *mal-à-propos* at a time when precisely that competition *within* each economic class—which, when generalised, has been supposed to be the saving feature of the situation—is conspicuously tending to disappear, and is doing so with, perhaps, results on the whole advantageous. In many trades, labourer no longer freely competes with labourer for employment; and, in the most advanced branches of modern business, producer no longer competes with producer for the larger sales to the consumer. Organisation and consolidation of interests in each class tend to be the rule; so that the competition which remains stands out all the more nakedly as a competition between economic classes as units. And, finally, to this latter sort of competition the usual argument of the economists is not in the least applicable. That argument never really faced the issue respecting inter-class competition as such; it merely pointed out that rivalry within a class was to the interest of those outside this class, and that each class, therefore, in so far as it was engaged merely in this internal competition, was benefiting all others."[1]

I have quoted Professor Lovejoy at some length because I agree with the substance of his remarks. I think, however, that he is guilty of one exaggeration. Although competition, in its proper sense, is proving less effective as a corrective of inter-class conflict, I cannot agree that it is "tending to disappear." The advent of the trust and the trade union do, indeed, limit its scope; but they by no means involve its gradual extinction. Even if we were to suppose all

1. "Christian Ethics and Economic Competition," *Hibbert Journal*, January 1911, 340-1.

the industry of the country to have passed under the control of trusts, and every wage-earner to be a member of a trade union, competition among wage-earners must still remain in various forms:—among applicants for work, among employees who are ambitious for a higher wage or for positions of responsibility, and among employees at the bottom of the ladder who have reason to fear being squeezed out of employment. In some American trusts competition is conserved between different plants by sharing with employees the results of the turnover. Speaking generally, a trust is likely to become somnolent unless it maintain an active competition in one form or another. What is more important, there are, in ways, which I shall illustrate later on, practical limitations upon the process of trust formation. The trust is only likely to succeed in industries where the business unit is large. Of course, the trust is only one form of class consideration. But as regards agreements between more or less independent concerns with a view to controlling prices, such concerns may still compete with one another in promptitude, civility, quality of goods, and other forms of serviceableness.

The economic doctrine that free competition is for the good of all classes was closely associated with another argument to which the *laissez faire* school attached importance. Under the influence of Darwinian theory, the sacrifice of human life that accompanied free competition was regarded as a beneficent cruelty—a sacrifice of the weak in the interest of the race. The argument has been justly discredited by later criticism; primarily on the ground that an unregulated, or inadequately regulated, system of industry does not work for the survival of desirable types.

"As long as we think of life as an end," remarks Mr. Hobhouse, "there can be no question of any kind of fitness, and this is precisely the biological view.

But if we conceive of one kind of life as intrinsically higher than another, and ask whether the type best fitted to survive is necessarily the type best adapted to that higher life, a perfectly new question arises, to which the biologist as such is not equipped with any answer."[1]

Social organisation should aim at maintaining such conditions as will tend to make the struggle for survival more and more a struggle in which the fact of survival is a proof of the possession of qualities of body, mind, and character that are socially valuable. If we consider the industrial scramble of the early nineteenth century, the biological argument in support of *laissez faire* appears a pernicious fatalism. Mill, in spite of individualistic predilections, expressed his own opinion in a passage that has become classic.

"If persons are helped in their worldly career by their virtues, so are they, and perhaps quite as often, by their vices; by servility and sycophancy, by hard-hearted and close-fisted selfishness, by the permitted lies and tricks of trade, by gambling speculations, not seldom by downright knavery. . . . It is as much as any moralist ventures to assert, that, other circumstances being even, honesty is the best policy, and that with parity of advantages an honest person has better chances than a rogue."[2]

Mill here attacks the character of those who triumph under a system of free competition. Some later investigators have much to say of those who go to the wall. Doctor Archdall Reid, in his recent and important work on "The Laws of Heredity," writes as follows:—

"To me it seems overwhelmingly probable that slum-dwellers, factory hands, and the like are physically inferior, not because they are as a class in-

1. "Democracy and Reaction," 99–100.
2. *Fortnightly Review*, February 1879. 226.

capable of developing as well as the best sections of the community, but mainly, if not solely, because their surroundings are such that they have not the chance of developing as well as they might."

The remarkable success of the late Doctor Barnardo's experiments with the London waif tends to justify this statement.

The failure of "free competition" to effect the survival of desirable types has discredited the biological arguments in favour of a policy of non-intervention. That argument, indeed, recalls the views of those who regarded sanitary laws for the prevention of cholera as an interference with the inscrutable ways of "Providence." Just as it was discovered that man can improve on "Providence," so it has been found that he can improve on "Nature." The biological form of the *laissez faire* argument assumes the universal application of a principle which is a generalisation from lower forms of life, and ignores the vast power of other agencies than "natural selection" where human life is concerned. Through the agency of the State, man can regulate competition in such a way as to encourage the survival of higher types; through manifold forms of associated effort, he is able to mitigate the cruelties of natural selection; and, by controlling the material conditions under which individuals live, he can improve the human race through changing the human environment.[1] It is scarcely possible to exaggerate the importance of the fact that man, as the architect of his environment, is to a large extent the controller of his destiny. He can so mould his environment as to bring out potentialities for good, and repress potentialities for evil, in the children born into

1. *Cf.* Archdall Reid, "The Laws of Heredity." "If we desire to improve a human race, two ways of attaining our aim are conceivable—(1) We may follow the plan of Nature and of plant and animal breeders, and alter by selection the racial capacity for growth in this or that direction; or (2) by altering the conditions under which the individuals of the race develop, we may alter the kind and amount of stimulus they receive."

it. If we assume, as I believe we must, that acquired characteristics are not transmitted from the parent to the offspring, the rational conclusion seems to be, not that we should desist from endeavours to effect an improvement of the human environment, but that we should persist in maintaining the improvement. The logical result of any other conclusion is to condemn sanitary laws, since they interfere with the process by which unaided Nature evolves a race of beings who shall be relatively immune from disease. Finally, as regards the more obvious forms of unfitness, man can aim at their elimination by other methods than those of non-rational Nature. Already men are beginning to ask whether it would not be less cruel, as well as more sane, to isolate or sterilise the vicious and diseased elements of society than to starve them out of existence.[1]

Professor Hobhouse, in his recent work on " Social Evolution and Political Theory," makes a suggestive contribution to the subject under discussion. He points out that, if natural selection is the foundation of all progress, mutual aid must be the enemy of progress. As a matter of fact, " it is the social type that inherits the earth." Although a community loses something by the preservation of members who are ill equipped, physically or morally, it gains more than it loses by compliance with rules of social order and justice. To understand the conditions of social progress, we have to take into account, not only the individuals with their capabilities and achievements, but the social organisation in virtue of which these individuals act upon one another and jointly produce social results. " While the race has been relatively stagnant, society has rapidly developed, and we must conclude that, whether for good or for evil, social changes are mainly determined, not by alterations of racial type, but by modi-

1. *Cf.* the remarks, in ch. viii. *infra,* on " The Right to Marry." Also, in ch. ix *infra,* on " The Problem of the Child."

fications of tradition due to the interaction of social causes. Progress is not racial, but social."[1]

(2) *Competition, in the sense of an efficient rivalry between individuals, is a condition of social progress.* The *laissez faire* doctrine maintained, in relation to the problems of industrial organisation, two propositions:—(*a*) Effective competition is indispensable to social progress: (*b*) In order that competition may be effective, it must be free from State interference. In rejecting the latter of these propositions, it is important not to overlook the truth and value of the former. While competition should be subject to State control, and while the forms of such control may possibly involve a radical reconstruction of the economic order, the need of maintaining the rivalry of individual against individual is indisputable.

The conclusion just stated is based upon one of the elementary facts of human nature. Man is a competitive animal—not in the sense that he will compete for the mere pleasure he may experience in doing so, but in the sense that his pursuit of an end is incomparably more eager if he finds himself in opposition to rivals with a like end in view. I shall venture to illustrate the fact by reference to a subject with which I have had some practical acquaintance—the discipline of the Universities. If students were super-human, such artificial stimuli as degrees, prizes, and scholarships might be dispensed with. Taking the student as he actually is, we find it useful to stimulate his pursuit of learning by the introduction of competition in many forms. We award honours; we draw up class lists in order of merit; we distribute money prizes and scholarships; and we refuse to grant a degree to students who fail to come up to a standard which is defined for practical purposes by reference to relative merits and demerits. Some ardent reformers—Mr. Frederic Harrison may be quoted as

1. "Social Evolution and Political Theory," 23–39. *Cf.* also *infra*, Chapter ix, "The Problem of the Child."

an example—would dispense with such expedients. They would trust to the will of each student to realise the best that is in him. Our knowledge of the character of the average student prevents us from sharing this faith. We know from experience that the vast majority work best where rivalry is most keen; and we seize every legitimate opportunity, whether in sports, examinations, or the discussions of the class-room or seminar, to stimulate the competitive instinct. To those who tell us that rivalry is not the highest motive to effort, we answer that it is the most efficient. We welcome the student who, for pure love of knowledge and in disregard of prize distinctions, ploughs a lone furrow. But we do not make the mistake of taking this exceptional student as a model for the purpose of determining our general system of discipline.

The State, no less than the University, must take men as it finds them. Whether its aim be the development of character or the maintenance of the standard of economic efficiency, it must utilise the combative instincts of men. If production is not to languish, if human worth is not to remain a mere potentiality, a keen rivalry is indispensable as a spur to habits of industry. It is also indispensable as a means to the discovery of that exceptional efficiency upon whose utilisation the success of any economic system must depend.

Some critics of competition, while admitting its value, declare that the price paid is too high. This general objection takes three forms which deserve separate consideration. In the first place, competition is said to involve a prodigal waste. But this assertion is not universally true: its validity depends upon the conditions under which, or the forms in which, competition is carried on. Competition for profits in the past has undoubtedly involved a deplorable waste of human effort and material resources. But industrial co-operation, the concentration of capital in the form of trusts, and even some forms of socialism, while they substitute rivalry among wage-earners for rivalry among profit-seekers, offer a means of avoiding the waste that takes place under an individualistic system of industry. Competition in these cases, though it may be less keen, is not eliminated; and, at any rate in the case of industrial co-operation, a compensating stimulus to effort may be found in the sense of community of interest. Whether this stimulus proves adequate must depend upon the form of industrial co-operation and the *morale* of the co-operating individuals.

In the second place, competition is said to be cruel. But this, again, largely depends upon circumstances. Even under existing conditions competition is far less cruel than it is often represented to be.

"Efficiency and inefficiency are relative terms. There are prizes greater and less for all, and these prizes are found all along the route, and not alone at some far-off terminus." [1]

But, even if the process were as cruel as it is often represented to be, the mitigation of such cruelty must be effected with a due regard to all the factors of the problem. It is even better that a few should suffer than that the many should be submerged. If a scheme of social reconstruction does not offer a reasonable guarantee that the best brains and the best workmen shall be brought to the top, it is *ipso facto* condemned.

In the third place, there are some who hold that under any conditions competition is essentially immoral. While I recognise the existence of higher motives to effort than those called into operation by rivalry, the view that competition is essentially demoralising appears to me to exhibit a strange ignorance of human character. I once read, in a French journal, a violent attack upon fox-hunting. A distressing picture was drawn of men and women,

1. Fell, "The Foundations of Liberty," 137.

riding furiously, and with their thought intent upon the shedding of innocent blood. To an Englishman, such a criticism only served to reveal the ignorance of the critic. Whether fox-hunting be defensible or not, no one who knows anything about the pastime can suppose that the dominant purpose of the hunter is to gratify a lust for blood. Many attacks upon competition reveal an equally absurd interpretation of the springs of human action. Men do not compete for prizes in order to gratify feelings of personal enmity. Even competition for profits is not necessarily vindictive. A. seeks to get as many customers as he can: B. has a like object. The competition may become immoral if one or the other is dominated by hatred, or endeavours to defeat his rival by the employment of unfair means. But neither of these conditions is essential to competition.

"When one producer or seller prospers as against another, it is by offering society the better product or the lower price. Viewed, therefore, from the point of view of society, competition is a rivalry in offering most for least—a contest in the rendering of largest service, a war in well-doing—where success is declared to the largest benefactor."[1]

The possibility that a trade rivalry may tend to unfair practices is less an argument against competition than an argument for its collective control.

(3) *One of the most important functions of the State is to ensure that competition shall be real.* So-called free competition is often no competition at all. Some classes still enjoy a monopoly of the learned professions; in some countries, hereditary houses have secured a practical monopoly of the land; and, in all advanced communities, great corporations have obtained, or are seeking to obtain, monopolies in trade, industry, and labour. Much as these forms of monopoly differ, they have one thing in common. They

1. Davenport, "Outlines of Elementary Economics," 187.

are attempts to restrict competition in the interests of particular classes—usually without any regard to the welfare of the community. Although the appropriate remedy may not always be found in legislative attempts to intensify or to restore competition, there are at least many cases of monopoly that should be dealt with in this way. I shall return to the question of industrial monopoly when discussing the theory of Socialism. Other forms of monopoly will receive consideration in chapters on "The Rights of the Individual."[1]

(4) *A no less important function of the State is to moralise competition.* This proposition does not conflict with that just stated. It may be illustrated by an analogy from the world of sport. The rules of football prohibit punching; the Marquis of Queensberry rules forbid kicking; and, according to the orthodox conception of the game of lacrosse, the lacrosse stick is not to be directed against the skull of the adversary. In all sports there are rules of the game, which define the forms in which rivalry between opponents may find expression. Such rules, in so far as they are good rules, do not enfeeble rivalry; they only regulate its character in accordance with a particular conception of the game. Certain muscular activities, proper in one sphere, may be brutal in another. Football is not a prize-fight; high kicking, however creditable on the music-hall stage, is out of place in the prize-ring; and cutting off the adversary's ear or splitting his cranium, admirable as it may be in swordsmanship, is no part of the game of lacrosse. The application of all this to political society is obvious. The true function of social regulation is not to eliminate competition, but to direct it along certain lines with the object of retaining its power as a stimulus to effort while removing or diminishing its undesirable consequences. In a passage quoted in a previous chapter, the poet Coleridge described "the free play of individual

1. *Infra*, ch. viii.

interests" as self-slaughter on the part of the poor, and soul-murder and infanticide on the part of the rich. Society recognised the justice of this censure, and devised new rules of the game, calling them Factory Laws. Such laws, so far from abolishing competition, had rather the effect of making competition more real. They rescued whole classes of the community from a condition of degradation in which competition had been free in name only. The history of law is to a large extent the record of attempts to control competition in accordance with higher conceptions of the meaning and purpose of life. While competition necessarily gives the award to the strong, the degree of civilisation that has been attained in any particular society may be gauged by reference to the nature of the qualities that make for strength.

The methods adopted by the State in its endeavour to moralise competition have usually been distinguished as legal control, administrative control, and public ownership. The dairy industry will serve as an illustration. Under a system of legal control, the customer who is served with impure milk may prosecute the vendor or may sue him for damages. Under a system of administrative control, the Government appoints inspectors to visit dairy farms and test the milk supplies. Under public ownership, the dairy farm becomes a governmental or municipal institution. In the last-mentioned case, it is apt to be assumed that competition is moralised out of existence. But this by no means follows. A Government which owns the farms may lease them to private individuals at a fixed rental. Here, of course, there is still a competition for profits. If, however, public ownership is accompanied by public management, there ceases to be a competition for profits; but amongst the employees of the Government or the municipality there may yet remain a competition for managerial offices and for higher wages.

The difference between the various forms of State

control may be illustrated by reference to the objections to which they are severally open. Legal control may fail to attain the end in view. Where, for example, the customers who receive impure milk are too ignorant to know good milk from bad, or are too apathetic to enter upon the troublesome business of a law-suit, legal control is likely to prove an inefficient check upon the malpractices of the milk vendor. On the other hand, an administrative control, though likely to prove less inefficient, will impose fresh burdens on the State. Public ownership, while it may prove to be the most efficient means of all for ensuring a supply of pure milk, limits the scope of competition and increases the responsibilities of the Government.

The attempts of legislatures to secure a minimum wage afford a striking illustration of the policy of moralising competition. While these attempts have been too recent to admit of a final pronouncement in favour of any one of the various schemes actually tried, none of the schemes with which I am acquainted can be regarded as involving a startling innovation. They are simply an extension to wages of a principle on which the factory legislation of the nineteenth century was based. Both the old factory legislation and the new are expressions of the will of the State to exercise a control over industry with respect to the conditions of labour. While the old legislation was concerned with the hours of labour and the sanitation of the factories, and the new legislation is more especially concerned with the rate of wage, it must not be forgotten that "prolonged hours of labour are in fact but a form of diminished wages."[1] The ends served by the old legislation and the new are the same—the protection of the workers, the care of womanhood and weakness, and the nurture of the childhood of the race. In both the old legislation and the new, these ends are effected by the same means—the elevation of the plane of competition among

1. Clementina Black, "Sweated Industry," 187.

employers. In the absence of State control, the capitalist who underpays his workman is able to undersell his rival. In other words, the rate of wage is ultimately fixed, not by the fair-minded employer, but by the unscrupulous employer. As Mr. Adams says,—" There must be conformity of action between competitors, and the only question is whether the best man or the worst man shall set the fashion." [1]

There is another respect in which we may trace an identity in principle between the old factory legislation and the new. Both originate in the proved inadequacy of any means, short of legislative action, to moralise the conditions of competition in the labour market. The argument used by T. H. Green to defend the factory legislation of the last century is so applicable to some of the legislative experiments of our own day that I venture to make a lengthy quotation.

" Left to itself, a degraded population perpetuates and increases itself. Read any of the authorised accounts, given before royal or parliamentary commissions, of the state of the labourers, especially of the women and children, as they were in our great industries before the law was first brought to bear on them, and before freedom of contract was first interfered with in them. Ask yourself what chance there was of a generation, born and bred under such conditions, ever contracting itself out of them. Given a certain standard of moral and material well-being, people may be trusted not to sell their labour, or the labour of their children, on terms which would not allow that standard to be maintained. But with large masses of our population, until the laws we have been considering took effect, there was no such standard. There was nothing on their part, in the way either of self-respect or established demand for comforts, to prevent them from working and living, or from putting

1. " The State in Relation to Industrial Action," *American Science Association*, i. 508.

their children to work and live, in a way in which no one who is to be a healthy and free citizen can work and live. No doubt there were many high-minded employers who did their best for their workpeople before the days of state-interference, but they could not prevent less scrupulous hirers of labour from hiring it on the cheapest terms. It is true that cheap labour is in the long run dear labour, but it is so only in the long run, and eager traders do not think of the long run. If labour is to be had under conditions incompatible with the health or decent housing or education of the labourer, there will always be plenty of people to buy it under those conditions, careless of the burden in the shape of rates and taxes which they may be laying up for posterity. Either the standard of well-being on the part of the sellers of labour must prevent them from selling their labour under those conditions, or the law must prevent it. With a population such as ours was forty years ago, and still largely is, the law must prevent it and continue the prevention for some generations, before the sellers will be in a state to prevent it for themselves." [1]

The contention that both the old factory legislation and the new find a justification in practical necessities may seem to be open to criticism, so far as some modern communities are concerned, in view of the increased power of the working classes to protect their own interests through the agency of the strike and the trade union. But such power as the working classes now have is subject to fatal limitation owing to lack of economic resources. As Mr. E. W. T. Cox remarks, men will as a rule be equal in bargaining so far as they are equal in resources.[2] Further, even if this were not the case, the adjustment of the rate of wage by industrial strife is costly to the community, and likely to prove in the long run very prejudicial to the interests of the workers themselves. A strike is a

1. "Works," iii. 376-7.
2. In "The Real Democracy," 99.

useful weapon under certain conditions. But, in proportion as political institutions are democratic, the workers who go out on strike endanger the usefulness of the infinitely superior weapon of legislative action. Australia affords a useful object lesson. The organisation of workers of all classes has advanced with great rapidity, and the force of collective opinion among the workers is at times irresistible. At the present moment, strikes are very frequent; and, whether legal or illegal, they are generally successful in leading to increased wages. While a powerful party in England are fighting for the Wages Board, an advanced wing of the Labour Party in Australia, where experience has been gained of the working of that institution, is speaking of it with contempt. A strike is much more exciting and picturesque; and it is proving a more immediately effective means of raising the rate of wage. But the conditions prevailing at present in Australia are exceptional; as a result of an unprecedented period of prosperity the demand for labour far exceeds the supply. Apart from this fact, even where legislative action is not necessary for the labourer, it is expedient for the community, and, in the long run, for the labourer also.[1] The more enlightened and representative members of the Labour Party in Australia recognise this; and they are actively engaged in an endeavour to discover a means for making strikes impossible. Although a revolutionary minority of the party is able to capture a majority in particular trades, the party as such is pledged to the adoption of constitutional methods of social amelioration. I believe that the future of labour as a political factor in Australia is largely dependent upon its loyal fulfilment of this pledge. If it allows its policy to be determined by the revolutionary section, it will alienate the support of a large body of opinion upon which it is at present dependent for political support.

In view of the great importance of Australian

1. *Cf.* the remarks, in ch. ix., *infra*, on "The Non-Living Wage."

experience in minimum wage legislation, I wish to refer to an article in the *Annals of the American Academy of Political and Social Science* for July 1913. The writer, Professor Hammond, discusses the results which have obtained in Victoria during an experience of sixteen years under the Wages Board system. The remarks of the learned writer are specially worthy of attention since he had made a careful and systematic investigation at first hand of minimum wage legislation throughout Australia. His chief conclusions may be briefly summarised:

(1) Sweating no longer exists, unless perhaps in isolated instances, in the industrial centres of Victoria.

(2) Industries have not been paralysed or driven from the State, as was at one time freely predicted.

(3) Although Victorian law does not forbid strikes, it would be hard to find a community in which strikes are so infrequent.

(4) In spite of occasional outbursts of feeling at meetings of the boards, the representatives of both parties go away from these meetings with an understanding of the problems and difficulties which the other side has to meet.

(5) That the minimum wage fixed by the board tends to become the maximum in that trade is often asserted but would be difficult to prove. "There seems to be no reason why under this system there should not be the same competition among employers as under the old system to secure the most efficient and highly skilled workmen; and there is no reason why such men should not get wages based on their superior efficiency." Victorian statistics are not available; but New Zealand statistics show that in the four leading industrial centres, the percentage of workers in trades where a legal minimum is fixed who receive more than the minimum vary from 51 per cent. in Dunedin to 61 per cent. in Auckland.

(6) Although the legal minimum wage does unquestionably force out of employment sooner than

would otherwise be the case a certain number of old, infirm and naturally slow workers, workers who feel that they cannot earn the minimum may apply for a special permit to work at a lower rate. Moreover, the percentage of men with permits is not high.

(7) There is much difference of opinion as to whether or not the increased wages have been to any considerable extent counterbalanced by an increase of prices due to the increased wages. The New Zealand Commission on the cost of living concluded that in the case of staple products, whose prices were fixed in the world's markets, the local legislation could have no effect on prices. In other trades the increased labour costs had served to stimulate the introduction of machinery and labour-saving devices; in still other trades it had not increased efficiency and accordingly labour costs had increased.

(8) Both employers and employees are now practically unanimous in saying that they have no desire to return to the old system of unrestricted competition in the purchase of labour.

Before I pass from the subject of Wages Boards, I wish to return to the article by Professor Lovejoy already referred to. The author distinguishes competition between individuals who offer in the social service the same commodity, in the form of labour, wages, goods, etc.—the competition with which I have been concerned in the present chapter—from the "competition" that exists between class and class, or between a member or group of one class and a member or group of another class.

"Distribution by bargaining places a premium upon an anti-social attitude. The rivalry between exercisers of the same economic function is, on the whole, a competition in serviceableness; he succeeds who produces most with the greatest economy of means, who does best some task which some third party desires to have done. But the competition between the two parties to a bargain is a competition in unserviceableness. For any person or group of persons having anything to sell, the way to success now lies through the establishment of some approach to monopoly conditions—in a small market or a large—and then the creation of a judicious degree of scarcity in the supply of the commodity sold."[1]

Professor Lovejoy appears to hold that no adequate remedy can be found for his second class of "competition" save through collectivism. But, so far as concerns the most important form of industrial conflict—that between capital and labour—the Wages Board system offers a means for the settlement of disputes on lines that are not inconsistent with the Christian ethic, if I understand that ethic aright. Critics of the Wages Board system have been impressed by its limitations; the impartial observer will recognise how much the system has achieved, and what possibilities it offers of further development. It brings capital and labour together under conditions that substitute friendly conference for open warfare. It moralises, not only competition among employers, but also "competition" between master and workmen.

The several propositions stated in the present chapter will be challenged by few. No one to-day will uphold the *laissez faire* argument in favour of "free competition." Nor, on the other hand, will any sane enquirer question the immense value of competition as a means to economic efficiency and to the development of individual character. It appears to me to be also beyond dispute that competition and State regulation are complementary factors of social progress, and that the general purpose of State regulation should be to preserve competition while moralising its character. I shall now venture on more debatable ground, and consider the bearing of these

1. "Christian Ethics and Economic Competition," *Hibbert Journal*, January, 1911, 335.

propositions upon some schemes for social reconstruction.

Many of the differences of opinion that exist to-day are the result of a failure to keep in view the dual aspect of the problem of State control in relation to competition. Disputants ignore either the *quantitative* or the *qualitative* aspects of the problem. While some people are so eager to maintain the effective power of competition that they dismiss any proposal for the elevation of its plane as Utopian, others are so eager to moralise competition that no scheme can be too Utopian for their acceptance. They take *au grand sérieux* imaginary commonwealths where co-operation supersedes competition and men work for the common good without any other stimulus than the consciousness of duty or the friendly rivalries of altruism. In Grant Allen's community of anarchists, each man labours when he chooses; if he feels so inclined he leaves off for the day and basks in the sun; each member of the community receives food and clothing; and at the end of each week, any surplus that may remain is divided amongst them as pocket-money. Such schemes of social reconstruction are not for the workaday world in which we live. They imply an exaggerated estimate of human worth. They do not eliminate competition altogether, but they enfeeble it by removing the stimuli necessary to its efficient working. Under existing conditions, competition penalises indolence and rewards diligence—in neither case with reasonable justice; and therein is the reformer's opportunity. But the first condition of wise reform is a sense of proportion which is lacking in those who propose to remedy existing ills by turning society into a communistic group.

Communism finds few advocates in Anglo-Saxon societies. But the objection just urged against communism applies also to socialism as interpreted by those who insist upon an equality of material rewards for service. This form of socialism retains competition for social distinction and administrative power; but I do not think that men have reached a stage, or are likely within the near future to reach a stage, when reliance can be placed upon the universal efficiency of these as stimuli to effort. If all workers in the socialistic State were to receive an equal remuneration for their labour—the energetic and capable no more than the idle and incompetent—it appears to me that the results would be fatal alike to economic efficiency and to the development of individual character. It is sometimes urged that the material rewards of the existing order derive their power as a stimulus to effort from the social esteem accompanying them, and that the equalisation of private incomes would only mean that men would seek distinction in other forms. But, in the first place, this argument does not represent existing facts. Large masses of men work because idleness is penalised; many work for the sake of material comforts; others, again, strive in order to secure the best conditions for their offspring. In the second place, the economic value of social esteem depends upon the qualities that are socially esteemed. The extreme socialist not only exaggerates the power of a certain motive to effort, but ignores the conflicting ways in which that motive works. As Professor Ely points out:

"It is the esteem of those about him, the esteem of his own class, which governs a man's conduct. . . . The prize fighter is animated by a desire for social esteem, and his conduct is that which meets with the approbation of a considerable proportion of the entire American community. . . . The achievements of scholars and statesmen, so far as the press of the day is concerned, fade into insignificance when brought into contrast with the encounters of a champion pugilist." [1]

If confronted by the facts to which attention has

1. "Socialism: Its Nature, Strength and Weakness," 230.

been drawn, the socialist who relies upon the power of social esteem as a stimulus to effort is driven to predict a swift transformation of human character when once the industrial order has been nationalised. That human character in some respects would be improved under socialism is more than probable; that any swift and fundamental transformation would be effected is extremely improbable. The experience of the past has demonstrated, again and again, the futility of expecting that some new faith, some new social scheme, some new invention or discovery, is going to revolutionise the character of man. The stubborn reluctance of Christendom to assimilate the ethic of the Gospels is one of the most significant facts in history. That reluctance cannot be attributed, solely or even mainly, to economic causes. While individual reform is often swift and enduring, a permanent elevation of the character of a race is a long and arduous process. But, apart altogether from the experience of the past, is it clear, when we look at the actual facts of the life of our own time, that to earn one's living by serving the State exercises any far-reaching influence upon the character of the employee? I have observed the civil servant in many lands; and I have not found him in any way remarkable for his courtesy or good-will. Nor does he display an exceptional industry. On the contrary, the term "government-stroke" is an epithet of abuse rather than of eulogy. If one man gains social esteem by the display of qualities that secure promotion, another gains the esteem of his fellow-workers by an excessive anxiety to avoid all suspicion of quickening the pace. We have learnt to despise the old doctrine of "the Deil take the hindmost." We have yet to realise the danger of a new doctrine:—"The Deil take the foremost!"

The equality of material rewards for service is, of course, not an essential element in the theory of socialism. Nor do the arguments that may be urged for or against socialism wholly turn upon the question of competition. But the propositions previously stated in this chapter predispose me to adopt towards socialism the attitude which I am about to indicate. It is necessary to begin with a definition. According to an eminent statesman, we are all socialists to-day. But, to take a concrete example, the man who believes in the need of more factory legislation is not necessarily a socialist. He is not necessarily a socialist even if he advocates the ownership of the factory by the community. The socialist advocates public ownership of the factory as a part of a general scheme for the complete ownership by public bodies of all the means of production, distribution, and exchange.

"The Alpha and Omega of socialism," says an impartial investigator, "is the transformation of private and competing capitals into a united collective capital."[1]

A socialist, declares Millerand, is one who believes in the necessary and progressive replacement of capitalistic property by social property.[2]

The importance of distinguishing between socialism and proposals for the extension of public ownership may be illustrated by a suggestive fact. The extensions of the sphere of public ownership in the past have not meant, as is commonly imagined, a corresponding diminution of the sphere of private enterprise. Just as law and liberty are not antithetical in the sense that the increase of law must necessarily mean the diminution of liberty, so public ownership and private enterprise are not antithetical in the sense that by the enlargement of the one the other is correspondingly diminished. Just as liberty may be promoted by State regulation, so the sphere of private enterprise may be enlarged by extensions of public ownership.

1. Schäffle, "The Quintessence of Socialism," 96.
2. *Cf.* Ensor, "Modern Socialism," 51.

"The contention that 'Socialism is already upon us,'" writes Professor Henry Jones, "is true, if by that is meant that the method of organised communal enterprise is more in use; but it is not true if it means that the individual's sphere of action, or his power to extract utilities, that is, wealth, out of his material environment, has been limited. It is being overlooked that the displacement of the individual is but the first step in his re-instalment; and that what is represented as the 'Coming of Socialism' may, with equal truth, be called the 'Coming of Individualism.' The functions of the State and City on the one side, and those of the individual on the other, have grown together. Both private and communal enterprise have enormously increased during the last century; and, account for it as we may, they are both still increasing. . . . The organisation of modern activities, of which the State is only the supreme instance, has placed in the hands of private persons the means of conceiving and carrying out enterprises that were beyond the dreams of the richest of capitalists in the past. The merchant in his office, the employer in his yard, can command far wider and more varied services, and make their will felt to the ends of the earth." [1]

I have dwelt upon the distinction between socialism and the extension of public ownership in order to prepare the way for a statement of my attitude towards socialism. While I believe that many institutions and some industries now in the hands of private individuals should be owned by the State or the municipality, I do not believe that the time has yet arrived when the theory of the socialist can be accepted as a guide in practical politics. I shall venture to state two among the many reasons that impel me to adopt this attitude. In the first place, since a partly-nationalised system of industry appears to me to offer more scope for competition, and to involve less interference with individual

1. "The Working Faith of a Social Reformer," 104, 109.

freedom, than a wholly-nationalised system, I am disposed to agree with those who regard public ownership as an expedient that should be limited to special cases such as the following: transport services, services vitally affecting the health of the community, and monopolies with regard to which there are no other means of adequate control by public authorities. In the second place, while proposals to extend the sphere of public ownership involve experiment on a relatively small scale, the advocate of socialism desires to experiment on a vast scale. In my opinion the general theory of socialism is in far too undeveloped and controversial a stage to justify such experimentation. I even doubt whether any conceivable advance in socialism as a system of thought will justify the assumption that the public ownership of all capital is preferable to private ownership. I believe that only the school of experience will determine whether, at some future date, it will be possible for the statesman to accept the socialist position as a starting-point for dealing with practical problems. Before that period arrives, the results of experiments in public ownership in various parts of the world will need to be submitted to a much more complete and impartial analysis than has yet been attempted. We shall have much to learn, also, from the success or failure of existing attempts to remedy the evils of private ownership, either by way of administrative control or through the various forms of industrial co-operation. In the meantime, I take my stand with those who prefer to consider each proposal for the extension of public ownership "on its merits." This does not mean an absence of general principle; but it does mean that each proposal to extend the sphere of public ownership should be carefully examined in the light afforded by the progress of thought and the lessons of experience. In thus refusing to identify myself either with those who regard public ownership as in itself good or with those who regard it as *per se* bad, I believe I am taking the position that will commend itself to prudent men. I even venture to suspect that most of those members of our representative legislatures who profess an absolute confidence in socialism, or an unconquerable aversion to it, have at least one thing in common—they have not given the subject a full and impartial consideration.

It is impossible to discuss the general question of socialism without referring to a fact that has been largely responsible for the extraordinary growth of the socialistic movement during recent decades. I allude to the concentration of capital in the form of trusts. The difficulty of organising an industry on a national scale has been one of the traditional arguments against socialism. The trust disposes of this argument. It is a conclusive demonstration, not only of the possibility, but also of the economic efficiency, of an industrial organisation extending throughout the whole of a State's territory. The failure to recognise the far-reaching significance of the trust explains the futility of much of the latter-day argument against socialism. While the socialist is adducing the trust as an argument to show that socialism is both desirable and inevitable, his opponent is too often content to re-state traditional arguments dating from a period when the trust was unknown.

In one way, however, the trust is an argument against the nationalisation of industry. If it may be used to show the possibility of socialism, it may also be employed to prove that socialism is unnecessary. "The milkman's cart converts me to socialism." The remark is typical of many discussions of the market-place, and reminds one of the man whose atheism was based on the textual difficulties of Genesis. The waste that has been involved in the friction of industrial warfare in the past is at least very materially lessened by the trust, if not eliminated by it. No doubt the trust brings great evils in its train; but experience has yet to demonstrate that the various classes at present exploited by the trust may not be protected by legislation that is quite compatible with the continuance of private industry.

While everyone agrees that the trust should be controlled by the State, and while most agree that different kinds of trusts call for different modes of treatment, the advocates of reform may be divided into three classes according as their preference is for prevention, regulation, or public ownership respectively. The policy of prevention seeks to maintain competition in its existing forms.

"There has never been a time," writes Mr. Howland, "when people were not more exercised over the conditions oppressing them than over the causes out of which the conditions had their growth. Everyone is hostile to the effects of monopoly; few will make the effort to penetrate to its cause. Our measures of relief must go straight at the cause. To prevent monopoly we must restrain the consolidation of corporate wealth by limiting corporate size; we should altogether forbid intercorporate stock-holdings, and should impose carefully chosen limitations upon the amount of capitalization and the holding of corporate assets. The limitation upon capitalization will depend upon the extent of the national market; if no corporation is allowed to grow big enough to fill this market, some competition at least within the nation is restored."[1]

Plausible as this argument may be, the policy of prevention finds few supporters. There are, indeed, obvious difficulties in the way of compelling individuals or groups to compete when they find it more profitable to combine. But even where an attempt to prevent the trust from coming into existence would be practicable, it would often be impolitic. Although in many industries there are limits to the efficiency of large

1. "Monopolies: The Cause and the Remedy," *Columbia Law Review*, February 1910, 106.

business organisations, in others the economies of production on a large scale enable a single business to supply an entire market without any other basis for its monopoly than the superior efficiency of its organisation. Where this is the case, the policy of prevention involves an interference with a legitimate and natural tendency towards increasing economic efficiency.

The policy of State regulation of the trust appears to me to be less impracticable. The policy may be illustrated by the Australian Commonwealth statute entitled "An Act for the Preservation of Australian Industries and for the Repression of Destructive Monopolies." The following clauses are sufficient to indicate the general purposes of the Act:—

"4. Every person who enters into a combination with other persons with the intent to restrain trade or commerce to the detriment of the public, or with the intent to injure Australian industries by unfair competition, is liable to a penalty of £500. Contracts entered into in pursuance of such a combination are illegal and void.

"6. Competition is *prima facie* unfair when it implies an inadequate remuneration for labour, or a disorganisation of industry, or an increase of unemployment, or any system of rebates offered upon the condition of exclusive trading.

"7. Any person who endeavours to gain a monopoly in any trade or commerce with the intent of controlling prices to the detriment of the public is liable to a penalty of £500. Contracts entered into, in pursuance of such a monopoly, are illegal and void.

"11. Any person, who is injured in his person or property by acts done in contravention of the preceding sections, may recover treble damages.

"13. Any person who is convicted a second time for acting in contravention of the preceding sections is held to be guilty of an indictable offence and is liable both to a penalty of £500 and imprisonment for one year.

"17. Unfair competition has in all cases reference to those Australian industries the preservation of which is advantageous to the Commonwealth, having due regard to the interests of producers, workers, and consumers."

Experience alone can demonstrate whether the foregoing act will prove efficient. Up to the present, however, despite the fact that the trust in Australia is in its infancy, the success of the measure has not been such as to warrant sanguine expectation with regard to this form of State control. Hence a tendency in many quarters to advocate the nationalisation of the trust.[1] Professor Ely, writing with special reference to American conditions, argues that the public ownership of the trust would lead to a better utilisation of productive forces, would produce a more stable equilibrium in industry, and would ensure a more equitable distribution of wealth.[2] To balance such advantages against the pleas that may be urged against the policy of nationalisation would be an elaborate and difficult process. But one thing may be pointed out. The policy in question is not necessarily socialistic. Sidgwick, whose point of view was avowedly individualistic, was no opponent of the public ownership of monopolies. On the contrary, he advocated such ownership, in certain cases, as preferable to the vexatious and inquisitorial legislation implied in attempts to control the trust by other means.[3] Even if *all* trusts were nationalised, there would remain a large number of businesses that were neither trusts

1. A proposed amendment of the Commonwealth Constitution, conferring on the Commonwealth Government the power to nationalise such trusts as it deemed expedient, was submitted in 1911 to the referendum. It was rejected; probably owing to the fear of an invasion of State rights. The opposition was based upon objections not so much to the policy of public ownership of monopolies as to the control of intra-State industry by the Federal government.

2. "Socialism: Its Strength and Weakness," 262 *et seq.*

3. "Principles of Political Economy," 508.

nor likely to develop into trusts. Those who imagine that the whole industrial system is tending in the direction of trust organisation overlook the limitations to concentrated capitalism that are involved in the nature of particular kinds of business. An eminent socialist, after discussing the persistent survival of the small business in certain fields of industry, remarks:

"All these small businesses in agriculture, the mechanical trades, mining, retail trade, the arts and professions survive because of certain features in the materials or processes involved which give importance to those personal qualities of skill, care, judgment and character incapable of being evoked, controlled, and applied effectively under the routine economy of the large business."[1]

I have referred to three ways of dealing with the trust—prevention, regulation, and public ownership. The socialist urges public ownership. In my own opinion, each of the policies is bad if regarded as a universal panacea; while each of them has value if regarded as a remedy for particular cases. The choice between them should depend upon the nature of the commodity in which the trust deals, and upon the social, economic, and political conditions of the country within which the trust operates.[2]

My reference to the trust has been parenthetic. I return to the question of the bearing upon socialism of the propositions stated in the earlier part of this chapter. Those propositions, together with a conservatism of temperament to which I must plead guilty, predispose me to prefer less drastic methods of social amelioration than those advocated by most socialists. Assuming, however, for the purposes of discussion, that the case for socialism could be established by

1. J. A. Hobson, "The Evolution of Modern Capitalism," 133.

2. Since writing the above passages on the subject of trusts, I have been engaged in the preparation of a work on "The Control of Monopolies." That work is now in the Press, and I take this opportunity of referring the reader to it for a more detailed treatment of a subject which becomes each year more important.

irrefutable argument, the propositions I have stated would predispose me to adopt the form of socialism which most conserved the merits of the traditional system. As I have already remarked, the public ownership of industry does not necessarily imply an equality of material rewards for service; it does not necessarily imply public management, since the State might own the factory or the farm and lease it to private individuals. Nor does socialism necessarily imply the ownership of all industry by the *State*. The smaller political units, such as the municipal governments in a Unitary State, or the municipal and "State" Governments in a Federal State, might be entrusted with the ownership or management of local industries. Such decentralisation of administrative responsibility should involve an important element of competition among the various local governing bodies. In all these ways, and in many others that might be indicated, it is possible to conceive of a socialistic State in which rivalry between citizen and citizen, municipality and municipality, and even to some extent between public management and private management, would exist in such a form as to suggest the term "competitive socialism." Whether such a scheme of social reconstruction would be superior to existing attempts at public regulation and tentative extensions of public ownership, is a question about which the prudent enquirer may feel sceptical. But two sound maxims of pathology have a direct bearing upon the question. (1) Drastic remedies should not be employed until milder remedies have proved inadequate. (2) The value of milder remedies depends upon their being employed in time. I do not wonder that in America, saturated though it be with the individualistic spirit, an increasing body of opinion looks upon socialism as the only real and enduring solution of existing problems.

CHAPTER VII.

THE RIGHTS OF THE INDIVIDUAL (I) —THEORY.

"The Forms of Action we have buried; but they rule us from the grave."—F. W. MAITLAND.

IN the preceding two chapters, I have endeavoured to re-state the doctrine of *laissez faire* in accordance with the progress of modern thought. This re-statement of a doctrine which sought to define the sphere of the State has prepared the way for an exposition of the rights of the individual. In the course of my argument I shall have much to say of the doctrine of the natural rights of man—partly because that doctrine is still a power in practical politics; and partly because the nature of the theory of individual rights towards which the thought of our time has tended can be best appreciated by showing in what respects it involves a departure from the earlier doctrine.

That the doctrine of natural rights is still a power in contemporary politics should surprise no one. As Sir Leslie Stephen remarked, philosophical theories survive long after their brains have been knocked out. Although the *natural right* has been derided as a superstition by generations of thinkers of widely divergent schools of thought, it is constantly reappearing—sometimes to justify proposals for reform, sometimes in defence of a traditional institution or policy. The following extracts, taken at random from recent issues of the daily press, speak for themselves:—

"The right of women to sit in Parliament is based upon higher considerations than social expediency; it is a necessary inference from the fact that women are human beings no less than men." "Nothing can justify the State in depriving a man of the product of his labour." "Man is born free; the only title a State can have to govern him must be based in the last analysis upon his expressed or implied assent." "Slavery is always unjust." "A man has a right to live; if he has a right to live he has a right to work; if he has a right to work, it is the clear duty of the State to find work for him when he cannot find it for himself." "All men have an equal right to freedom—in particular an equal right to earn their own livelihood in their own way—the free labourer no less than the trade unionist. It follows that Wages Board legislation, which prevents a man from working for what wages he chooses, is an unjustifiable denial of his equal right to freedom." "It is the manifest duty of the State to secure an equality of opportunity to all its citizens." "If self-government be so good a thing for the Anglo-Saxon, it can scarcely be a bad thing for the Hindu. The Hindu, not less than the Anglo-Saxon, is a human being, capable of rights and duties, and equally entitled to a voice in the control of national destinies."

It is not in the daily press alone that we find such conclusions and arguments as those just stated. Much of the literature that affects to expound a theory of the rights of woman is still in the natural-rights stage, and the occasional extravagance of its conclusions is largely traceable to this fact. In many other departments, the ancient doctrine displays a strange vitality. We can trace its presence and influence in the survival of the formula of the happiness of the greatest number, with the suggested implication that society is constituted of individuals who are equal and similar; in the tendency to accept the verdict of majorities as a final interpretation of truth and justice; in the notion, which is undoubtedly gaining ground, that the promotion of State officials should go by mere seniority; and in the movement which, in various forms, seeks to substitute a direct democracy in the place of representative institutions.

In part, no doubt, this stubborn survival must be attributed to the enduring value of the ideas the doctrine sought to express. The doctrine, like that of *laissez faire*, was a protest against governmental despotism. The dangers of such a despotism have not ceased to exist with the change in the form of our political institutions. Whether the citizen be regarded as a mere means to the furtherance of the interests of a governing class or be looked upon as a mere organ of the democratic community, the complete and harmonious development of his nature is challenged. In the extracts which I have quoted from the daily press, and in the political tendencies to which I have referred, we can trace the influence of ideas that are true and socially valuable. Unfortunately, those ideas suffer from their association with false doctrine; and their advocacy—if not in its conclusions, at least in the argument by which those conclusions are supported—serves to exemplify the penalties waiting upon the disputant who " drags his case through the swamps of nonsense."

Political philosophers have long recognised the need of formulating a theory of the rights of the individual which shall preserve the truths that underlay the doctrine of natural rights, while avoiding the errors with which those truths were associated. Nor has the recognition been barren of practical results. In the present chapter, I propose to illustrate the trend of speculative opinion. I shall refer to the defects of the older doctrine and to the attempts made to remedy them. Incidentally, I hope to be able to show that the defects are the result of a disregard, or distortion, of the fundamental principles that have been stated in earlier chapters.

A brief word may be permitted as to historical origins.

"A recognition of the existence of the inborn and indestructible rights of the Individual," writes Gierke, "may be found in the mediæval philosophy of Right when it attributes an absolute and objective validity to the highest maxims of Natural and Divine Law." [1]

The statement seems to imply a fully-developed doctrine of the natural rights of man. But that doctrine was ill-adapted to the general scheme of mediæval thought, which, if it was conscious of the claims of the individual, was also conscious of the unity of society. Post-Reformation thought, however, in its protest against Authority, enthroned the Individual. The political philosophy of later centuries followed on the same lines. That philosophy was an important factor in the political changes of the eighteenth century, when the doctrine of natural rights became at once a theory of politics and the watchword of revolution. The rights themselves, solemnly expressed in the American Declaration of Independence of 1776, received their classic statement in the manifesto in which the National Assembly of France justified the Revolution. According to that manifesto, men are born, and always continue, free and equal in respect of their rights; those rights are natural, imprescriptible, and inalienable; they relate to liberty, property, security, and the resistance of oppression; and their exercise has no other limits than those necessary to secure to every other man the free exercise of the same rights.

Several implications in this creed deserve consideration. (1) If men have equal rights, we must assume that men themselves are potentially equal. (2) If men are born, and always continue, free and equal in respect of their rights, these rights belong to the individual as such, and are independent of the existence of a social order. (3) These rights can be determined by an appeal to *a priori* conceptions of

1. "Political Theories of the Middle Age," 81. *Cf.* Dubois, *L'évolution de la notion du droit naturel antieurement au physiocrates.* Paris, 1908.

justice. (4) Inasmuch as these rights are independent of a social order, they cannot be overridden by the interests of that order. (5) Inasmuch as they are innate, inalienable, and imprescriptible, the control exercised by society over the individual can only be justified by the fact that he assents to such control. I propose to examine these several positions from a theoretical point of view, and to consider to what extent they have been abandoned by later thought. In the succeeding chapter I shall illustrate the trend of opinion by reference to concrete examples.

I.—Human Equality.

The equality of men is not expressly asserted by the French Declaration; but the statement that men are free and equal in respect of their rights suggests, if it does not assume, that the congenital differences between men are so slight that we may disregard them.

"The French Revolution," declares a recent writer, "was in essence an attack on privilege, based on the idea, not of the *absolute* equality of man, but of the equality of man in the essential things that make him to be a man." [1]

The "essential things" must necessarily include mind, will, and character. If so, the idea of human equality, though not expressed in terms, is implicit in substance.

"Of all the principles of 1789," wrote Maine, "equality is the one which has been most strenuously assailed, which has most thoroughly leavened modern opinion, and which promises to modify most deeply the constitution of societies and the politics of States."

When we remember to how large an extent the power of a political principle depends, not upon its logical justification, but upon the magnitude of the

1. J. H. B. Masterman, "Parliament and the People," 47.

evils it attacks, and when we reflect upon the persistence of grave economic inequalities despite the tendency towards an equality of electoral privilege, we may be tempted to concur in Maine's forecast. It has been said that one per cent. of the population of the United States of America owns half the wealth of the Republic! No one can suppose that in the present structure of society the acquisition of riches is any guarantee of high character in the person who acquires them. Nor can any one doubt that the descendants to whom the multi-millionaire bequeathes his gains are, more often than not, quite unfitted to cope with the responsibilities of colossal wealth. Conditions so revolting to man's sense of justice do not justify a dogma of equality; but they give that dogma a plausibility and a power which have to be reckoned with. The belief in equality is largely responsible for certain very dangerous tendencies to which I referred at the beginning of this chapter. It even appears in the views of those to whom one might hope to look for a sane and reasoned expression of the democratic faith.

"Any claim," writes Mr. J. H. B. Masterman, "to equality of social condition, or equality of political rights, or equality of economic status must be founded on a real, definite, convinced belief in that deeper equality that lies under all these things."[1]

Mr. Masterman no doubt means well. But he would certainly be puzzled to explain in what this "deeper equality" consists. Is it equality of body, mind, or character? Why, in the name of Heaven, should men seek to refute one error by asserting another? Why should they oppose to the pretensions of privilege the assumption of equality? That assumption implies that one Anglo-Saxon is as good as another, that the Anglo-Saxon of the ninth century is the equal of his descendant in the twentieth, and that

1. J H. B. Masterman, "Parliament and the People," 55

the Australian aboriginal is the equal of either. It implies, in a word, that men are not only equal in fact but are in nature unchangeable. To state such absurdities is to confute them. Yet it is necessary to dwell upon them. If the reformer, in his zeal to abolish the tyranny of a class, overlooks the infinite variety of individual claim and potentiality, he fights for social betterment with the weapon of false doctrine, and encourages the multitude to disregard or belittle the value of wise direction, alike in legislation, administration, and industry. The way to true progress is not to be found in the abolition of aristocracy, but in the substitution of an aristocracy of mind and character for one that is based on rank or wealth.

Not the fiction of equality, but the fact of human worth is the true basis for a sound theory of the rights of the individual. The position thus adopted not only possesses the merit of recognising facts: it is adequate for the purposes the reformer may be supposed to have in view. It embraces, for example, that equality, before the law which has been a useful object of legislative policy in the past; it may even embrace, under modern conditions, a complete equality of voting power; and it sanctions, within due limits, the legislative policy of dealing with men *as if* they were equal. It does these things, not on the ground that men are equal in fact, but on the ground that in a world of endless complexity, imperfect machinery, and finite intelligence the adjustment of the claims of individuals can only be effected in a rough and ready way. A critic may be tempted to deny that there is any difference between postulating the equality of men and admitting the expediency of treating men as if they were equal. But in the one case we are trifling with facts, whilst in the other case we merely adopt a maxim of legislative practice which is trustworthy *so long as its justification is kept in view.* In the one case we assert a dogma that experience has shown to be productive of dangerous fallacies; in the other case we merely sanction an equality of treatment in so far as it tends to promote the conditions that on the whole tell for the development of individual lives.

II.—Rights Apart from Society.

In our consideration of the doctrine of natural rights we must next examine the assumption that man's rights, if not historically prior to the existence of society, are logically independent of society. This assumption may, perhaps, seem harmless, and its discussion academic; but it involves important consequences to which I shall refer at a later stage in my argument. Before it can be profitably discussed, several terms require definition. A right is a claim enjoyed by one man to acts or forbearances on the part of others. If it denotes a privilege it connotes an obligation. Further, both right and duty imply a law of some sort—divine, civil, or moral—which defines their nature and scope. The theory of natural rights makes its appeal to a Natural (or Moral) Law. By natural rights are meant the fundamental moral rights which the State ought to enforce. So far, there is no occasion for controversy. But the doctrine under examination asserts the existence of rights that belong to the individual as such, and are independent of the existence of a social order.

The assertion is not lacking in plausibility; its fallacy consists in forgetting that man is by nature so essentially a social being that it is impossible to define his position in terms of rights and duties except by considering him in relation to others with whom he is associated in some kind of social order. The state of nature is a fiction of the imagination. If, however, such a state may be conceived to have existed, the transition from it to a state of society would be a transition from a condition where each has a claim to everything, to a condition where duties correlate with rights and where the claims of each are limited by reference to the claims of others. It is only in the latter case that we can speak of the claim as a moral right. The claim of man in a state of nature would be like the claim of an animal to take the food its nature demands. It would be neither moral nor immoral, but simply pre-moral. So long as the claim of each is only limited by the power of each, we can have nothing of the nature of a right. But when that claim is limited and defined by reference to the claims of others, we have rights; and we have also, though perhaps only in an elementary stage, society. The society may not exhibit all the qualities we associate with the modern State. But the patriarchal family, or the primitive horde, is a State in embryo. The State and the Individual grow together.

The absurdities resulting from the confusion between the rights of man as a moral being and the claims of man in an imaginary state of nature have been exposed by Huxley in an essay on "Natural and Political Rights." As Huxley points out, the appeal to nature would justify us in attributing rights to tigers.

"A tiger has a natural right to eat a man; but if he may eat one man he may eat another, so that a tiger has a right of property in all men, as potential tiger-meat. Men are as much the 'gratuitous offering' of nature to tigers for their subsistence, or part subsistence, as fruits are to men. But any one tiger has no more natural right of property in men than any other tiger. All tigers are free to eat any man they can seize; and if two tigers are sneaking along through the jungle on opposite sides of a foot-path, their rights to the villager, who, travelling thereby, fondly imagines he is going home, are equal. So that we may safely enunciate the conclusion that all tigers have an equal natural right to eat all men. . . . But here we stop. If the advocate of the 'rights of tigers' attempts to drive us into the further admission that, as tigers have a right to eat men, it is wrong of men to put obstacles in the way of their having their rights by refusing to be eaten, we protest against the doctrine.

. . . The champion of the 'rights of tigers' has, in fact, made a convenient, though unwarrantable jump from one sense of the word 'right' to another—from 'natural right' to 'moral right.'" [1]

T. H. Green occasionally uses language that suggests an imperfect emancipation from the fallacies of earlier doctrine. While he asserts that no one can have a right except as a member of some society,[2] he also asserts that the right to free life belongs in principle to *man as man*. He refers to the value of Roman law, Stoic doctrine, and the Christian conception of universal brotherhood, as influences that have been instrumental in effecting the recognition of rights in the individual as independent of particular citizenship. He then proceeds:—

"The admission of a right to free life on the part of every man, as man, does in fact logically imply the conception of all men as forming one society in which each individual has some service to render, one organism in which each has a function to fulfil." [3]

If we regard these conclusions together and put such a construction upon them as will make them mutually consistent, the statement that a man has *rights merely as a man* must be interpreted to mean less than was intended by earlier writers, and less than the words themselves suggest. It is better to allow exponents of the doctrine of natural rights to enjoy a monopoly of an expression which, from the point of view of the reconstructed doctrine, stands for a fiction of the imagination.

The fallacies inherent in the doctrine of natural rights are the result, as I have said, of a distortion or disregard of the principles stated in previous chapters. The dogma of equality is a distortion of the principle of individual worth. The conception of rights inher-

1. "Method and Results," 346-7.
2. "Works," ii. 350.
3. *Ibid.*, ii. 462-5.

ing in individuals as such implies a disregard of the principle of social unity. It finds no place for either the reality or the continuity of the social life, although these are indispensable factors without which no determination of the rights of the individual is possible. Every one will admit, for example, that the present generation is called upon to consider the claims of future generations. But when we seek to determine what particular sacrifices the present ought to make in the interests of the future, we are confronted by a problem whose solution is only possible on the condition of recognising the continuous life of society.

III.—The *a priori* Determination of Rights.

The view that rights inhere in individuals as such is partly responsible for the belief that the nature of the rights can be determined once and for all by *a priori* logic. If we ignore the reality and claims of the social life, we exclude a factor which has a long past and which cannot be understood apart from that past, and we have only to deal with a factor (*i.e.*, the individual) which, since it came into being to-day or yesterday, can be investigated at first hand.

"Governments," exclaimed Paine, "are ever leading men to the sepulchre of precedents."[1]

"The sacred rights of mankind," declared Hamilton, "are not to be rummaged for among old parchments or musty records. They are written, as with a sunbeam, in the whole volume of human nature, by the hand of the Divinity itself, and can never be erased or obscured by mortal power."[2]

"From whatever standpoint the question is approached," writes a latter-day exponent of natural rights, "there results the conviction, that, though there may be additional guidance for individual conduct, there is only one clear, safe and infallible guide for collective conduct, the conduct of the State. That

1. "The Rights of Man," 104.
2. Quoted, Acton, "History of Freedom and Other Essays," 587.

guide is justice, the recognition of equal natural rights inherent in every member of the State, and entitling each to equal opportunities with all others for the achievement of his own happiness."[1]

The dangers of an appeal to reason divorced from history and experience have been so frequently dwelt upon by eminent writers that an apology may seem necessary for referring to them; but they are being constantly exemplified in contemporary politics. The ideal of Justice needs no defence; but the interpretation of that ideal in terms of laws and institutions is a difficult task which demands a patient examination of questions which the *a priori* investigator is apt to ignore. If, for example, we work out by rigorous logic a theory of man's rights without reference to the processes of social development in the past, we shall fail from sheer inability to understand the material with which we are dealing. Man is the result of a long process of evolution, and cannot be understood apart from the study of that process. Nor can the nature of his rights be determined once and for all without reference to changing conditions of time and place.

"To know whether it would be more for the advantage of society that this or that should be abolished," said Bentham, "the time at which the question about maintaining or abolishing it is proposed must be given, and the circumstances under which it is proposed to maintain or abolish it."[2]

Bentham was speaking of the advantage of society; but, with equal justice, he might have said the same thing concerning the advantage of the individuals who constitute society. Finally, even if it were true that the individual could be understood apart from the history of man in society, and that the nature of the rights of the individual were independent of time

1. Max Hirsch, "Democracy *versus* Socialism," 194.
2. "Works," ii. 501.

conditions, the difficulties of ascertaining these rights by an appeal to *a priori* conceptions of justice are insuperable. If we reject the lessons of experience and disdain to enquire with respect to any particular system of right how it has worked or is likely to work in practice, we dethrone reason in order to follow the will-o'-the wisp of speculative opinion. The French Revolution, said Acton, "taught the people to regard their wishes and wants as the supreme criterion of right." [1]

IV.—Rights as Superior to the Interests of Society.

The belief that the individual possesses rights that cannot be overridden by the interests of society has an historical explanation in the very extended interpretation given to such interests by political rulers. Logically, however, its origin must be sought in a certain way of regarding society, and in a very inadequate recognition of the correlativity of rights and duties. A society, whether or not organised as a State, was regarded by the advocate of the doctrine of natural rights as a mere aggregate of atoms. The interests of this aggregate were conceived of as a mere aggregate of the interests of individuals. It followed that society did not exist in any distinctive sense, and therefore as such could have no claims. Closely associated with the total failure to recognise the organic character of the social structure was a tendency to look upon rights as a heap of material goods, which had only to be divided equally in order to secure justice to all. As soon, however, as we realise that rights are meaningless apart from duties, and that we cannot attribute a right to one man without imposing a duty on other men, we are impelled to find a warrant for imposing this duty. If a man has a right that cannot be denied to him by others without committing a wrong, it is clear that we can only determine the

1. "History of Freedom and Other Essays," 271.

nature of this right by reference to the interests shared by him in common with others. We may define these interests in terms of the best life, or in terms of general happiness; but, in either case, to suppose the individual to possess a right that is superior to a common interest is to disregard the only possible criterion for determining rights.

Two objections, however, deserve mention. In the first place, exponents of the doctrine of natural rights allege that it offers the only adequate expression of the protest of the individual against the tyranny of majorities. If natural rights are denied, says Max Hirsch,

"that only is right which the majority for the time being has empirically adjudged to be socially advantageous; and wrong is only that which the majority for the time being considers to be socially disadvantageous." [1]

An excuse for loose argument of this description may be found in the language of some distinguished opponents of natural rights. The theory of natural rights, writes Professor Burgess,

"did its practical work when the State was a single person, or a few persons, indistinguishable from the government, and, in its formulation of rights, was acting in utter disregard of the popular ethical feeling. Where the State is the people in ultimate organisation, the theory can only mean that the State should act rationally in its construction of the principles of liberty; but of their rationality, *the State, again, is the final interpreter*." [2]

While these authors arrive at opposite conclusions, both overlook the existence of an important distinction between moral and legal rights. Legal rights are

1. "Democracy *versus* Socialism," 178.
2. "Political Science and Constitutional Law," i. 88. The italics are my own.

ascertainable by a final authority, while moral rights are not. When we speak of the State as a final interpreter of rights, we can only be referring to legal standards. In truth, there is no final interpreter of rights, unless indeed it be Time. The interpretation of any generation or civic power is only a provisional interpretation. There may be occasions when, in the interest of the moral rights of all, a minority ought to resist to the uttermost the enforcement of the legal rights of the majority. It is quite possible to assent to this proposition without asserting the existence of natural rights.[1]

In the second place, advocates of the doctrine of natural rights allege that their opponents, in determining rights by reference to the common interests of a social group, can find no place for the claims of any one outside that group. Surely, it has been asserted, an English citizen travelling in Africa would be under a duty to rescue a drowning Hottentot whom he could save without risk to his own life. If so, the duty implies a recognition of the Hottentot's right to be rescued. That right must be a natural right, independent of membership of a society. "I love my family better than myself"; said Fénelon; "my country better than my family; mankind better than my country."

The objection just stated involves issues whose discussion would take me beyond the scope of the present work. I venture, however, to make two observations. (1) Politics is concerned with the claims of individuals who are members of a society organised as a State. It is quite possible to deny that the citizen can have against the State any claim contrary to its interests, without, at the same time, denying that the members of the State, and the State itself, may be under a *moral* duty to the alien. (2) When we attempt to determine the nature of the obligations of a citizen or political community to the alien, we are compelled

1. *Cf.* ch. viii., *infra*, sect. viii., "The Right to do One's Duty."

to recognise the fundamental principle that the rights of the alien can only be ascertained when we regard him in relation to some social whole whose interests are superior to those of its particular members. Our common humanity can be the basis of no right that is contrary to the interests of mankind as a whole. Absurdities too palpable for refutation would be involved in any endeavour to define the obligation of superior races to inferior races by regarding humanity as a mere aggregate of individuals endowed with equal rights.

If the preceding argument be sound, we must substitute, for the idea of absolute rights, *the idea of rights as relative to a common good which is also a personal good.* The appropriate weapon with which to oppose a despotism in the name of a common good is to be found, not in a theory of natural rights, but in the fact that the good of society is also the good of its individual members. The healthy life of society, as of the individual, is only possible where the elements of which it is formed are also healthy.

"Our ultimate standard of worth," said T. H. Green, in a familiar passage, "is an ideal of *personal* worth. All other values are relative to value for, of, or in a person. To speak of any progress or improvement or development of a nation or society or mankind except as relative to some greater worth of persons, is to use words without meaning." [1]

But the position that the common good is also a personal good has a deeper meaning—a meaning that will be familiar to students of the author just quoted or of the school of which he is the greatest English exponent. When we say that the common good is a personal good, we mean something more than that society is composed of individuals. We mean that the individual is so related to the social group that his good is bound up with, and completed in, the good of

1. "Prolegomena to Ethics," 193.

others. Their good is not something alien to his own; it is something that is a part of his own good. The common good is his, not merely because he is one of the many, but also because it is through the common life that he realises himself. The higher that life, the nobler are the possibilities of his own life. It is by losing himself in the life of worthy citizenship that he most truly finds himself.

"The Athenian citizen," said Pericles, "should be ready to die for Athens, because Athens offers so glorious a life of freedom to the individual citizen."

"The good," writes Professor Maitland, "is not merely personal *and* social. It is the one precisely so far as it is the other. It is just in so far as a man is able to set aside merely private ends and identify himself with the larger purposes of society that his life becomes rounded into the unity in which personality in the full sense of the word consists."[1]

While the theory of natural rights ignored the Unity of Society, the reconstructed theory has the merit of recognising that unity without sacrificing the life of the individual. It does not defend the fictitious unity to which Lord Acton refers as overruling the just claims of the individual for the purpose of vindicating itself.[2]

V.—The Sovereignty of the Individual.

No examination of the doctrine of natural rights would be complete without some reference to its relation to theories of the sovereignty of the individual. If man has innate rights apart from society and superior to its claims, the State derives its authority from the consent of those who are subject to its jurisdiction. If the individual has a good which is wholly and exclusively his own, by what right can an

1. "The Service of the State," 36-7.
2. "The History of Freedom and Other Essays," 288–90.

external authority determine for him in what that good consists, unless he assents to such determination?

"Men being by nature all free, equal and independent," said Locke, "no one can be put out of this estate, and subjected to the political power of another, without his own consent."[1]

The association between natural rights and theories of individual sovereignty is illustrated in Herbert Spencer's "Man *versus* the State." The author, believing that the assertion of natural rights is the appropriate answer to the apologists of legislative despotism, reduces the State to the level of a joint stock company whose members are subject to the will of the majority in no other matters than those for which they are incorporated. In order to discover what these matters are, we are told to have recourse to the question, "What would be the agreement into which citizens would now enter with practical unanimity?" Such a theory of government is closely related to Anarchy. Herbert Spencer, it is true, expressly sanctions the coercion of an insignificant minority, and when he insists upon the importance of consent it is as a means of defining what matters the State shall deal with rather than of determining what the State shall do within that sphere when once it has been defined. These qualifications of anarchist doctrine, however, are only made at the sacrifice of logical consistency. If the consent of individuals is substituted for the common good as the justification for the exercise of political authority, there is no logical escape from a conclusion that is indistinguishable from the theory of Anarchy. Herbert Spencer does not quote, though the position which he adopts would have justified his doing so, the language of an intellectual forerunner.

"It is impossible that such governments as have

1. "Of Civil Government," ii. 95.

hitherto existed in the world could have commenced by any other means than a total violation of every principle, sacred and moral. . . . It could have been no difficult thing in the early and solitary ages of the world, while the chief employment of men was that of attending flocks and herds, for a banditti of ruffians to overrun a country and lay it under contributions. Their power being thus established, the chief of the band contrived to lose the name of Robber in that of Monarch; and hence the origin of Monarchy and Kings. . . . what at first was plunder, assumed the softer name of revenue; and the power originally usurped, they affected to inherit."[1]

Such extravagances find their proper place in the propaganda of Anarchy. In the reconstructed doctrine of individual rights, the common good takes the place of consent as the justification for the exercise of civil authority. To base government on the sovereignty of the individual is to ignore the unity of society. To base it on the common good is to find a place both for the just claims of society and for the just claims of the individual. The case for any particular form of government stands or falls by reference to the degree in which it serves to promote the complete development of the life of its subjects. Democratic institutions, for example, depend for their justification, not upon any abstract right of the individual to self-government, but upon the guarantees they may offer for ensuring the due consideration of the claims of all classes of the community, and upon the educational value of the life of active citizenship.[2]

1. Paine, "Rights of Man," 87.
2. *Cf.* ch. viii. *infra*, sect. vii., "The Right to Self-Government."

CHAPTER VIII.

The Rights of the Individual. (II)

Illustrations.

In the preceding chapter I have contrasted two theories of the rights of the individual. While the later of these theories may not be beyond criticism— and what human theory can be said to be beyond criticism?—it expresses the general trend of the thought of our time; and its relative superiority may be indicated by the following summary of difference. (1) The fact of human worth is substituted for the fiction of human equality. (2) The proof of the existence of a right is held to depend, not upon *a priori* conceptions of justice, but upon such practical considerations as the consequences that may be anticipated to follow from the recognition of that right. (3) For the static idea of a right as immutable in nature and scope is substituted the dynamic idea of a right as the claim of the citizen in communities at varying stages of development, and therefore as relative to conditions of time and place. (4) The idea of society as a mere sum of individuals who are equal and similar is superseded by the idea of society as having a common life organically related to the life of the individual. (5) So far from the citizen having claims superior to a general interest, his claims are held to be ascertainable only when we regard him in relation to a common life of which the good is at once social and individual. For practical purposes, it matters little whether legislative effort be directed to the common good or the individual good, so long as a sufficiently wide interpretation is given to these respective ends. That interpretation must recognise that the State is a means to individual salvation, and that the individual is a means to the common good. Or, as Professor Bernard Bosanquet says, the State and the individual as they exist are means to the perfection of the State and the individual as they may be. (6) Finally, the justification for the exercise of governmental authority is found, not in the consent of the individual to such exercise, but in the purposes that it serves.

In the present chapter I propose to illustrate the extent to which the differences just stated affect our arguments or conclusions when we come to consider concrete cases—the right to life, to liberty, to marry, to the land, to work, to equality of opportunity, to self-government, and to do one's duty.

I.—The Right to Life.

The difference between the earlier and later doctrines as regards the right to life may be illustrated by the question of capital punishment. Most opponents of the death penalty contend that the State has no right to take the life of a citizen on any ground whatsoever. The position is suggestive of, if not a necessary deduction from, the earlier doctrine. It is wholly untenable from the point of view of the later. Whether that doctrine justifies the existing usage as to capital punishment is another and more difficult question. The arguments that call for examination are numerous and complex. We have to consider, for example, the moral character and potentialities of a certain type of criminal, the deterrent value of the death penalty, the advantages of a scale of punishment which discourages a man who commits rape or burglary from seeking to escape detection by murdering his victim, the merits of retributive justice, and the attitude of popular opinion, together with the degree of security actually existing in the particular community where the merits of capital punishment are under discussion. We can only give a judgment on the general question after due consideration of each and all these factors. So far, most thinking people will be in substantial agreement. The real difficulties begin when we come to examine the several factors in detail. Some people, for instance, contend that the man who commits homicide seldom belongs to the class of habitual criminals; and that, if his life were spared, he would prove to be a useful and law-abiding citizen. A conflict of expert opinion, moreover, exists as to the precise value of the death penalty as a deterrent influence. Some writers maintain that the person who would be restrained from committing murder by fear of the death penalty but would not be restrained by any other form of punishment is too exceptional to be taken into account in the framing of general laws. Even the attitude of public opinion with respect to capital punishment is doubtful. Obviously, if the State abolishes the death penalty when public opinion supports it, the citizens are likely to take the law into their own hands; whilst, if the State retains capital punishment in the teeth of public opinion, the result is to corrupt juries and to evoke public sympathy on behalf of the criminal.

Any one who has reflected upon such difficulties will admit the need for caution in expressing an opinion upon the merits of the general question. The Royal Commission of 1864, after taking the opinion of the judges of the United Kingdom and other eminent authorities, recommended the restriction of the death penalty to high treason and murder in the first degree; the modification of the law as to child murder, so as to enable certain cases of infanticide to be punished as misdemeanours; and the abolition of public executions.[1] Parliament has acted upon none of these recommendations, except the last. This may be due either to the absence of any marked trend of public opinion or to the disinclination of political parties to arouse the hostility of an energetic minority. My own opinion, which I submit with great diffidence, is

1. *Parliamentary Papers* (1866). Cd. [3590] (vol. xxi. p. 1).

favourable to the retention of the death penalty. I do not believe that the conscience of the community demands its abolition. Proposals for abolition are made from time to time; sometimes as the result of journalistic enterprise in search of the sensational; sometimes as a result of misguided sympathy for a particular criminal. Whether I interpret public opinion aright, and whether in upholding capital punishment I have given due weight to the other considerations to which I have referred as essential to the formation of a sound opinion, may be doubtful. But I am less concerned to decide such questions of practical politics than to indicate the methods of reasoning by which, as I believe, they ought to be decided.

Does the right of the individual to life include a right to take one's own life? English law formerly denied this right. It even went so far as to brand suicide with ignominy, and to impose various penalties on the offspring. Blackstone upheld the law, primarily for the reason which sounds unconvincing to modern ears, that the individual who took his own life was "invading the prerogative of the Almighty." Existing law does not punish a man or his offspring if he chooses to commit suicide, but it sanctions the imposition of penalties for an unsuccessful attempt. In other words, punishment follows from the fact of having bungled! This does not seem logical; but it may be expedient. In discussing the general question, it must be remembered that I am now primarily concerned with those moral rights which are fit for political enforcement. The recognition of a right to take one's own life would imply a duty on others not to interfere. It should be apparent that whether or not the individual has a moral right to take his own life, he has not a right which the State would be justified in expressly recognising.[1]

1. *Cf.* the interesting discussion in Sir Roland Wilson's "Province of the State," 168–70.

II.—The Right to Liberty.

I shall discuss at a later stage some aspects of the right to liberty that call for separate consideration. At present I shall deal only with its relation to slavery —a subject which deserves special examination in view of the inconsistencies of two eminent thinkers who have written about it. *Prima facie*, if the right to liberty is conditional upon the social welfare, slavery may have been justifiable among primitive peoples as a step towards a better order of things; whilst, if man has a natural right to liberty, slavery must be wrongful always and everywhere. Curiously enough, however, the most distinguished modern champion of natural rights has sought to justify slavery; while the apostle of the gospel of the common good has condemned it under all conditions.

"There is constantly made the erroneous assumption," wrote Herbert Spencer, "that there may exist in early stages the same system of free labour as that which we have; whereas, before money comes into existence, payment of wages is generally impracticable; nothing but food, clothing, and shelter can be given to the worker. . . . It is taken for granted that as among ourselves free labour is conducive to social welfare, it is everywhere and at all times conducive to it; but in early stages the undisciplined primitive man will not labour continuously, and it is only under a *régime* of compulsion that there is acquired the power of application which has made civilization possible."[1]

T. H. Green, on the other hand, declares:—

"That capability of living in a certain limited community with a certain limited number of human beings, which the slave cannot be prevented from exhibiting, is in principle a capability of living in community with any other human beings, supposing the necessary

1. "The Principles of Sociology," iii. 457.

training to be allowed; and as every such capability constitutes a right, we are entitled to say that the slave has a right to citizenship, to a recognised equality of freedom with any and every one with whom he has to do, and that in refusing him not only citizenship but the means of training his capability of citizenship, the state is violating a right founded on that common human consciousness which is evinced both by the language which the slave speaks, and by actual social relations subsisting between him and others."[1]

Neither of these writers, however, is consistent. Herbert Spencer, writing as a sociologist, employs arguments directly opposed to those used in his political pamphlets. The logical scheme of "Man *versus* the State" would condemn slavery under any conditions. The passage from Green, on the other hand, invites comparison with the same author's definition of rights as "powers which it is for the general well-being that the individual (or association) should possess."[2] If we base rights solely upon the capacity for them, and apart from considerations of a social good, we have gone far to restore the doctrine of natural rights in its traditional form. Green might have answered that the social good necessarily implies the recognition of rights in all who have the capacity for them. But such a contention seems to involve an indifference to the logic of circumstance—an indifference of which Green is rarely guilty. That the slave has claims must be conceded; but to assert that their nature can be determined in such a way as to justify the postulate that man has a right to freedom at all times and places, is to assert a conclusion that could only be maintained after a much more elaborate investigation of past conditions than was attempted by Green.

"To the scientific student of human history," says

1. "Works," ii. 451.
2. "Principles of Political Obligation," par. 206.

Ritchie, "it seems almost certain that slavery was a necessary step in the progress of humanity. It mitigated the horrors of primitive warfare, and thus gave some scope for the growth, however feeble, of kindlier sentiments towards the alien and the weak. It gave to the free population sufficient leisure for the pursuit of science and art, and, above all, for the development of political liberty; and in this way slavery may be said to have produced the idea of self-government. By contrast with the slave the freeman discovered the worth of freedom. Thus slavery made possible the growth of the very ideas which in course of time came to make slavery appear wrong."[1]

While this eulogy of slavery may be open to some criticism in detail, it has the merit of recognising the futility of judging the institutions of a primitive people by reference to the ideals and conditions of a civilised epoch. I incline to the opinion that it is the inhuman treatment of the slave, not the institution of slavery itself, that is open to unanswerable criticism. While slavery has served useful purposes, the callous disregard of the slave's welfare during particular periods was altogether bad. It degraded the master as well as dehumanised the slave. No doubt slavery was liable to cruel abuses; but if we condemned every institution that was open to this accusation, the history of the past would be one long chronicle of censure.

While a sound doctrine of individual rights may admit that slavery was justified at a particular stage in human progress, it must repudiate slavery under modern conditions for the sufficient reason that any need that may once have existed for the institution has been outgrown. The recognition of the relativity of institutions to conditions of time and place, so far from being hostile to progress, is in truth a weapon in the hands of the reformer. It enables him to emancipate himself from the superstition that existing

1. Ritchie, "Natural Rights." 103-4.

institutions, if they have served useful purposes in the past, are for that reason still entitled to his allegiance. The same spirit of historical-mindedness that enables him to hold slavery justified in a past age will also lead him to criticise any institutions of our own time that involve slavery in a more or less modified form. It will condemn, for example, such freedom of contract as finds expression to-day in the sweater's den. It will also have something to say about the relation of superior to inferior races in tropical regions—a subject of menacing portent for the future, and calling in an exceptional degree for the qualities of a wise statesmanship which will be on its guard, alike against those who would restore the reality of slavery under the pretence of discipline, and against those who advocate the undiscriminating extension of the institutions of progressive communities to communities that are relatively stationary.

III.—The Right to Marry.

The right to marry (including the right to have offspring), is seldom enumerated among natural rights, but its existence as a natural right is implicit in popular ideas. From the point of view of the reconstructed doctrine, this right is relative to considerations of the social good. While such considerations impel the legislator to respect public opinion, even where it may be wrong, they justify the reformer in insisting upon the relativity of the right in order to prepare the way for legislative action in the future. When modern communities determined to limit the operation of natural selection by caring for the unfit, they implicitly pledged themselves to the adoption of other means to the improvement of the species. Among such means, none is more obvious than the control of marriage. The present custom of permitting reproduction among idiots, the insane, habitual criminals, and deaf mutes, is suicidal. "In America, deaf mutes are increasing in numbers, and are founding a deaf and dumb race."[1] Some difference of opinion may exist with respect to certain other classes. A memoir, recently issued from the Galton Laboratory, and based upon an examination of children attending elementary schools in Edinburgh and Manchester, affirms that the child of alcoholic parents, so far as concerns his intelligence, physique and liability to disease, is apparently no worse off, if not a little better off, than the child of non-alcoholic parents. The conclusion gives some support to the view, generally held among biologists, that acquired characteristics are not transmitted. But the memoir does not challenge two facts which appear to me indisputable, and are relevant to the present question. (1) The child of alcoholic parentage is severely handicapped by his environment. It is even possible that this handicap may account for the startling conclusions of the memoir. If the operation of natural selection is more ruthless among the infants of intemperate parents, the character of those who reach the school-going age would naturally bear a favourable comparison with the character of the children who come from homes where the infant mortality is lower. (2) While it is probable that a taste for excessive drinking is no more transmitted to the offspring than is the specific microbe of tuberculosis, there is likely to be transmitted in either case a vulnerability to the disease from which the parent suffered. The mere fact of a man's becoming a dipsomaniac is *prima facie* evidence of his unfitness for parentage. I therefore conclude in favour of the prohibition of marital right to the habitual drunkard. The marital right, like every other right, is not an absolute privilege that can be claimed by human beings as such. It inheres in the individual so far as its possession is in accordance with a social welfare of which the well-being of each is but a constituent part.[2]

1. E. A. Fay, "Marriages of the Deaf in America."

2. *Cf. infra*, chap. ix., the remarks on "The Problem of the Child."

But modern doctrine, as interpreted by some capable thinkers, goes much further than to qualify the right to marry: it even challenges the right to abstain from marriage.

"No problem," asserted Professor Armstrong in his Presidential address to the chemistry section of the British Association in 1909, "can compare in importance with that of the future of our race. To consider it is the one plain duty before us, and the need becomes daily a more urgent one. Not only do we encourage deterioration at the lower end of the scale of intelligence; we are now, through our system of higher education, courting failure also at the upper end. . . . The subject has been brought before the chemical world in England recently by the application of a number of women to be made Fellows of the Chemical Society. Many of us have resisted the application because we were unwilling to give any encouragement to the movement which is inevitably leading women to neglect their womanhood, which is in itself proof that they do not understand the relative capacities of the two sexes, and the need there is of sharing the duties of life. If there be any truth in the doctrine of hereditary genius, the very women who have shown ability as chemists should be withdrawn from the temptation to become absorbed in the work, for fear of sacrificing their womanhood. They are those who should be regarded as chosen people, as destined to be the mothers of future chemists of ability."

Most advocates of the Rights of Woman will regard Professor Armstrong's conclusion as belated. The chief end of woman, they contend, has been defined in the past by her male oppressor. She has existed to serve man and to perpetuate the species! The modern revolt against a conclusion so obviously open to criticism is apt to find expression in an extreme form of individualism. As I have already remarked, much of the modern literature that purports to elaborate a theory of woman's claims is in the natural-rights stage. The advocate is so concerned to prove the existence of rights that duties are practically ignored; so possessed by the consciousness of woman's potentialities for what may be regarded as a higher life, as to deem it superfluous to enquire how far the recognition of these potentialities in social and legal institutions would be in accord with racial good.

While I dissociate myself from the arguments often employed by advocates of the cause of woman's enfranchisement, I am not disposed to challenge the conclusion generally adopted by those advocates with respect to the matter under immediate discussion. The argument of Professor Armstrong, in the passage quoted, is open to several criticisms. In the first place, the alleged sterility of the educated woman has never been proved. Mr. C. F. Emerick sums up as follows an able and judicious discussion of the question:

"The conclusion of this study is chiefly negative. It is apparent that the statistical tables which we have examined fail to establish any causal nexus between higher education on the one hand and the frequency of marriage and maternity on the other."[1]

In the second place, even if the higher education of women in the past has been hostile to maternity, we cannot assume that in the future it will continue to be so. Is it not conceivable that a mistake has been made in submitting women to an academic discipline that was developed with a single view to the education of men? When our Universities have once recognised that physical life is the basis of all other life, and have learnt to keep in view the physical, moral, and æsthetic, as well as intellectual, aspects of the complex problem of the education of women, I venture to believe that a high development of the feminine mind will be found to be compatible with the

1. *Political Science Quarterly*, June 1909, 283.

interests alike of the individual and the race. In the third place, there is no likelihood that the admission of women to certain occupations will result in those occupations meaning to women as a class what they mean to men. The emancipation of women consists less in the fact of competition with men than in the freedom to compete if they choose to do so; for this freedom reacts upon the position of women as a class. It is the expression of a policy whose root idea is that women, not less than men, have a claim to be considered as something more than a mere means to the good of others.

Some might argue that the principle which justifies the isolation of the unfit will also justify the State in discouraging the celibacy of those women who are specially adapted to enrich the race by passing on their qualities to future generations. But the cases are not parallel. Marriage and reproduction by a dipsomaniac are forms of self-indulgence; a woman who chooses a scientific or professional career in preference to wifehood and motherhood chooses one form of social service in preference to another. To deny her the power of choice on the ground of advantages that might possibly accrue from her marriage, would impose a despotism in the name of the common good. On the other hand, a woman who marries and deliberately and selfishly refuses the responsibilities of motherhood is just as blameworthy as the dipsomaniac who has offspring for a reason that is not essentially dissimilar. She is, of course, more difficult to deal with; but she is exercising a power which is not a right; and the State would be justified in bringing pressure to bear upon her with a view to inculcating a sense of responsibility to the race. "It is one of the entirely unforeseen consequences that have arisen from the decay of Normal Social Life," writes Mr. H. G. Wells, "that great numbers of women while still subordinate have become profoundly unimportant. They have ceased to a very large extent to bear children, they have dropped most of their home-making arts, they no longer nurse or educate such children as they have, and they have taken on no new functions to compensate for these dwindling activities of the domestic interior."[1] The justification for these remarks, at any rate so far as they are pertinent to the subject under immediate discussion, will be admitted. We hear much to-day of a tax upon bachelors; we may hear something in times to come of a tax on the childless. Our whole scheme of taxation calls for readjustment on lines which shall involve a recognition of the social value of parentage.[2]

IV.—The Right to the Land.

"The right of any one to the exercise of his faculties being limited only by the equal right of every one else," writes a recent exponent of natural rights, "and the exercise of any faculty being dependent upon the use of the earth, it follows that the right of any one to use the earth is limited only by the equal rights of every one else. The natural right to the use of the earth, therefore, is an equal right, inherent in all. If there were only one man upon this earth he would obviously be free to use the whole earth; the right of any second man to do the like must be equal to that of the former. Nor can further multiplication bring about any change in this relation. Of all the millions inhabiting the earth to-day, each is free to use the whole earth or any part of it, provided he infringes not the equal right of any other man. And conversely, it is equally true that no one of them may so use the earth as to prevent any other from similarly using it."[3]

Huxley has exposed, with cogency and felicity, the absurdity of approaching the urgent question of the reform of the land laws from this point of view. If all men have natural and equal rights as men, then

1. "The Great State," 44.
2. *Cf. infra,* chapter ix, remarks on "The Problem of the Child."
3. Max Hirsch, "Democracy *versus* Socialism," 228-9.

the dominion of the earth belongs to the aggregate of human beings, each man to count as one and no man as more than one.

"My free and equal fellow-countrymen," exclaims Huxley's imaginary orator, "there is not the slightest doubt that not only the Duke of Westminster and the Messrs. Astor, but everybody who holds land from the area of a thousand square miles to that of a table-cloth, and who, against all equity, denies that every pauper child has an equal right to it, is a ROBBER. (Loud and long-continued cheers; the audience, especially the paupers, standing up and waving hats.) But, my friends, I am also bound to tell you that neither the pauper child, nor Messrs. Astor, nor the Duke of Westminster, have any more right to the land than the first nigger you may meet, or the Esquimaux at the north end of this great continent, or the Fuegians at the south end of it. Therefore, before you proceed to use your strength in claiming your rights and take the land away from these usurping Dukes and robbing Astors, you must recollect that you will have to go shares in the produce of the operation with the four hundred and odd million of Chinamen, the hundred and fifty millions who inhabit Hindostan, the——(loud and long-continued hisses; the audience, especially the paupers, standing up and projecting handy moveables at the orator)."[1]

Assuredly, in considering the contention of a natural right to the land, we may concur with a sage observation of Bentham:—

"In regard to most rights, it is as true that what is every man's right is no man's right, as that every man's business is no man's business. . . . From *real* law come *real* rights; but from *imaginary* laws come *imaginary* rights, a bastard brood of monsters, 'gorgons and chimeras dire.'"[2]

1. "Method and Results," 381-2.
2. "Works," ii. 502. *Cf.* "Works," ii. 501, 508, 523.

From the standpoint of the later doctrine, the rights of the individual to the land may be defined as the right to demand that the land shall be employed for the good of the community of which the individual is a member. This may involve at one time public ownership and at another time private ownership. But at no time is the title of the individual absolute. A tax upon landowners, which is for the common good, imposes moral as well as legal duties, even though it be so large as to be equivalent to confiscation of the land. Obviously, however, the amount of the tax is always relevant to the question whether the common good justifies its imposition. The advocate of the single tax proposes to simplify the problem of national finance by throwing all the burden of taxation upon the land-owning class. This proposal, generally defended on the ground of the claim of the individual to equal and inherent rights, is sometimes defended by an appeal to the welfare of the community. How such an appeal can justify the State in discriminating between classes in this way is not apparent to me. Nor can I see how the State can be justified in ignoring those rights of property which individuals have acquired in the past with its express approval and positive sanction. The State may have erred in parting with the freehold of the land; some people may possess too much land and some people too little: and the time may have come to substitute public for private ownership of land. But, in seeking to effect reforms in these directions, the State must be loyal to the moral obligations it has incurred in the past. The difficulties of a modern State, when it finds itself confronted by a conflict between the claims of vested interests and the need of social and economic readjustments in the interests of the community at large, can only be overcome by the adoption of a *via media* which will satisfy absolutists in neither camp. To attempt to state in detail what this means, so far as England is concerned, would lead me into highly controversial topics. My objects in discussing the right of the individual to the land have been to illustrate the futility of the argument from natural rights and to point out the dangers of a crude application of the argument from the common good. The statesman has to consider, not only the question whether public ownership of the land would be for the good of the community, but also, assuming that question to be answered in the affirmative, how he may bring about the desired result while avoiding grave injustice to existing owners. He has to recognise that society, like most individuals, has a past—a past that cannot be ignored when problems of reconstruction are under consideration. No doubt it would be easier for him if he had a clean slate. In point of fact he has not; to act as if he had might be magnificent; but it would not be politics.

V.—The Right to Work.

The right to work has two aspects. The first raises the question whether the State ought to recognise a right in the individual to earn his own livelihood in his own way without regard to the effect of his action upon the well-being of workers as a class. Those who assert the existence of such a right assert by implication the equal right of men to freedom. Those who deny the right appeal to the common good. But, just as in the case of the land, so also in the case of labour, we must be on our guard against crude applications of the argument from the common good. That good undoubtedly justifies the general policy of Factory Laws that qualify the right of the individual to work as he chooses. At the same time, the State protects the labourer's freedom of action so long as he does not act in contravention of particular laws. It protects, for example, the free labourer who chooses to work for lower than union wages. Nor can its action in this respect be impugned. Circumstances may arise —in my opinion they exist to-day—when the State should legislate with a view to maintaining a minimum wage. But until this responsibility is undertaken, the State is just as bound to recognise the free labourer's claim to work as it is bound to recognise the claim of the members of a trade union to combine for the purpose of raising the rate of wage.[1] The trade unionist may employ suasion; but, if he employs force, he becomes a rebel to the community. While his action may be morally justifiable under particular circumstances of time and place,[2] the duty of the State is clear. The State should amend laws that involve injustice to its citizens; but it cannot, without abdicating its most essential function, permit the violation of those laws prior to their amendment.

But the right to work, as it is ordinarily understood to-day, involves more debatable issues. Most of those who affirm the "right to work" mean that the individual has a right to demand employment of the State at the customary wage if he fails to find employment for himself. In recent sessions of the House of Commons, several attempts have been made to secure for this claim a statutory recognition.

Clause 3 of a "Right to Work Bill" provides:—

"Where a workman has registered himself as unemployed, it shall be the duty of the local unemployment authority to provide work for him in connection with one or other of the schemes hereinafter provided, or otherwise; or failing the provision of work, to provide maintenance, should necessity exist, for that person and for those depending on that person for the necessaries of life: provided that a refusal on the part of the unemployed workman to accept reasonable work upon one of these schemes, or employment upon conditions not lower than those that are standard to the work in the locality, shall release the local unemployment authority of its duties under this section."

1. *Cf.*, however, the remarks in ch. vi. on "The Moralisation of Competition."
2. *Cf. infra.*, "The Right to do One's Duty."

Some advocates of the Bill within the House, and many advocates of the Bill outside of the House, have defended its essential principle by an appeal to natural rights. The controversial advantages of approaching the subject from this point of view must be admitted. There is then no need to prove that the recognition of the right in question would be in accord with social good; and the advocate who relies upon *a priori* principles is enabled to disregard the lessons taught by the experience of the past. Mr. John Burns, in replying to the speeches delivered in the House of Commons in 1911, in support of the right to work, remarked:

"All precedents have been ignored; universal experience has been ignored; and any reference to recent attempts to apply the underlying principle contended for has been most discreetly avoided. The cost has not been estimated; the consequences have been left to sentimental speculation; and the effects upon industry have not even been referred to."[1]

Assuming the impracticability of *a priori* methods of determining the rights of the individual, the question whether the State ought to recognise a claim in the individual to demand public employment can only be answered in the affirmative after an examination of several objections. These may be grouped as historical, economic, and psychological. The historical objection is far from conclusive, since it may be met by the rejoinder that in the instances quoted the conditions were different. But the objection has nevertheless some weight. The establishment of the French *ateliers nationaux* of 1848, and the less ambitious attempts that have been made at different periods in England to provide relief work, have shown that such experiments are likely to be followed by an increase in the number of the unemployed, a gradual drift of labour from private employment to public employment,

1. *Times*, 11th February 1911. I have taken one or two verbal liberties with the text of the report.

and a deterioration in the character of the workmen. Large bodies of workers, who would have remained in normal occupations under sterner conditions, have yielded to the allurements of "the softer job" when once those conditions have been relaxed. A Local Government Board inspector, speaking in 1905 of the effect of the establishment of relief works in the West Riding of Yorkshire, said: "There is every likelihood of a stereotyped class of men being evolved who will be content to live on three days' work a week." Another inspector declared: "Irregular relief work has such charms that numerous instances have been noted of men throwing up regular wages at eighteen and nineteen shillings a week to earn from five shillings to seven shillings in a stone-yard."[1]

"Relief works," remarked Mr. John Burns in 1911, "are like opiates: the more one takes the more one wants."[2] Truly we are reminded of Fuller's caustic reference to the ancient monastery: "These abbeys did but maintain the poor which they made." Although the abuses to which I have referred could be mitigated by the payment of a low rate of wage for all relief work and the application of penal discipline in the case of "shirkers," such safeguards are not popular with those who affirm the right to work, and are inconsistent with its general principle.[3]

Apart from the failure of experiments in the past, there are two economic objections to the legislative recognition of a right to work. The first of these is based upon financial considerations. In the very nature of things, relief works are foredoomed to be economically unprofitable. This has been amply demonstrated by recent experience.

"The net cost of relief in London," writes Mr. Beveridge, "has been three times the allowance which

1. Quoted, *Quarterly Review*, January, 1908, 212.
2. *Times*, 11th February 1911.
3. As to the experiment of *ateliers nationaux* in 1848, see the article of Mr. Marriott in *The Nineteenth Century and After*, June 1908. *Cf.* also, Beveridge, "Unemployment: A Problem of Industry," 190-1.

the best organised trade unions think necessary for their unemployed members."[1]

Road work, under the control of the Norwich Town Council, cost six times what it ought to have done.[2] An experiment in rural colonies showed that it would have been as cheap to the Central (Unemployed) Body to have paid the men twenty-five shilling a week for doing nothing in London.[3] The Finance Committee of the Paddington Borough Council, in discussing relief works, reported: " It would really be cheaper to the ratepayers, who have to find the money in any case, if relief were given to the men themselves direct."[4] No doubt such failures may be attributable in part to defective administration. But the difficulties in the way of finding suitable work for a heterogeneous body of applicants, the general inferiority of the unemployed in physique and *morale*, and the impracticability of reducing the wage beyond the minimum required for subsistence, combine to make relief work highly unprofitable from the purely economic point of view.

The costliness of relief works may be met by the argument that the unemployed must be maintained somehow, and that they had better be maintained in work than in idleness. A more serious objection to relief works is the industrial dislocation they involve. This takes several forms. (1) The Poor Law Commissioners have drawn attention to the fact that relief works, undertaken by municipalities, are often a mere arrangement by which some men are deprived of their regular employment in order that others may be given, in rotation, a " three days' turn."[5] (2) " It would in practice prove impossible," writes Mr. Beveridge, " to make any system of State employment act as a reservoir

1. " Unemployment," 190.
2. " Minority Report of the Poor Law Commission," edited by S. and B. Webb, ii. 124.
3. *Ibid.*, 141.
4. *Ibid.*, 125.
5. *Ibid.*, 126.

for the ordinary labour market. The men might flow in; they would not naturally flow out again unless the State employment was made in some way less attractive than ordinary employment. Yet this is just what it could not be made without being made either degrading or inadequate for a living. . . . In so far as State employment in any way served the object for which it is here supposed to be started—that of affording a universal refuge for men in involuntary idleness—it would be a support to the methods making that idleness inevitable."[1] (3) Since relief works prove economically unprofitable, the taxpayer has to pay for their support with funds that would otherwise be spent in the purchase of goods whose production and distribution would afford employment to the normal worker. In other words, by increasing the taxation imposed for the purpose of carrying on unproductive works, the State tightens the purse-strings of the taxpayer, limits the demand for commodities, and secures work for some men by means that involve squeezing other men out of employment.

Two further objections to the legislative recognition of a right to work may be described as psychological. (1) The proposed remedy must weaken the incentive to habits of industry. As Mr. Cross once said before the House of Commons, " It is not possible to teach a worse lesson than this, that if you do not take care of yourself, the State will take care of you." While no one doubts that unemployment is often unavoidable, and while few will deny that the State has a duty to perform with regard to the workless of all classes, the admission of an absolute right to demand work of the State is likely to develop in the mind of the weaker worker a debilitating sense of security. To seek to relieve or prevent the distress resulting from unemployment is a defensible policy. To make the mere fact of inability to find work a passport to the civil service is to court disaster.

1. " Unemployment," 195-6.

(2) The proposed remedy ignores the variety of individual characters within the unemployed class. Many are unemployed, not through any personal demerit or disinclination, but through fluctuations of supply and demand, the progress of machinery, the caprices of fashion, or the accidents of fortune. Even within the class that is described as unemployable, many lack work, less from disinclination than from congenital inferiority. This is true even in communities where the unemployed problem is relatively non-existent. The Director of the New South Wales State Labour Bureau writes:

"There are many who, by reason of old age, physical infirmity, incapacity, unworthiness, etc., are never likely to be employed under normal conditions. These form a class of unemployable. . . . Only to meet some emergency would any one seek their services; and they must always largely live on some system of charitable relief, as work in ordinary channels cannot be found for them. . . . With the utmost sympathy for their infirmities, and even for their shortcomings, they are most difficult to deal with. Nearly all are without initiative of any kind, many without energy, almost without capacity, and frequently without hope."

On the other hand, there is the class typified by the individual whom Mr. John Burns described as "the gentleman who gets up to look for work at mid-day and prays that he may not find it." A leader of the Bradford unemployed, on a "hunger-march" in 1909, attributed the failure of the march to the fact that so many of the men did not intend to look for work, and had never looked for it in their lives.

"They had joined the hunger-march for what they could make out of it. Some refused corned beef and butter, or grumbled at boiled bacon and beefsteak pudding. Others took to drink at every opportunity. At Stoke they went to church, but some of them had been 'fresh' the night before, and, when a meeting was called, were not fit to be seen. . . . After that," continued the leader, "I did not think I was justified in appealing to the public for help, and I left them." [1]

But if the unemployed include such a variety of classes, the differences between them must be carefully observed if remedial measures are to prove effective. No single panacea can be found. To assert that all men who are out of employment have a right to demand employment by the State is to disregard the complicated character of the material with which the State has to deal.

The preceding argument has been negative. I have stated certain objections—historical, economic, and psychological—to the legislative recognition of "a right to work." While these objections illustrate the danger of certain methods of dealing with the problem of unemployment, they are not inconsistent with a recognition of the urgency of the problem or with the need of State action in relation to it. I shall return to these aspects of the problem in Chapter IX when discussing the evils of unemployment. In the meantime I may remark that the duty of the State is especially evident in view of the fact that modern industry requires a surplus of labour for its efficient functioning. There are always *some* workers, and at times of industrial crisis there are *many* workers, who are quite unable to find work for themselves. Mr. Ramsay Macdonald, when speaking in the House of Commons in support of the Bill already referred to, said:

"If we are to have unemployed, not because the men are inferior to the employed but because of the very nature of the organisation of industry, it is a logical and humane corollary that the burden of unemployment should not be placed on the backs of these weak men, should not be left to charity or the odds and ends

1. *Times*, Weekly Edition, 8th January 1909.

of ill-assorted legislation, but should be dealt with more and more on the lines of Clause 3 of the present Bill."

While I dissent from this conclusion, I *do* think that the State has a grave responsibility to the unemployed of all classes. The practical question is to define the nature of that responsibility.

Some useful hints towards the solution of the problem may be obtained from an examination of practice in other countries. In particular I may refer to experiments in dealing with the unemployed in Switzerland. These have been described with admirable lucidity by Miss Edith Sellers, to whose investigations I am indebted for the present summary.[1]

Swiss practice draws a broad distinction between two classes of the unemployed. Unemployment due to laziness or misconduct is treated as a form of criminality. The offender is detained at a reformatory institution, under military discipline, for as long as may be deemed necessary. In return for his work he receives board and lodging, together with a wage that varies from a penny to threepence a day. On the other hand, the honest seeker after work is helped without being subjected to any sort of humiliation. The help may take several forms:—for example, grants in money or in kind; or the provision of employment at regular wages which are lower than a private employer would pay for similar work; or board and residence at home-inns, where a man may stay with his wife and children for a limited time at a trifling expense; or assistance at a relief-in-kind station, where a man who is on his way to find work may receive temporary board and lodging. Any one who lives in Berne, provided that he is able to work and is not above sixty years of age, may insure against unemployment in the municipal Bureau. By the payment of seventy centimes a month, he obtains a right to an

1. See article in *The Nineteenth Century and After*, November 1908.

allowance on his becoming unemployed. Before an applicant receives such an allowance, however, the manager of the Insurance Bureau, who is also manager of the Labour Bureau and is in close touch with the employers in the canton and the various Labour Bureaux throughout the country, will seek to find work for him. The allowance is granted only in cases where work cannot be found, and only until it can. The man who receives it must present himself at the Bureau waiting-room twice every day, to see if the manager is able to find work for him. The subscriptions paid to the Insurance Bureau by its members are supplemented by a fixed municipal grant and voluntary subscriptions from employers. It acts in co-operation with the State, which allows members of the Bureau, when in search of employment, to travel on the State railways at half fares. It also acts in co-operation with a municipal board of works, which gives priority of claim to members of the Insurance Bureau, and arranges that municipal works shall be carried out as far as possible in December, January, and February.

Perhaps the most interesting feature of the Swiss practice consists in the effort to cope with the causes of unemployment. Bureau statistics show that, except during periods of industrial crisis, the vast body of the unemployed belong to the class of unskilled workmen. Such national conditions as tell for the multiplication of the number of *unskilled* workmen tell for the manufacture of *unemployed* workmen. In the more important Swiss cantons, the recognition of this fact has resulted in a popular crusade with the aim of ensuring that every citizen shall become a skilled worker. Parents who neglect their children, and masters who are indifferent to the welfare of their apprentices, are amenable to civic penalties. In some places, masters are required to see that their young employees go to a night school. Another common source of unemployment is intemperance. This evil, too, is being effectively dealt with. At the first signs of alcoholism, the patient is liable to be sent to a home for inebriates. When the *Bundesrat* surrendered the yield of the spirit monopoly to the Governments of the several cantons, it stipulated that a tenth should be devoted to the cause of temperance. Every temperance society that is doing good work receives a grant from the spirit monopoly. The definition of a temperance society is comprehensive: it includes, for example, every institution that indirectly combats alcoholism by endeavouring to improve the conditions of home life. As the Swiss regard decent housing and good food as the most effective weapons in the struggle against intemperance, they encourage the promotion of peoples' kitchens and the teaching of cookery.

"Social reformers," writes Miss Sellers, "go forth into the highways and byways, and literally force girls and women to come in and be taught how to cook. They try to teach them, also, how to take care of their babies, and how to make their homes comfortable. All Switzerland is now alive to the fact that if men, whether unemployed or employed, are not to become unemployable, they must be kept from drink; all Switzerland is alive to the fact, too, that it is hopeless work trying to keep them from drink unless they are properly fed." [1]

I have dwelt at some length upon the Swiss practice in relation to unemployment because I believe that we have much to learn from it. Its general object is to help men to help themselves. While public institutions may supply work in cases of emergency, the provision of such work is ancillary to the action of various agencies that enable a man to find work for himself. If he does not want to find work, he is subjected to penal discipline. Moreover, the fund for insurance against unemployment is obtained by the co-operation of employers, employees, and municipal

1. *The Nineteenth Century and After,* November 1908.

bodies. Finally, the nation, acting in co-operation with the workers themselves and with various philanthropic agencies, recognises that prevention is better than cure. It deliberately and persistently seeks to cope with the causes of unemployment. It endeavours—by the education of the citizen, by the improvement of the conditions of home life, and by the encouragement of the habits of thrift and temperance—to eliminate the problem of the unemployable, and to develop in every citizen a capable and resourceful manhood.

The ameliorative legislation of one country is seldom adequate to the necessities of other countries. In England, with its larger population and vast industrial centres, voluntary agencies can do relatively less than in Switzerland, and graver responsibilities are imposed on the State. But already the influence of continental example is reflected in the trend of opinion and legislation. Writing in 1908, Mr. Beveridge, in his admirable work on Unemployment, advocated the following measures of reform:—(1) The establishment of labour bureaux and other agencies for promoting the fluidity of labour:

"Fluctuations of demand are now provided for by the maintenance of huge stagnant reserves of labour in varying extremities of distress. There is no reason in the nature of things why they should not be provided for by organised reserves of labour raised beyond the reach of distress."[1]

(2) Greater elasticity of working hours:

"Half-employment as a normal condition is nothing but bad; as a method of meeting an emergency it has everything in its favour."[2]

(3) Further extensions of the principle of insurance

1. "Unemployment: A Problem of Industry," 236. For a criticism of the working of Labour Exchanges in England, see an article by Mr. H. W. J. Stone, in *The Fortnightly Review*, October, 1913

2. *Ibid*, 222.

against unemployment.[1] (4) The more systematic distribution of public work:

"the steadying of the labour market by making demand in one direction—that of public bodies—expand or contract as the demand in other directions contracts or expands."[2]

(5) A reformed poor law, which shall not admit of relief works masquerading as industry, and shall be adapted to the varying needs of different classes—providing, for some, sustenance till they can recover employment; for others, restorative or educational treatment; and for others, again, disciplinary treatment under detention.[3]

Most of these proposals for reform appear to me admirable. Many of them are approved in the report of the Poor Law Commissioners of 1909. Some are being tentatively adopted in legislation such as the Labour Exchanges Act of 1909 and the National Insurance Bill of 1911. Mr. Beveridge did not purport to deal, however, with all of the deeper causes of unemployment. In addition to the reforms suggested by him or adopted by later legislation, much remains to be done through popular education. According to the report of the minority in the Poor Law Commission,

"this perpetual recruitment of the Unemployable by tens of thousands of boys who, through neglect to provide them with suitable industrial training, may almost be said to graduate into Unemployment as a matter of course," is "perhaps the gravest of all the grave facts which this Commission has laid bare."[4]

Moreover, I believe that legislation against intemperance, on lines similar to the Swiss, would have a

1. "Unemployment: A Problem of Industry," 223-30. *Cf.* Mr. Chiozza Money's "National Insurance and Labour Unrest," *Fortnightly Review*, October 1913.
2. *Ibid.*, 230-1.
3. *Ibid.*, 232-4
4. Edited by S. and B. Webb, ii. 223.

useful effect in preventing unemployment.[1] Many other reforms of a useful character might be suggested. The State is under a duty to effect such reforms. Correlatively, the unemployed have a right to demand that the State should recognise its responsibilities in this direction. In a sense, this may be termed a *right to work*; but it is a right that is relative to, in harmony with, and justified by, the well-being of the community as a whole.[2]

VI.—The Right to Equality of Opportunity.

In asserting the claim to equality of opportunity the advocate of the doctrine of natural rights is fighting in his last ditch. This claim is a special form of the demand for equal rights to liberty. Plausible as it may be, it involves consequences such as few men desire and none can justify. Not only must all capital be State-owned—a consequence about the expediency of which there is room for difference of opinion—but the family must be abolished. Equality of opportunity, between the offspring of parents of varying degrees of capacity and influence, could only be secured by removing the child from the parental control. No doubt many advocates of equality of opportunity have not this consequence in contemplation; but that only goes to show the danger of adopting a phrase without realising its implications.

If, however, we reject the phrase in question, how shall we express the right of the individual in respect to opportunity? The answer involves a consideration of the evils out of which the demand for equality of opportunity has grown. In brief, the demand is a protest against the prevailing monopoly of careers.

1 But *cf. Ibid.*, 233-5.

2. Since writing the above I have read the chapter on "The Problem of the Unemployed," in Mr. Percy Alden's "Democratic England." The author refers *inter alia* to the New Zealand Co-operative Gang system. Local authorities, acting in behalf of the government, employ a gang to work on its own responsibility. The gang accepts a contract to accomplish a specific amount of work for a fixed price, elects its own foreman, and shares the proceeds.

Nominally, every citizen may choose his own calling. As a matter of fact, the career the youth is to follow, the trade, profession, or calling he is to enter, are determined less by reference to his capacity than by reference to the wealth or position of his parent. "The majority of labourers," said Mill, "have as little choice of occupation as could exist in any system short of actual slavery." Mill's dictum still remains true in substance. Multitudes find the career for which they are most adapted as rigidly closed against them as if it were guarded by iron bars. They have to stifle the impulses of their nature lest they lose their daily bread. Moreover, restrictions upon the free choice of careers involve a loss to the community as well as an injury to the individual. The State needs to-day, more than ever, to discover and utilise the best talent in every branch of life, if it is to hold its own in the conflict of the nations. At an early stage in the history of the modern demand for freedom in the choice of careers, the question was fought out between the aristocratic and the middle classes. At a meeting in Drury Lane Theatre, an exponent of middle-class views said:

"I have recently discussed this question with a peer of the realm. He asked me what would become of their younger sons if our reform should be accomplished? I answered that question by another. What would become of our younger sons if the reform should not be accomplished?"

To-day, the question of freedom of careers is often discussed as if related solely to the relative claims of the middle and working classes. But it calls for dispassionate discussion from the point of view of the community as a whole. The interests of the community demand the full and free development of each citizen, a constant regard for the material, intellectual and moral well-being of every child, and a persistent effort to discover talent and to secure to it the fullest and freest scope.

I have tried to show that the reformer of to-day who upholds the right to equality of opportunity is fighting evils that are grave in their character, widely diffused in their influence, and inimical in the last degree to a sound system of national economy. But the right of the individual, which is infringed by the prevailing monopoly of careers, would be better expressed as a right to *equity of opportunity*. This terminology, if less definite and attractive, expresses an ideal that is less revolutionary and unpractical, since it admits of a due regard to the inherited structure of society and to the importance of maintaining the integrity of family life. The ideal involves, as I believe, two things. In the first place, it involves the progressive amelioration of material conditions. "The home of thirty-seven out of every hundred families in Dublin is a single living-room." To suppose that equity of opportunity can exist under such conditions is absurd. Not in Dublin merely, but throughout the industrial centres of the United Kingdom, the home life of multitudes of children is deplorable. At the very basis of every sound proposal for achieving an equity of opportunity is the question of the material condition of the people. In the second place, equity of opportunity demands a prolongation of the period of free education, together with such an extension of the scholarship system as will enable the poorest child of more than average talent to climb to the station of life for which he is fitted. We could not neutralise all the differences resulting from the fortune of birth without undertaking social experiments of a most perilous character; but we can at least remedy the graver injustices, and so minimise the artificial handicaps imposed by existing conditions upon whole classes of the community.

VII.—The Right to Self-Government.

The preceding chapter concluded with some observations upon the relation of the doctrine of natural rights to theories of the sovereignty of the individual. While I hold that civil authority is only to be justified by the purposes it serves, I include among those purposes the maintenance of conditions conducive to the government of the individual by himself. It will be evident that any one who adopts this position means far less by the right to self-government than the term implies when employed by the anarchist, or even by the advocate of natural rights. At the same time, he means something more than the right of the individual to share in the life of active citizenship. He suspects parental laws no less than autocratic institutions. I have already discussed the subject of parental laws. In the present place I limit myself to an examination of the right of the individual, in a modern community, to share in the life of active citizenship.

To many, the statement that the British elector has a right to determine the laws he lives under will seem a truism. In reality, it is a truism of yesterday which is to-day being called in question. It is the expression of a democratic faith which has suffered in two ways. In the first place, there has been a reaction from exaggerated expectations. Human possibilities are not to be actualised in the course of a few decades. The failure to recognise this fact accounts in part for unjustifiable pessimism—a disposition to proclaim that democratic institutions have been weighed in the balance and found wanting. In the second place, the democratic faith has suffered because men have not made allowance for the difficulties with which democratic institutions have had to cope. Scientific and mechanical progress, by increasing the facilities for making great fortunes, has lured the souls of men into the pursuit of gain; the growing complexity of affairs and the rapid development of urban populations have increased the number and difficulty of our economic problems; and the competition of the nations for world dominion, due to the opening up of new continents, is imposing a great strain upon national finance and threatening the world with the evils of chronic militarism. Democratic progress is not responsible for these things; but democratic institutions have had to cope with them.[1]

The impartial student, if he makes allowance for the short time during which democratic institutions have existed and for the difficulty of the problems with which they have had to deal, will be less impressed by the failures of democracy than by its relative success. That success would have been impossible but for a circumstance which affords at once an explanation of past achievement and a ground for indulging a reasoned hope with respect to the future. As Professor Maccunn remarks, in his essay on Carlyle, the difficulty of our problems is no conclusive argument against their submission to the electorate, since they come before the electorate in a simplified form.

"The people are not called upon to play their decisive part till, by much discussion elsewhere, in press, platform, Parliament, private life, the questions *sub judice* have been threshed out and reduced to board issues. . . . The one point worth discussing is whether beneath the defects, which need not be disputed, there cannot be found in the members of *all classes* in the State those positive qualities that make the citizen. These qualities are not intellectual merely; nor is it difficult to specify what they are. One is the ability to set sufficient value upon the broad public ends upon which all political effort is directed, and among these the very ends to which Carlyle himself has so opened the eyes of his countrymen that they cannot again be closed. One has but to think of personal independence, tools to the man who can use them and wages to the man who can earn them, good sanitation, accessible education, the maintenance of law and order, an efficient public service, national defence—these are the very ends which Carlyle proclaimed upon

1. *Cf.* Jethro Brown, "The New Democracy," 19–21.

the housetops; and not in vain, because in truth they are ends that stare even the average man in the face and cross his life and his interests in manifold inevitable ways. A second quality, and it goes closely with the first, is sufficient superiority to selfish and (to use Bentham's favourite term) 'sinister' interests. But, then, these 'sinister' interests are not the peculiar bane of a democratic electorate. They are the bane of all classes in the State, and they are not least the bane, as Bentham would remind us, of those classes who are peculiarly tempted towards them by social privilege and political monopoly. Still another quality is that experience of the transactions of public business which, as we have seen, filled so large a place in the educational outlook of Mill, and which comes of actual contact with the affairs of workshop, friendly society, trades-union, co-operative association, political organisation, not less surely than it comes in other walks of life. Lastly, and above all else important, there is that sagacity, shrewdness, common sense (call it what we may) which is the cardinal quality of the practical man in all conditions of life."[1]

That capacity for the life of active citizenship, upon which Professor Maccunn insists, will reveal itself more clearly when our educational system has been more fully developed. The errors of the electorate are due, in so small measure, not to any incurable unfitness of the voters themselves to express an opinion worthy of expression, but to a culpable neglect of which our educational institutions have been guilty. We turn our youths into the polling booth, to exercise a grave and responsible duty, without having provided them with any training to help them to discharge that duty wisely. I believe the time will come when the unwisdom of this policy will be recognised. The rudiments of political and economic science could be taught in the school without infringing upon the domain of

1. "Six Radical Thinkers," 153-6.

party controversy; and, if they were so taught, the pupil would not only gain a few useful ideas as to the principles upon which the questions at issue between political parties should be decided, but—what is still more important—he would leave the school *prepared to learn.* I do not think that at any of our educational institutions, whether primary, secondary, or university, we have yet learnt to appreciate the special claims of those subjects in which the student is likely to continue to be interested in after-life if his mind has once been directed to them by a capable teacher. Politics is pre-eminently such a subject. If the citizen has acquired while at school an elementary knowledge of the principles of legislative action, he is much more likely to take an interest in the study of those principles when he is called upon to consider the particular problems submitted to his judgment as an elector. We hear much to-day about the training of the individual for life; but, in a democratic community, such training cannot ignore the part the individual is called upon to play as the arbiter of the national destiny.[1]

In recent literature, I know of no work which offers a more plausible criticism of democratic institutions than M. Faguet's " The Cult of Incompetence." The distinguished author urges that modern democracy, acting in despite of the elementary fact that the best society is one where the division of labour is greatest and specialisation is most definite, is essentially amoebic. The author does not quote, but he appears to subscribe to the dictum,

> " Where everybody's somebody,
> Then nobody's anybody."

The electors, it is urged, choose the impassioned representatives of their own passions. They may *think* they choose their candidates on moral grounds. In reality, they impute a high morality to those who share their own passions, and who express themselves

1. *Cf. infra* the remarks in chapter ix. on " The Problem of the Child."

thereon more violently than others. The people favours incompetence not merely from its own incapacity to judge competence, but because it desires above everything that its representatives shall resemble itself. The resemblance is a kind of protection against the simulation of popular passion. It also satisfies an instinctive demand for equality. Finally, democracy, not content to exclude competence, wishes to do everything itself. Hence the manifold forms of the appeal, destined to become increasingly insistent, for a *direct* democracy in politics and industry.

If M. Faguet's diagnosis of existing facts be correct, I should incline to the opinion that democracy as a form of government is doomed. But I cannot for a moment accept that diagnosis, at any rate as regards the Anglo-Saxon community. Not that the diagnosis is wholly false, but that is grossly partial. I believe that the author very much underrates the capacity of the average elector. He appears to be guilty of that confusion between ignorance and stupidity which has so often vitiated the plausible syllogisms of the learned. He even exaggerates the ignorance of the masses. He seems to regard them as having no ideas but their own, whereas their ideas far more often than otherwise come to them from more enlightened individuals who belong to classes with which they may have very little social relation. Again, I do not think that the author realises the distinction between a jealousy of economic inequality and an aversion from intellectual superiority. The former is fostered by the glaring and unjust disparity of existing economic conditions. The latter is incidental. The reason why claims to intellectual superiority are apt to be viewed with popular suspicion is largely the result of the fact that in the past the educated classes have so largely identified themselves, as a result of the very circumstances of their origin and environment, with the forces of conservatism. The antidote to the pessimism of M. Faguet may be found in the philosophy of Carlyle as expressed in "Heroes and Hero Worship." Both these writers make useful contributions to popular psychology; but those contributions complement and correct one another. Speaking at any rate of the Anglo-Saxon community, the evidences do not justify the affirmation of a persistent and instinctive preference for the incompetent legislator. The masses of the people are slow to recognise greatness; but they are quite prepared to bow to it when they see it. They often mistake the false for the real; and they pay heavy penalties in consequence. But I cannot admit for a moment that there is a direct preference for mediocrity and incompetence as such. No doubt one of the dangers of the future will be an *inadequate* recognition of the value of enlightened guidance. The consequence would only be a natural reaction from the superseded assumption that the multitude were born to be the passive material of autocratic manipulation. But, taking into consideration the improving standards of education, the multiplication of agencies for the dissemination of knowledge, and the reality of the penalties which wait upon passion divorced from reason, I believe that the sane democrat of to-day may look to the future with a reasonable confidence in the ultimate triumph of his faith.

The right of self-government does not rest solely (1) upon the ground of the citizen's capacity to express an opinion upon the broader issues of national policy; or (2) upon the ground that this capacity develops with opportunities of its exercise, and that its development is an end of sufficient importance to justify the payment of a liberal price in the form of blundering legislation; or (3) upon the ground that the claims of the multitude are unlikely to receive an adequate consideration unless the multitude has a voice in framing the laws under which it lives. All these are important elements in the case for self-government; but deeper than any of them lies the fact that the really valuable achievements in life are not those that have been won *for* men, but those that have been won *by* men. We hear much to-day, in certain circles, of "efficiency" and "expert guidance"; and such things are undoubtedly of great importance. But impatience to get things done overshoots the mark when it ignores the importance of securing the co-operation of those for whom things are to be done. Such effort to bring about social amelioration as is prompted by community of aspiration and will may seem to promise less than could be effected by a complete delegation of power to the capable and intelligent few; but, if it achieves less, what it does achieve is of incomparably greater value and of more enduring quality. There is no royal road to social progress. Such progress is from within men. It implies the gradual emancipation of the human spirit, the slow accumulation of petty gains which are valuable and enduring because they are sought and won by men for themselves.

"The man who moves with the people," writes Miss Addams, "is bound to consult the 'feasible right' as well as the absolute right. He is often obliged to attain only Mr. Lincoln's 'best possible,' and then has the sickening sense of compromise with his best convictions. He has to move along with those whom he leads toward a goal that neither he nor they see very clearly till they come to it. He has to discover what people really want, and then 'provide the channels in which the growing moral force of their lives shall flow.' What he does attain, however, is not the result of his individual striving, as a solitary mountain-climber beyond that of the valley multitude, but it is sustained and upheld by the sentiments and aspirations of many others. Progress has been slower perpendicularly, but incomparably greater because lateral. He has not taught his contemporaries to climb mountains, but he has persuaded the villagers to move up a few feet higher; added to this, he has made secure his progress. . . . Associated effort toward social progress, although much more awkward and stumbling than that same effort managed by a capable individual, does yet enlist deeper forces and evoke higher social capacities."[1]

VIII.—The Right to do One's Duty, including the Right of Resistance.

"The individual," writes Professor Henry Jones, "has no right which can compare with his right to do his duty, which is to fulfil his part as a member of society."[2]

This assertion, in the emphasis it lays upon human duty, indicates the advance that has been made in the general theory of individual rights. It involves, however, an ambiguity that has been responsible for much confused thinking. On the one hand, a man is surely under a moral duty to do what, after all reasonable consideration, he believes he ought to do. On the other hand, since rights and duties are correlative and the existence of a right to act on certain ways implies a duty in others not to interfere, the individual has not always a right to do what he thinks he ought to do. Hence it would appear that a man may be under a duty to do what he has no right to do.

The apparent conflict is the result of confusing two entirely distinct standards, each of which is valid within its own sphere and for its own purposes. In a world of finite intelligences, it is the moral duty of men to act up to the light they have. But that light may be defective. A man's duty as he sees it may differ from his duty as he would have seen it had he been more enlightened. If we are discussing his moral innocence or blameworthiness we are compelled to judge him by reference to an internal standard; but if we are seeking to determine whether his action is in harmony with an ideal system of moral rights, we are compelled to appeal to a standard that is external.

1. "Democracy and Social Ethics," 151-3.
2. "The Working Faith of a Social Reformer," 248.

The distinction between the question of rights and that of personal innocence applies to group conduct as well as to individual conduct. A concrete illustration may be suggested. A besieged city is at the mercy of an invader. The invader demands the surrender, for exemplary punishment, of one of two persons. One of these is a saint; the other is a criminal. The city decides, after due consideration, that the saint (being, we will suppose, something of a fanatic) shall be surrendered. But the saint, believing himself to stand for ideals of great social value, goes into hiding. As a consequence, the city surrenders the criminal. What are the rights and wrongs of this case?

The society fulfils a moral duty in endeavouring to carry out a decision that has been reached after a full and impartial deliberation. At the same time, since the question of moral right must be determined by an external standard, the society has no moral right to surrender the saint, even though, arguing on mistaken grounds, it thinks otherwise. Whether the saint has a right to evade the decree is a further question. If he thinks, after due consideration, that he ought to go into hiding, he is under a moral duty to do so. But the question whether in hiding himself he is exercising a moral right can again be determined only by the application of an external standard. In the application of that standard, some weight must be attached to the mere fact that the society, having exercised its judgment according to its lights, has decided that he ought to be surrendered. But this is the utmost that can be said in favour of denying to the individual a right to disobey the society which has decided on inadequate grounds to sacrifice him. All this may savour of casuistry; but in point of fact many discussions on individual rights are vitiated by a failure to recognise the elementary distinction I have attempted to illustrate.

The practical importance of the distinction is most readily seen when we consider the question of the right of the citizen to disobey the laws or rebel against the government. The problem presents itself in the attitude of the Passive Resister to the Education Rate, and in the more militant methods of the suffragette. Most thinking people will agree that the suffragette who is sincerely acting up to her light is discharging a moral duty. Whether she is exercising a moral right is another and more difficult question. At least one thing may be said. The question cannot be answered in the affirmative simply on the ground that the suffragette may be animated by the best intentions. To justify the affirmative answer, it would be necessary to show that disobedience to law is in accordance with social good as rightly interpreted. There have been occasions in the past—and similar occasions may arise in the future—when disobedience to law, and even active rebellion, could be justified on this ground. But, in the first place, the right to resist the law, or to rebel, is obviously one that cannot receive legislative recognition: it is a merely moral right. In the second place, the conditions under which the right arises are unlikely to exist under democratic institutions. As T. H. Green observes, the public interest, on which all rights are founded, is more concerned in the general obedience to law than in the exercise of the powers which unjust laws may withhold. The citizen has no right to disobey the law unless it be for the true interest of the State, and such interest can hardly exist save where the law is obnoxious to claims which are acknowledged by the conscience of the community.[1]

1. Green, "Philosophical Works," ii. 454-6.

PART III.

THE OUTLOOK.

CHAPTER IX.

PROBLEMS OF TO-DAY AND TO-MORROW.

THE separation of Church and State and the secularisation of politics find a place among the accredited triumphs of the modern era. But although politics claims to be emancipate from theology, the spirit within the letter of the creeds has permeated the thought of our statesmen and thinkers, and the separation of Church and State has been accompanied by a progressive tendency on the part of the State to undertake duties that were formerly a function of the Church. Education, once a sacred charge of the priest, is now the grave responsibility of the statesman. A like transference of function can be seen with respect to works of charity, the defence of the weak against the strong, and the care of the moral character of the citizen. Public assistance, in manifold forms, takes the place of the ancient monastery; the strong arm of the law and the keen eye of the ubiquitous inspector are employed in the guardianship of the weak; and public libraries, institutes, art galleries, State Children departments, and a growing body of law, aim at the development of character.[1]

The trend towards an increase of State responsibility and control is further evidenced in the enlarged sphere of public ownership. The age of private prisons, private lunatic asylums, private workhouses, and private coinage is long since past. In our own day public authorities discharge industrial functions or social services that were formerly undertaken by private individuals or companies—post and telegraph; railways and tramways; the supply of gas, electricity,

1. Cf. *International Journal of Ethics*, April 1907, 336–47.

and water; systems of drainage; hospitals, reformatories, and social insurance; schools and universities, and institutions of popular culture and recreation. All these involve extensions of the sphere of public ownership. They are expressions of a general movement, which, whether wise or unwise, is the most momentous fact of our time.

I.—The Pressure of Social and Economic Problems.

When we turn from an examination of the realities of a recent past to reflect upon the probabilities of the future, one thing at least seems certain. The movement towards an increase in the activities and responsibilities of the State is destined to continue. In the present chapter I shall endeavour to state the grounds of this conclusion. The first of them is the pressure of social and economic problems. Whether the problems are new or old, and whether they owe their driving power to the growing sensibility of the social conscience or to the democratisation of our political institutions, they are the material out of which the political future of the race is to be fashioned. I select for special consideration the Trust, Unemployment, the Inadequate Wage, and Child Life. I have discussed, in previous chapters, some attempts that have been made, or proposals that have been suggested, in solution of these problems. I wish now to state the data as briefly and dispassionately as I can, with a view to considering how far they afford a ground for anticipating a period of exceptional legislative activity in the near future.

(1) *The Trust.*[1]

I have referred in an earlier chapter to the revolution effected in the conditions of modern industry by

1. I have left the remarks on this subject as they were in the first edition of this work. Since writing them, however, I have given to the Trust Problem a systematic study of which the results are now in the Press in a work on "The Control of Monopolies." This work, however, deals *mainly* with the question of means of controlling trusts and combines.

the progress of mechanical and scientific discoveries. The relation of master and apprentice gave way to a relation of employer and employee, and the new economic conditions demanded new forms of State regulation. In our own day, the isolated manufacturer is being superseded by the corporation. This concentration of capital finds no parallel in the history of the past; and it promises to prove as fertile a source of legislative action as the factory conditions in the nineteenth century.

In its ultimate form, the concentration of capital means the organisation of industry in the form of trusts. A trust may be defined as a consolidation of capital in a particular industry, or in a system of related industries, with a view to the establishment of a monopoly. The various stages of development between the typical company and the trust are indicated by such institutions as Pools, Conferences, Corners, and the German Cartel. The developed trust implies two things. In the first place, it implies a consolidation of capital, which is operated as a business unit and is therefore distinguishable from looser combinations by the subordination of each part to a central control. In the second place, it implies the control, by this consolidation, of a predominating share of the output of a commodity. Mr. J. A. Hobson, whose lucid and impartial account of the trust is the basis of the present summary, writes:

"In England it is a common maxim of business that a minimum of 70 per cent. of the trade is indispensable to the success of consolidation, and in almost every instance of a strong trust the proportion is considerably larger than this. The Wall Paper Manufacturers, for example, claim to control 98 per cent. of the trade."[1]

The evils incidental to the concentration of capital in the form of trusts are found in varying degrees of intensity according to the magnitude of the trust, the

1. "The Evolution of Modern Capitalism," 218.

nature of the commodity in which it deals, and the industrial and political conditions of the country within which it operates. Its powers of exploitation require to be examined from the points of view of the several classes most concerned: producers, competitors, employees, and consumers. The first of these classes includes those who are engaged in either the earlier or the later processes of production. The various ways in which the class is exploited are illustrated by the operations of the American Standard Oil Company. Formerly, this company left the oil lands, and the machinery for extracting crude oil, in the hands of others; but its position as the largest purchaser of crude oil enabled it to dictate the price of the raw product. In 1870, the price of crude oil was quoted at 9.15 cents. From 1881, when the trust was formed, to 1890, the price was maintained at about 2.30 cents. With regard to the refined article, wholesale or retail dealers who attempted to buy from other companies than the Standard Oil were warned that local stores would be opened to undersell them. If a new patent for the treatment of oil was placed on the market, the trust could generally effect a compulsory purchase at its own price. It might even take the patent without paying any price at all, since its great wealth enabled it to ruin a patentee who might choose to refer the matter to the dubious and expensive arbitrament of the Courts of Law.

The attitude of the trust towards competitors in its main line of business is one of war *à outrance*. If necessary, goods will be sold at less than they cost to produce. Whether the underselling is confined to a limited area or extends over the whole area of the trust's market, the superior staying powers of the trust enable this policy to be continued until the ruin of the rival is complete. If the rival business is strong, the trust may endeavour to buy it out; but in such a case the price is determined, not by reference to the earning capacity of the business, but by reference to the amount of damage the business is capable of inflicting upon the trust. Some writers maintain that in such cases the trust is only seeking to do what every business firm is attempting, *i.e.*, to get as much trade as it can. But there appears to be a real distinction between the ordinary trade policy and a resolute and systematic endeavour to crush rivals out of existence.

The power of the trust in relation to its employees is despotic. Its despotism is often benevolent. The economies effected by the trust enable it to pay high wages; its control of the market enables it to assure a greater regularity of employment than is attainable under competition; the superior intelligence of its administration is not unlikely to recognise the economy of high wages; and its fear of legislative interference will naturally predispose it to seek the favour of the working classes. Since 1903, the Standard Oil Company has retired its men on half-pay at the age of sixty-five, and on quarter-pay at seventy. Other trusts have followed this excellent example. But a benevolence based upon prudential considerations cannot be regarded as an adequate safeguard of the interests of the working classes. Under the system of competitive industry, a workman may leave one employer for another, either to secure a higher wage or to obtain better conditions of employment. Where the trust is the only employer, the workman must come to terms with it or abandon his trade. If he elects to do the latter, he must either enter the ranks of the unemployed or secure employment as an unskilled labourer. It often happens that even the alternative of accepting or rejecting work on the trust's terms will not be offered to him. One of the chief economies effected by the trust is an economy of labour. When the Whisky Trust was formed, sixty-eight of the eighty constituent distilleries were closed and three hundred "travellers" were dismissed. Not less important than the power of determining whom the trust shall employ is the power of determining the wages and general conditions of employment. An employee who ventures to complain will probably be informed that he can go elsewhere. If he be young, he may choose to go elsewhere. But more workers are over thirty than under it; and a man of more than thirty does not easily find work of another class than that to which he has been accustomed. Speaking broadly, then, the trust possesses an enormous power over its employees; and there is no guarantee that this power will be exercised with a due regard to the interests of the working classes.

"The normal result of placing the ordering of an industry in the hands of a monopoly company," writes Mr. Hobson, "is to give them a power which it is their interest to exercise, to narrow the scope of industry, to change its *locale*, to abandon certain branches and take up others, to substitute machinery for hand labour, without any regard to the welfare of the employees who have been associated with the fixed capital formerly in use. When to this we add the reflection that the ability to choose its workmen out of an artificially made over-supply of labour, rid of the competition of other employers, gives the trust a well-nigh absolute power to fix wages, hours of work, to pay in truck, and generally to dictate terms of employment and conditions of life, we understand the feeling of distrust and antagonism with which the working classes regard the growth of these great monopolies on both sides of the Atlantic."[1]

The power of the trust, in relation to the general public as consumers, is scarcely less despotic; though here, too, the despotism may be tempered by prudence or controlled by practical necessities. Where the demand for a commodity admits of indefinite expansion, the trust may even profit by lowering prices. Even where the demand is relatively fixed, the dangers of

1. "The Evolution of Modern Capitalism," 225-6. *Cf.*, however, Mr. J. B. Clark's "The Problem of Monopoly," 60 *et seq.* Also the articles in the *Annals of the American Academy of Sciences,* July 1912, pp. 3-62, 122-3.

potential rivalry and the fears of legislative interference impose important restrictions upon the trust's freedom to fix its own price. But, with due allowance for such facts, no one can deny that the power of the trust to control prices is greater than is consistent with the public welfare. The trust will naturally charge the price that pays best, and the absence of effective competition deprives the public of any security that this price will be a fair one.

"The 'cost of living,' instead of being an expression of the needs and resources of society adjusting themselves through multitudinous transactions, is fixed by central authorities."[1]

Where, as in the case of railroads, the commodity in which the trust deals is indispensable, or where, as in the case of the supply of ice during a heat wave, the urgency of the need enables the trust to charge famine prices, the general public is likely to be "fleeced" just so far as the fleecing can be done without provoking legislative action. The consumer who grumbles at the price may be reminded that the trust is not a philanthropic institution. When Mr. J. D. Rockefeller was before the Courts of the United States in 1908, he assessed his profits for a single year as a member of the Standard Oil Trust at the enormous sum of £3,000,000! The estimated earnings of the Standard Oil Trust and the Standard Oil Company during twenty-seven years amounted to £200,000,000 on an original investment of £13,800,000; and the percentage of net earnings to capital stock between the years 1901-1909 varied from 57 to 84![2]

The trust, as we have just seen, makes enormous profits. How are these profits invested? The answer to this question reveals what is, perhaps, the most sinister form of the antagonism between the trust and

1. Howland, "Monopolies: The Cause and the Remedy," *Columbia Law Review*, February 1910, 92.
2. Cf. *Times*, weekly edition, 9th April 1909.

the community. While a part of the profits of the trust is spent by its members as consumers, an ever-increasing portion is conserved in the form of capital. If the employees and the general public were admitted to a larger share of the profits effected by the trust, there would be an increased demand in the home market for home-made goods. This increased demand would enable the results of the investment of fresh accumulations of capital to be consumed in the country within which the trust operates. But since the profits of the trust are absorbed by a very limited number of individuals, capital is impelled to turn to foreign markets to discover a field for its investments. Hence, the trust organisation of industry aggravates one of the gravest of the industrial anomalies of the age. Large masses of capital cannot find investment in the home market, because the demand there is inadequate. The multitudes of consumers who should have created the requisite demand are unable to do so, not because their need is small but because they have not at their disposal the means to give expression to it. From the point of view of the community, the undesirability of this condition of things is too evident to require demonstration.

"If," writes Mr. Hobson, "competition was displaced by combinations of a genuinely co-operative character, in which the whole gain of improved economies passed, either to the workers in wages, or to large bodies of investors in dividends, the expansion of demand in the home markets would be so great as to give full employment to the productive powers of concentrated capital, and there would be no self-accumulating masses of profit expressing themselves in new credit and demanding external employment. It is the monopoly profits of trusts and combines, taken either in construction, financial operation, or industrial working, that form a gathering fund of self-accumulating credit whose possession by the financial class implies a contracted demand for commodities and a correspondingly restricted employment for capital in American industries."[1]

The evil is not peculiar to the trust, for it exists under concentrated capitalism in any form; but it is intensified in proportion as the capital of the country passes under the control of trust organisations.

The trust, then, has several means of profiting at the expense of other sections of the community. It can "squeeze" producers; ruin competitors; "fleece" consumers; and dictate the wages, the hours of work, and the general labour conditions of employees. These powers are effective just in proportion as the trust organisation is complete. They illustrate the dangers following on the cessation of industrial competition. The resulting despotism is tempered in many ways; for example, through the endeavours of the trust, by sharing a portion of monopoly profits with its employees, to secure industrial peace as a means of more effectually fleecing the general public. Finally, the absorption of the profits of the trust by a very limited group of individuals is inconsistent with a system of sound national economy, stimulating, as it does, recourse to foreign markets for the sale of goods needed at home.

The trust is sometimes described as a parasite, which preys upon the community in general. Or it is compared to an octopus, whose gigantic arms encircle one class of the community after another in a grip as remorseless and inexorable as fate. Such analogies overlook the important functions that the trust discharges with economy and efficiency. At the same time, if the community is to profit by the trust's efficiency without sacrificing the interests of producers, employees, and consumers, it must find some way of protecting those classes. While the means may be a matter for debate, the necessity for protection admits of no question. If

1. "The Evolution of Modern Capitalism," 263-4.

the State did not control the trust, the trust would soon control the State.

(2) *Unemployment.*

Unemployment, whether we consider the evils due to it, the complexity of its causes, or the difficulty of devising effective remedies, is one of the gravest problems the statesmanship of our time has to solve. My present object is to bring into relief some of the data of the problem, in order to illustrate the probability of legislative action. I shall begin by considering briefly what unemployment means from the points of view of the worker, the home, and the community. "A man willing and unable to find work," said Carlyle, "is, perhaps, the saddest sight that fortune's inequality exhibits under the sun." Many of the unemployed are *not* willing to work; but the demoralising influence of unemployment is independent of the causes of its existence. The "shirker" grows more confirmed in the habits of idleness, and the worker who has sought employment without finding it becomes disinclined to seek it any longer. The degeneration of the honest unemployed is one of the most distressing of the facts demonstrated by the recent Poor Law Commission.

"This misery does not, like the temporary hardships of work or adventure, produce in those capable of responding to the stimulus, greater strength, energy, endurance, fortitude, or initiative. On the contrary, the enforced idleness and prolonged privation characteristic of unemployment have, on both the strong man and the weak, on the man of character and conduct and on the dissolute, a gravely deteriorating effect on body and mind, on muscle and will."[1]

The problem of unemployment is sometimes discussed as if it related solely to the persons who are themselves out of work. But a large section of the un-

1. "The Minority Report of the Poor Law Commission," ed. by S. and B. Webb, part ii. 241-2.

employed are the breadwinners of a home. While the fact cannot be questioned, its significance is seldom realised. The procession of the unemployed is a familiar spectacle; but the privation and possible demoralisation of the home do not appear in official statistics, and are invisible to the eye of the casual observer. As I write, the morning paper lies before me. Here is one of its items of news:

"George Brown, a collier, living in Conisborough, Yorkshire, had been out of work for eleven months, and, together with his large family, was reduced to such sore straits that in a mad frenzy he attempted to murder his eight children. While the little ones were asleep, their father closed all the apertures in their room, turned on the gas, and then committed suicide. The children are in a serious condition from gas poisoning, but will probably recover."

This report serves to illustrate, in an extreme form, something of the suffering that lies behind the official reports. Such a case is, of course, exceptional. Far more frequently, the family keeps starvation at bay by making breadwinners of either the mother, who should be engrossed in the care of the home, or the child, who should be at school or play.

"We have, in increasing numbers (though whether or not in increasing proportion is not clear), men degenerating through enforced Unemployment or chronic Underemployment into parasitic Unemployables, and the burden of industrial work cast on pregnant women, nursing mothers, and immature youths." [1]

The degradation of an individual however weak, the misery of a home however humble, affects the community of which the individual and the home are integral parts. But the community suffers in ways

1. "The Minority Report of the Poor Law Commission," ed. by S. and B. Webb, ii. 243-4.

that are more apparent to the average sense. According to the Report from which I have just quoted, the chronic underemployment of certain classes of the community is responsible above all other causes for the perpetual manufacture of paupers.[1]

" It is from the casual labour class," declares the Secretary of the Charity Organisation Society," that those who fall upon the Poor Law, Relief Works or Charitable Funds are mostly drawn." [2]

From the point of view of the community, the primary aspect of the fact just mentioned is the increased burden on the taxpayer. But there are secondary aspects no less important and scarcely less obvious. Further, in measuring the extent of a social evil, we have to take into account, not merely those upon whom it falls, but those upon whom it *may* fall. It is a bad thing that there should be so many unemployed; it is also a bad thing that there should be a much larger class possessing no reasonable security against becoming unemployed. Within limits, the fear of losing one's work is a useful stimulus to effort. But under existing conditions it is far in excess of the requirements of economic efficiency. An accident, an illness, a dismissal, a new invention, foreign competition, the failure of a capitalist, a change in the fashion of silk, or indeed any one of an indefinite number of such possibilities—and the blow has fallen. He upon whom it falls may recover his foothold; but there is no adequate security that he will do so. Indeed, too often, his fate is comparable to that of the man overboard whom Victor Hugo describes. He watches in despair the vessel and crew, which are indifferent to him, and are fast disappearing in the night. Happy is it for him in that hour if there are none who depend upon him!

The gravity of the evils of unemployment varies

1. "The Minority Report of the Poor Law Commission." ed. by S. and B. Webb, ii. 243.
2. Quoted, *Ibid.*, 196.

in proportion to the number of unemployed. In the United Kingdom, the number suffering from privation due to unemployment amounts in the best of times to hundreds of thousands, whilst in years of trade depression it must exceed a million.[1] If all this distress with its attendant evils—its burden of taxation, its deteriorating influence upon individual character, and its desolation of home life—were inevitable, its continuance would have to be accepted with stoical endurance. But it is not inevitable, as will be admitted by any one who carefully considers the passages quoted above from Mr. Beveridge's "Unemployment."

In an earlier chapter, I have referred to the lines along which, as it appears to me, immediate reforms may be effected. All that I wish to insist upon here is the gravity of the evils of unemployment and the resultant necessity for State action. The time has passed for indulging in the superstition that every man can find work if he wants it. The time has passed for supposing that any adequate remedy can be found in a system of occasional State doles supplemented by the irregular and capricious efforts of private philanthropy. The complexity of modern industry, the fluctuations (cyclical, seasonal, or casual) of supply and demand, and the manifold nature both of the causes of unemployment and of the types of unemployed character, impose upon the State new responsibilities which can no longer be ignored. While I cannot agree with all the recommendations of the Minority Report of the recent Poor Law Commission, I can at least subscribe to the following:—

"The eighteenth-century citizen acquiesced in the horrors of the contemporary prison administration, and in the slave trade; just as, for the first decades of the nineteenth century, our grandfathers accepted as inevitable the slavery of the little children of the wage-earners in mines and factories, and the incessant

1. "The Minority Report of the Poor Law Commission," ed. by S. and B. Webb, ii. 247

devastation of the slums by 'fever.' Fifty years hence we shall be looking back with amazement at the helpless and ignorant acquiescence of the governing classes of the United Kingdom, at the opening of the twentieth century, in the constant debasement of character and physique, not to mention the perpetual draining away of the nation's wealth, that idleness combined with starvation plainly causes." [1]

(3) *The Non-Living Wage.*

What a living wage is, and what steps should be taken by the State to ensure it, are matters about which a wide difference of opinion is possible. I am here concerned only to show that the evils of the inadequate wage are of such a nature as to justify the belief that further legislative action is inevitable. There is a large proportion of the home and factory workers in Great Britain in receipt of wages which, so far from admitting of a provision for periods of unemployment, sickness, or old age, are insufficient for decent subsistence. The problem has many aspects: it demands examination from the points of view of the worker, the home he may represent, the employer, and the community in general. So far as the worker and his home are concerned, the evils are comparable with those already indicated in my comments on the problem of unemployment. There is, however, one important difference. The class of the underpaid is much larger than that of the unemployed, and the distress and degradation resulting from underpayment are in consequence more widely diffused. As regards the position of the employer and of the general community, a more detailed consideration of the problem will be necessary.

Unless the rate of wage is directly or indirectly fixed by law, the employer, under the system of industrial competition, must often choose between underpaying his workmen and ruining his business.

1. Edited by S. and B. Webb, ii. 324.

I believe this dilemma is felt as a real grievance by an increasingly large class of employers and in an increasing degree of intensity. It is pertinent in this connection to quote a remark made by Mr. Verran, at the time Labour Premier of South Australia, when addressing in 1910 the House of Assembly of that State.

"It has been found necessary," he said, "after a long struggle to secure some machinery to regulate wages and conditions of labour; and it is no longer requisite to plead for the appointment of Wages Boards for the purpose of testing their usefulness. So popular have the Wages Boards become that it is now usually the employer who asks for their appointment, either as a means of securing industrial peace or for the purpose of protecting himself against unscrupulous competitors."[1]

Finally, although ill-paid labour may enrich particular employers, it is inconsistent with a sound system of national economy. It tells for inefficient labour; it entails heavy burdens upon the taxpayer; and it involves a restricted demand for commodities in the home market. The last-mentioned evil illustrates the close connection between the problems of the unemployed and the underpaid. According to Mr. Hobson, the main cause of unemployment is under-consumption. If the wage-earners took a larger share of the profits of production,

"not merely would the volume of consumption be enlarged by diverting 'surplus' into wages of efficiency, but the character of the consumption would be steadier. . . . Indeed, one of the most important results of this reform would be that the more stable character of national consumption would react upon industry, making the employment of capital and labour more regular and calculable, and reducing the relative

1. *South Australian Register,* 21st September 1910.

importance of the fluctuating trades engaged in satisfying shallow tastes and trivial needs."[1]

Only those who have worked among the poor can realise the extent of the evils to which I have drawn attention. In a recent volume Miss Black has presented a dispassionate picture of the sweated industries in Great Britain. The classes of individuals immediately affected are divided by her into five groups:—"The Poorest of All; Workers in Factories and Workshops; Shop Assistants, Clerks, and Waitresses; Traffic Workers; and Wage-Earning Children."[2] No open-minded reader of Miss Black's book can escape the conviction that the evils of the inadequate wage are appalling. As regards the question of the number of workers affected, it is difficult to speak. The statistics of human misery very inadequately discriminate between the responsible causes. But the insufficient wage is first among the reasons why so large a proportion of the population is living below the poverty line. It is not very long since an economist of repute declared:—

" It may be well the case, and there is every reason to fear it is the case, that there is collected a population in our great towns which equals in amount the whole of those who lived in England and Wales six centuries ago; but whose condition is more destitute, whose homes are more squalid, whose means are more uncertain, whose prospects are more hopeless, than those of the poorest serfs of the Middle Ages and the meanest drudges of the mediæval cities."[3]

Sir Robert Giffen estimated that not less than 8,000,000 of our population exist under conditions where the family income is less than one pound per week. Mr. Charles Booth's analysis of London disclosed the fact that over 30 per cent. of the population

1. "The Industrial System," 296.
2. "Sweated Industry."
3. J. E. Thorold Rogers, "Six Centuries of Work and Wages," ch. vi.

(about 1,300,000 persons) belong to classes on or below the poverty line of earnings not exceeding a guinea a week per family. Mr. Rowntree's investigations into the conditions of life at York showed that the position of London among industrial centres was not exceptional. He wrote:—

"The wages paid for unskilled labour in York are insufficient to provide food, shelter, and clothing adequate to maintain a family of moderate size in a state of bare physical efficiency. And let us clearly understand what 'merely physical efficiency' means. A family living upon the scale allowed for in this estimate must never spend a penny on railway fare or omnibus. They must never go into the country unless they walk. They must never purchase a halfpenny newspaper or spend a penny to buy a ticket for a popular concert. They must write no letters to absent children, for they cannot afford to pay the postage. They must never contribute anything to their church or chapel, or give any help to a neighbour which costs them money. They cannot save, nor can they join sick club or trade union, because they cannot pay the necessary subscriptions. The children must have no pocket-money for dolls, marbles, or sweets. The father must smoke no tobacco and must drink no beer. The mother must never buy any pretty clothes for herself or for her children, the character of the family wardrobe as of the family diet being governed by the regulation: 'Nothing must be bought but that which is absolutely necessary for the maintenance of physical health, and what is bought must be of the plainest and most economical description.' Should a child fall ill, it must be attended by the parish doctor: should it die, it must be buried by the parish. Finally, the wage-earner must never be absent from his work for a single day." [1]

Of course, the inadequate wage is not the only

1. "Poverty," 133-4.

cause of failure to rise above this level. But in the list of causes it stands easily first. Here is Mr. Rowntree's analysis of the causes of "primary" poverty in York:—

Section.	No. of House-holds affected.	Immediate Cause of "Primary" Poverty."	No. of Children affected.	No. of Adults affected.	Total number affected.	Percentage of Total Population living under "Primary" Poverty line.
1	403	Death or desertion of chief wage-earner	460	670	1130	15.63
2	146	Illness or old age of chief wage-earner	81	289	370	5.11
3	38	Chief wage-earner out of work	78	89	167	2.31
4	51	Irregularity of work	94	111	205	2.83
5	187	Largeness of family, *i.e.*, more than four children	1122	480	1602	22·16
6	640	*In regular work but at low wages*	2380	1376	3756	51.96
Totals	1465		4215	3015	7230	100.00 [1]

There are some who regard a low rate of wage as the inevitable corollary of the pressure of population upon the means of subsistence. As a matter of fact, the wealth of the population per head has nearly doubled within quite recent times. The vast multitude of our London East End lives at the very gates of the greatest centre of wealth and luxury that the world has known. It is even said that one million persons among the wealthy of our country receive twice as much of the total annual produce of the national labour as the twenty-six millions constituting the manual labour class.[2]

There are some who find a consolation for existing ills in reflecting that things are not so bad as they

1. "Poverty," 120.
2. A. R. Wallace, "The Wonderful Century," 342-4.

have been. The period selected for comparison is generally the terrible thirties of the last century. It would be easy to show a real advance without going so far back as that. The extent of recent achievement, however, is frequently exaggerated. While wages have risen and hours of labour have shortened, whole classes of the community have failed to receive any share of these gains, and the total bulk of poverty has in all probability increased—and that despite a period of great if not unexampled prosperity and of unparalleled private and public philanthropic effort, despite slumming, settlements, funds, General Booth's schemes, and the like. As a people, we are slow to recognise the need of reform, more especially when reform requires the action of the State. But it is becoming increasingly clear that, as long as the policy of the Factory Acts is limited to the hours and conditions of labour and is not applied also to the rate of wage, some of the gravest evils that prey upon our national life will never be overcome.[1]

(4) *The Child.*

In an earlier chapter I have referred to the increase, during the nineteenth century, in the sense of responsibility to childhood.[2] In spite of this improvement the problem of the relation of the State to the child is still unsolved. In the present place I shall merely indicate the more important data of the problem as it presents itself to-day.

(*a*) *Home training and conditions.*—Whether from the poverty, ignorance, or vice of the parents, child life and character are sacrificed to an extent which no patriot can regard with complacency. Dr. Playfair estimated that infant mortality up to the fifth year may be placed at 18 per cent. for the upper class, 36 per cent. for the tradesman class, and 55 per cent. for

1. For a brief review of some recent legislation in various countries, the reader is referred to Mr. Alden's "The Condition of England," 62 *et seq.*
2. *Supra,* ch. ii.

the working class. Such figures imply a slow slaughter of the innocents. What happens to the children who survive? Mr. H. G. Wells writes:

"I have already quoted certain facts from the London Education Committee's Report, by which you have seen that by taking a school haphazard—dipping a ladle, as it were, into the welter of the London population—we find more than eighty in the hundred of the London children insufficiently clad, more than half unwholesomely dirty—11 per cent. verminous—and more than half the infants infested with vermin! The nutrition of these children is equally bad. The same report shows clearly that differences in clothing and cleanliness are paralleled with differences in nutrition that are equally striking."[1]

(*b*) *The exploitation of child labour.*—Modern machinery enables the child to do much that was formerly done by the adult; and new forms of child labour are being evolved as a result of the greater complexity and variety of modern demands. Whether the parent is needy or simply callous, and whether employers are impelled by greed or by the competition of unscrupulous rivals, the fact remains that our industrial army still includes multitudes of children who should be at school. Unfortunately we have to reckon, not only with premature employment, but often with revolting conditions of labour. When we read of forty little girls engaged in licking adhesive labels, at the rate of thirty gross a day, with tongues that have acquired "the polished tips characteristic of label lickers,"[2] it is difficult to believe that we live in the twentieth century of the Christian era. Miss Jane Addams, writing of conditions in Chicago, declares:

"Almost every day at six o'clock I see certain factories pouring out a stream of men and women and boys and

1. "New Worlds for Old," 29. For an interesting summary of recent ameliorative legislation, the reader may be referred to Mr. Percy Alden's "Democratic England," the chapter on "The Child and the State," 28–59.

2 Quoted, C. F. G. Masterman, "The Condition of England," 161.

girls. The boys and girls have a peculiar hue—a colour so distinctive that one meeting them on the street, even on Sunday when they are in their best clothes and mingled with other children who go to school and play out of doors, can distinguish them in an instant, and there is on their faces a premature anxiety and sense of responsibility, which we should declare pathetic if we were not used to it. . . . In a soap factory in Chicago little girls wrap bars of soap in two covers at the minimum rate of 3,000 bars a week; their only ambition is to wrap as fast as possible and well enough to pass the foreman's inspection." [1]

The conditions in Chicago are not without parallel in England. Miss Black, in her work on "Sweated Industry," discusses in detail the various forms of children's work—babies' shoe-making, all-night work, matchbox-making, string-bag making, tooth-brush making, kid-belt making, wood chopping, wood polishing, steel covering, fish-basket sewing, laundry work, errand running, street trading, work in the bake-houses, brick-fields, potteries, etc., etc.

"Most of us," she writes, "are still very little awake to the sacrifice of childhood that is daily being made in our midst. We pass a pale child in the street, carrying a long bundle in a black wrapper, and the sight makes no impression. But, to those of us who have seen the under side of London, that little figure is a type of unremunerative toil, of stunted growth, of weakened vitality, and of wasted school teaching." [2]

(*c*) *The uneducated character of child labour.*—The premature employment of the child is a bad thing; it is a worse thing that the character of the work done by the child so seldom prepares him for earning a livelihood in maturer life. He toils in a *cul de sac*.[3]

1. "Newer Ideals of Peace," 155-6, 174.
2. "Sweated Industry," 141.
3. *Cf.* the passage quoted in chapter viii. (when discussing the Right to Work) from the Minority Report of the Poor Law Commission.

(*d*) *The growing responsibility of the Teacher.*—Two conclusions emerge from the welter of controversy on the subject of education. One is the infinite importance of the subject in relation to national well-being. The other is the urgent need for a policy of persistent, systematic and far-reaching reform. I do not propose to discuss the lines along which reform should be effected; but, since reform must obviously be the result of State action of one kind or another, I shall review the more essential data of the problem. I shall do this at a length which may seem disproportionate to the general scheme of this chapter. But I wish to bring together in one connected argument scattered hints and conclusions which I have expressed in earlier parts of this work. And I wish to place in clear relief certain questions which are profoundly important from the point of view of the future of the race.

The teacher receives into his hands the youth of a nation. He has a great opportunity; and upon the use which he makes of it depends to a large extent the character of the people and the destiny of the nation. I say "to a large extent." Other powers are at work, acting in alliance with the teacher—the discipline of the Church and the family, the spirit of authority, the laws and institutions of the State. But to-day some of these powers, though at work, are not so potent as they have been; and the increase in the activity of the State throws upon the teacher a responsibility of which the extent has yet to be appreciated.

I wish to draw attention to these changed conditions. I do not speak of them in terms of praise or censure. I speak of them simply as material which bear upon the question of the position and responsibilities of the teacher. I make no apology for quoting, in the course of my argument, an occasional extract from an article which I wrote for the *Hibbert Journal* on the "Passing of Conviction." [1] I begin with an

1. In 1904.

expression of opinion which may provoke dissent. But it is my opinion. I give it for what it is worth. It is that the value of the Church as an ally to the teacher is growing less and less. The most conspicuous causes at work have been the progress of scepticism in thought, the increase in man's material possessions, and the multiplication of forms of pleasure or entertainment which are unassociated with the Churches, and often in unavowed rivalry with them. The results of the combined influences of these causes are revealed in the waning efficacy of religious belief. We are, I believe, in a transitional period, when old faiths have lost much of their authority and power, and revisions or reconstructions of that faith, while they may be potent with a few, have not a controlling influence over the many. The great mass of individuals have relaxed their hold upon an ancient creed without replacing that creed by any conviction or faith of comparable power. The teacher has to work under these changed conditions. His responsibility is increased. I do not mean that he should expound religion. But I do mean that the material with which he has to deal comes to him less equipped in some important respects than formerly, and that he must make good the deficiency as best he can.

There is a second and possibly more serious way in which the responsibility of the teacher has been increased. The value of parental discipline as an ally in the training of the youth of the nation is declining. This is partly because the family itself, as a social institution, though not dying, is surely declining. The reasons are many. The decline in the power of religious conviction has weakened for many the sanctity of the marriage tie. Migrations, social instability generally, divide the family and destroy its continuity. Supremely, the age of the great cities is upon us; and the whole atmosphere of the modern city is charged with influences which are hostile to the family. In the civic community the bonds which unite the family group are relaxed. The lodging house, the flat, the factory, the streets, and the various forms of social activity or dissipation, weaken the family tie and destroy the family tradition. Other causes work towards the same end. We have only to glance at the statute book. Modern legislation, by making the State responsible for education, has appreciably weakened the sense of parental responsibility; by facilitating divorce has strengthened the contractual at the expense of the sacramental conception of marriage; and by protecting womankind has created a rival to marriage in the shape of a career for women. I am not condemning such legislation. On the contrary I approve of it, but it has its drawbacks. The drawbacks may be transitional, but they exist to-day. While the family will continue, it seems destined to have less than its old power of giving to men and women the sense of something to live for.

The decline of the family as a social institution must be regarded for present purposes in association with a decline in the spirit of authority. For one thing we have lost belief in rank: in some respects a gain; in others a loss. "I would rather be a peasant and reverence a lord, than be a politician and reverence nothing." To-day the social value of rank sinks to insignificance. The spread of knowledge and the growth of plutocracy have undermined the foundations of class supremacy. Although we are far from social equality, although we still have social classes, the power of class to train men to reverence is lacking. Envy, not reverence, is the plant that thrives in the soil of a challenged but still dominant plutocracy. We dream to-day of a new aristocracy which shall be based not on birth or wealth, but on mind and character. Unfortunately, while the old aristocracy has lost its power, the new aristocracy is but a vision of a future that may be. As a result, aristocracy as a school of reverence is non-existent.

From the point of the education of the youth of

the nation, all this is significant. I have said that the discipline of the family and of the spirit of authority have been in the past important allies of the teacher. I have tried to show that the value of these allies has been weakened in many ways. But if this be so, an added responsibility is thrown upon the teacher. The teacher has always recognized that mind and character are the objectives of education; but his special contribution to education has been to inform the mind, to nurture latent potentialities of thinking, to awaken curiosity, to encourage a love for knowledge, to discipline the mind as an instrument of thought, and to inculcate right methods of reading and study. These are elements in character but not the only elements. In many ways, direct or indirect, the teacher has recognized the fact. My point is that the recognition involves a graver responsibility to-day than in time past. The moral education of the pupil, his manners, the discipline of his will—these great objects make an ever increasing demand upon the teacher. I don't mean that they involve didactic discourse. They are ends to be pursued by ways more indirect, more subtle, and more burdensome. But, however they are to be pursued, the conditions of our time demand that they shall receive from the teacher more consideration, more systematic and sustained effort, than has been deemed necessary in the past.

In the foregoing remarks, I may seem to have taken a gloomy view of recent progress. I have ignored those aspects of modern life which reveal progress in a real sense—for example, the triumphs of Democracy, and the growth of a sense of corporate responsibility, of social solidarity, and of human brotherhood. As a matter of fact, however, when we turn to these aspects we shall find that they involve a direct increase of the teacher's responsibility. In the first place, the teacher in a democratic community is not merely training citizens; he is training the arbiters of the national destiny. It appears to me to follow, as I have already stated in Chapter VIII, when discussing the Right to Self-Government, that a school curriculum with any pretension to completeness should find some place for the teaching of the elements of politics. The child who leaves the school should already know a little, and *want* to know a great deal more, of the principles which guide legislative action. The teacher can deal with no more than the merest rudiments of the subject; but it is within his power to evoke the child's interest in those grave responsibilities which he will have to discharge as an enfranchised citizen of a democratic community.

In the second place, the growth in the sense of corporate responsibility, of social solidarity, and human brotherhood, implies above all things a deeper recognition of the claims of human weakness. This in itself is a good thing, a real achievement, something to be proud about. Yet when viewed in relation to the teacher it implies an addition to his responsibilities which exceeds in significance any fact or condition to which I have previously referred. The most conspicuous agency in the maintenance of the racial type has been natural selection. Natural selection has eliminated the relatively weak and thus secured the breeding of the race from the relatively strong. The result has been only clumsily attained. There has been much cruelty in the process. Undesirable forms of inferiority have survived. Desirable forms of superiority have been sacrificed. The "fit" have indeed survived; but the fitness has meant a fitness to survive in a particular environment. Still, making all due allowance for such qualifications, the operation of natural selection has worked steadily and persistently in the direction of maintaining the racial standard.

In the popular mind there persists the belief that, independently of selection, we can improve a race by improving the environment of that race. Of course environment is extremely important; but its operation affects the individual, rather than the racial type. I use environment in the broadest sense. I mean by it much more than physical and climatic conditions. I include the complexus of beliefs, opinions, knowledge, social, economic and political conditions. I need not say that environment so defined is of the utmost importance. But there are certain things which it can effectively do, and certain things which it cannot effectively do. Let us consider for a moment the things which it can effectively do.

In the first place, social and economic institutions may be of such a nature as to affect the forms of fitness upon which natural selection operates. The fitness, for example, instead of being dependent upon a capacity to survive in a free fight may be in part dependent upon the possession of mental or moral qualities which belong to a higher plane. In the second place, an environment may bring out the potentialities for good, and repress the potentialities for evil, in the children which are born into it.

But it is just at this point that the popular belief, to which I referred just now, becomes dangerous. It is commonly believed that if we provide an ideal environment for a child, say, of criminal tendencies, or defective physique, we not only improve him as an individual, but also improve him as a breeding stock. The weight of scientific opinion does not countenance this belief. As an individual, we may have made a man of him; as a breeding stock, he remains what he was. Of course this cuts both ways. If an individual who might have grown up good, grows up bad, while he deteriorates as an individual, as a breeding stock he remains what he was. All this is expressed in scientific terms as the doctrine of the non-transmission of acquired characters. The individual transmits *inborn,* not *acquired* characters. Now, on the face of it, this seems ridiculous, impossible. But the very fact that it seems ridiculous and impossible only tends to make its endorsement by the weight of scientific opinion more significant. Speaking for myself, I feel bound to accept that opinion. If the reader is sceptical on the subject, I must refer him to Thomson's great work on Heredity—a work of which the reasoned, sane, and judicial outlook must be apparent to everyone. The writer sums up his general conclusions as follows: "There seems to be no convincing evidence in support of the affirmative position (that acquired characters can be transmitted); and there is a strong presumption in favour of the negative." On the whole, then, it seems that we must assume that even if under some circumstances an acquired character is transmitted, the fact should be regarded as exceptional, rather than normal. If it were normal, the scepticism as to the *possibility* of transmission would not exist.

But if this be so, it has an immense significance for the social reformer. Many social reformers have imagined that they could save the race by providing an adequate nurture for the children of the race. By this means the next generation would be born with a clean heritage. But we cannot shed the past in this way. We can only secure a clean heritage by the process of breeding from the superior stocks. The child of the slum may be taken out of the slums; he will breed the stock from which he comes despite his changed environment.

All this may seem remote from my subject. On the contrary it is most relevant. I referred just now to our deeper consciousness to-day of the claims of human weakness. That consciousness has had, and is destined to have, a far reaching influence upon the efficiency of natural selection as a factor in maintaining the racial type. The spirit of our time has been distinguished by a progressive desire to qualify the operation of natural selection. Natural selection operates; it must always operate. But it operates in an ever decreasing degree. Preventive and remedial medicine is partly responsible. But a potent factor is the resurgent will of man rising in revolt against the ruthless cruelties of Nature.

"So careful of the type she seems,
So careless of the single life."

Much of the legislation of our time illustrates this resurgent will at work. Public Health Acts, Social Insurance Acts, Industrial Legislation, as well as the multiplication of public and private philanthropic institutions, qualify in many and diverse ways the operation of natural selection. Nature, as we generally understand the term, would eliminate the weak; but Man rises in revolt against this law. As a result the relatively weak survive. But they not only survive; they marry; and they have a posterity which perpetuates their weakness despite any improvement in the parental environment. Now this fact, taken in conjunction with the fact that breeding is on the whole more prolific in inferior stocks, involves a grave consequence. Unless other agencies are at work, we shall save the single life at the expense of a persistent degradation of the average life.

I submit three practical conclusions. In the first place, it is the duty of statesmanship to control social and economic institutions in such a way that the fact of survival becomes increasingly a proof of the possession of really desirable qualities. In the past, such institutions have too often told for the survival of undesirable rather than desirable types. In the lower strata of society, many individuals have been precluded from any fair and reasonable chance to demonstrate a real fitness to survive. In no class has there been even an approximation to a coincidence of the fit and the successful.

In the second place, there is such a thing as artificial selection. I presume that all sane people who are at all acquainted with the results of modern researches on heredity believe more or less in eugenics. But we must not expect too much of eugenics. Extreme forms of unfitness may be dealt with. The habitual criminal, the insane, the unemployable may be drafted, in one way or another, out of the marriage market. But there appear to me to be insuperable obstacles to dealing in these drastic ways with any but extreme forms of unfitness.

In the third place, however, man's environment may be such as to bring out potentialities for good and repress potentialities for evil, in the children born into it. I have already pointed out that this of itself will not save the racial type; but it may at least save the individual. And we must not, in our enthusiasm for the race, overlook the claims of the individual. As Thomson says, in his work on Heredity, "Though modifications due to changed nurture do not seem to be transmissible they may be reimpressed on each generation. Thus nurture becomes not less but more important. . . . Although what is acquired may not be inherited, what is not inherited may be acquired. Thus we are led to direct our energies ever more strenuously to the business of reimpressing desirable modifications. . . . To secure a good nurture for our children is one of our most obvious and binding duties." [1]

I hope I have said enough to justify my excursions into science and politics. Man has declared for a progressive qualification of the operation of natural selection. He has resolved to secure the nurture of every child, strong or weak. The resolution should be accompanied by a recognition of the price to be paid. That price includes the strengthening of all the influences which I have grouped under environment—conspicuously a recognition of the importance of the teacher to the community. There are some people to-day who want to be virtuous without paying the price of virtue. But the thing cannot be done. Logically and morally, having decided in favour of the nurture of the unfit as well as of the fit, the decision becomes a curse not a blessing unless we are prepared to make all the sacrifices that may be necessary in order to ensure for the whole youth of the nation the best

1. 245-9

possible material, mental and moral environment—conspicuously the best and completest system of education that our ingenuity can devise. We have undertaken, perhaps without realising our full responsibilities, a decision to weaken one factor in the maintenance and development of the national life. Good; but we must shoulder the responsibilities. The task is stupendous. It demands the best brains and the highest character that the nation can devote. If, as I believe, the religious discipline of time past has lost much of its old power, if the discipline of the family has relaxed and the spirit of authority has weakened, and if the progressive qualification of natural selection throws an ever increasing importance upon environment, then the teacher of to-day finds his responsibilities multiplied indefinitely. I do not ask how he is going to discharge these increased responsibilites. I am content to indicate their existence. They demand the serious thought of the legislator no less than of the teacher. The community which ignores them, or trifles with them, is doomed.

Summary of Preceding Argument.

My object, in the preceding part of the present chapter, has been to justify the statement that the pressure of social and economic problems is likely to tell in favour of increased State activity in the future. When we consider the extent of the evils to which I have referred, the suffering they involve, the lives they cost, and the characters they degrade, we realise something of the nature of the material out of which the politics of the future will be fashioned. There are still some who, while admitting the gravity of the social problems of our day, urge that their solution by means of legislation is neither necessary nor desirable. They proclaim a gospel of individual reform in opposition to a programme of legislative action. But, under the complicated conditions of modern life, the reform of the law is an indispensable means to the reform of the individual. Any one who doubts this should reflect upon the history of industrial amelioration in the last century. He might, further, consider with advantage the relative futility of the attempts that have been made to secure a fair wage by moralising employers, or to abolish sweating by establishing consumers' leagues. The problems of modern industry can only be solved by the action of the organised community. On the precise form that action should take different people may hold different opinions. On the need of legislative action of some sort impartial thinkers are in agreement.

II.—The Advent of Democracy.

The pressure of social and economic problems is only one among several reasons for anticipating an increase in State activity and responsibility. A second reason is to be found in the progress of a movement which, whether we consider its intrinsic importance or the rapidity of its development, is one of the most remarkable in history. In the early nineteenth century, the democratic form of government was practically confined to a few communities on the eastern shores of the United States. In the early twentieth century, more than fifty countries, containing in all more than a quarter of the population of the globe, possess constitutional governments, in which taxation and legislation are controlled by the people or their representatives.[1] The influence of this movement upon the course of legislation in the past may easily be exaggerated; but no one can doubt that it has been considerable. What of the future?

In answering this question, two facts demand consideration. (1) The spread of popular education, the discipline of experience, and the magnitude of the issues at stake tell for an increasingly effective organisation of the masses for the purposes of collective

1. *Cf.* Parsons, "The White Light of Civilised Democracy," *The Arena*, xxvi, 374.

action. (2) The tendency of modern industrial organisation is to draw a sharp line between employers and employees, and to increase the numerical ratio of the latter to the former. The workers, instead of being masters in the making, remain workers throughout their lives; and their numbers include an increasingly large proportion of the population. We have become a nation not of profit makers, but of hired men. The authors of "Problems of modern Industry" tell us that "the hired men already form three-fourths of the population in the United States, Western Europe, and Australia." The significance of this change in the industrial order will be at once apparent. If political power is vested in the hands of the many, and if in an increasing degree the many compose a relatively homogeneous class of wage earners, the organisation of the multitude for political purposes becomes more easy, and the demand for legislation as a remedy for industrial ills is likely to prove irresistible. It can no longer be said that King Demos is dumb.

An interesting illustration may be found in the position of the Labour Party in Australia. That party has learned, as it was bound to learn, the lesson of organisation for political purposes. At the present moment, it directs the course of legislation in several of the States and dominates the Senate in the Parliament of the Commonwealth. Its ablest leaders speak of the strike as an antiquated weapon of industrial warfare. They say, in effect, "We can get what we want through legal or constitutional channels; *and we mean to get it.*" The party may legislate unwisely; no one can doubt that it will legislate upon a quantitatively liberal scale.

Mr. H. G. Wells, speaking of European conditions, remarks that in a community where nearly every one reads extensively, travels about, sees the charm and variety of prosperous and leisurely people, no class is going to submit permanently to modern labour conditions.

"Things are altogether too stimulating to the imagination nowadays . . . For a time, indeed, for a generation or so even, a labour mass may be fooled or coerced, but in the end it will break out against its subjection even if it breaks out to a general social catastrophe."[1]

III.—The Sense of Corporate Responsibility.

As factors in the present situation, the pressure of social and economic problems and the democratisation of political institutions derive an additional significance from the progress of moral ideas. Only the growing sense of collective responsibility can explain the extent of the influence now exercised upon the course of legislation, and likely to be exercised upon it in an increasing degree, by several of the problems to which I have referred. If the electorate were actuated by purely selfish motives it would lack the fighting power that comes of the consciousness of high purposes. But "thrice is he armed that hath his quarrel just." The growing demand for legislative reform becomes the more significant when we remember that, among increasing numbers of the people, it springs from motives that possess the intensity and power of a religious faith.

IV.—Conclusion.

If, then, we take the various factors already mentioned and regard them in combination—the pressure of social and economic problems, the democratisation of our political machinery, and the growth in the sense of collective responsibility—we must conclude that the supreme problem of the future will be, not how to thwart the movement towards State control, but how to direct it in such a way as to achieve legitimate ends without sacrificing the individuality of the citizen. He who clings blindly to the *status quo* in legislation, while economic, political, and moral

1. "The Great State," 37.

conditions are rapidly changing, is a menace to the very social order he affects to defend. If I were asked to name the worst enemy of the existing social order, I should point to the man who opposes any and every proposal for social amelioration. There are, I fear, many men to-day, men often of great ability and even of exemplary private character, whose political opinions are based upon an unalterable conviction that every new idea or proposal in politics is impracticable. These very men may be quite open-minded when it is a question of applying new machinery or new discoveries within the sphere of the particular form of industry with which they are themselves associated. But they dismiss any new idea in politics as impracticable if it does not square with preconceptions which they have never submitted to the test of serious examination. Such men are unassailable by argument; and, by their attitude of uncompromising opposition to reform, they are the unconscious instruments of social catastrophe. By combining with other forces, they may succeed in delaying reforms; but the ultimate result of their effort, if successful for a time, must be to give a plausibility and an irresistible power to the demand for revolutionary change in the near future. We may learn a lesson in this matter from the experience of the past. Speaking of a critical era in Roman history, Lord Acton remarks:

"The old and famous aristocracy of birth and rank had made a stubborn resistance, but it knew the art of yielding. The later and more selfish aristocracy was unable to learn it. The character of the people was changed by the sterner motives of dispute. The fight for political power had been carried on with the moderation which is so honourable a quality of party contests in England. But the struggle for the objects of material existence grew to be as ferocious as civil controversies in France. Repulsed by the rich, after a struggle of twenty-two years, the people, three hundred and twenty thousand of whom depended on public rations for food, were ready to follow any man who promised to obtain for them by revolution what they could not obtain by law." [1]

When I reflect upon the power of the forces that to-day impel toward legislative action; upon the peril that the action thus taken may be injudicious and harmful; upon the need of the co-operation of all classes, of mutual sympathy, of comprehensive views, and of wise statesmanship—when I reflect upon these things, I cannot but feel that we are on the eve of a great crisis in the nation's history. We have reached a stage when the ignorance of the citizen is a menace and his apathy a crime. Among the many disturbing facts with which we have to reckon, one stands out pre-eminently. Each of us has gone too much his own way. Education, for example, has never become with us a really national question; and the subject has only awakened a general interest under the stimulus of sectarian conflict or of the loss of foreign markets. Our employers, as a class, have gone too much their own way, lacking even the generosity that is based on sound policy. The employed have borrowed from their masters the ruthless principle of getting as much as possible by giving as little as possible, and threaten to pass under the leadership of the fanatical reformers who hope for social salvation through the propagation of a class war. The air is full of remedies more or less deserving of attention. But the one supreme need is that, as a nation, we pull together. When I think of the proud position of our nation in the past, its victories by land and sea, its trade and commerce, its achievements in the spreading of Freedom and the building up of Empire, its example of political and civic institutions—I cannot help asking myself whether it is not possible that we, who are of a race that has so often led the van, may yet prove ourselves worthy

1. "History of Freedom and Other Essays," 14.

to uphold the traditions we inherit. If in the past our country has led the way to free institutions, why should it not to-day be the first of all the nations to realise that new interpretation of social justice for which the conditions of the modern world cry aloud? If as a nation we can grapple honestly, firmly, intelligently, with the problems of our time; if we can realise that a slum in a city is a stain upon the fair name of every rate-payer; if we can turn to practical account the growing sense of kinship with the despised and rejected; if, in a word, we can approach social problems in a social spirit and with an enlightened judgment, we need have little fear for the kingdom of the markets. But if we fail in these things we shall have ourselves to blame. When I look at the horizon of the future I see the dark menace of grave dangers which are rapidly taking shape. I see a great people passing through strange ordeals, which will put its intelligence and its virtue to tests so severe that the ultimate issue is impossible to foretell. And I turn from this vision of the future to ask what the citizens of to-day are doing to prepare themselves to cope with the problems that lie before them—problems that will demand clear heads as well as loyal hearts, enlightened statesmanship no less than reforming zeal. I ask a question: the answer I leave to the judgment of the reader.

THE END.